COMPANY COMMANDER

VIETNAM

COLONEL JAMES ESTEP (U.S. Army, Ret.) rose from sergeant to captain during four tours of duty in Vietnam between 1962 and 1973. Estep is now retired and lives with his family in Florida.

COMPANY COMMANDER VIETNAM

BY

JAMES ESTEP

ibooks
new york
www.ibooks.net

DISTRIBUTED BY SIMON & SCHUSTER

ibooks, inc.
24 West 25th Street
New York, NY 10010

The ibooks World Wide Web Site Address is:
http://www.ibooks.net

Originally published as
Comanche Six: Company Commander, Vietnam
Copyright © 1991 by James L. Estep
Reprinted with permission of Presidio Press
All Rights Reserved

Cover Design: J. Vita
Cover Photograph Courtesy the National Archives

ISBN: 0-7434-5250-X
First ibooks printing September 2002
10 9 8 7 6 5 4 3 2 1

Share your thoughts about *Company Commander Vietnam*
and other ibooks titles in the ibooks virtual reading group at
www.ibooks.net

For those who didn't return,
who, like the centurions and their soldiers, deserved
better from the republic they served.

And especially for
William "Billy" McCarty.
He made us laugh, and we miss him.

Contents

Preface

This is a story of American soldiers who fought in a faraway place, for an elusive cause, for eleven long years.

Historians now tell us our country's military involvement in Indochina can be chronologically divided into three distinct phases. The early 1960s was the period of the advisor, a period in which we tried to turn the tide in a relatively small insurgency, employing only a modest expenditure in men and material. This phase ended with the introduction of North Vietnam's armies into the fray and the subsequent arrival of our ground forces in 1965. For the next three years, we sought to end the war by judicious use of our military might and would have probably succeeded in doing so had our national will not collapsed in the aftermath of the enemy's 1968 Tet offensive. During the final and most costly phase, from the spring of 1968 until the Paris Accords were signed five years later, we simply looked for a way out.

Many fine books tell the story of America's soldiers at war in each of these periods; however, most provide only a snapshot of our country's exposure to this the longest of its military struggles. Having served four tours of duty in Vietnam during the years from 1962 to 1973, I had a unique opportunity to study the war's changing face as our part in it evolved from a low-level advisory effort to the massive employment of over half a million men, before once again becoming what was essentially an advisory campaign.

Moreover, my postings as a Special Forces noncommissioned and commissioned officer, a U.S. rifle company commander, and an ARVN advisor provided a dimension of diversity other than time alone from which to observe our soldiers' many-faceted participation in the conflict. I hope, therefore, to have succeeded in furnishing a broader appreciation of what some of these men experienced over the war's long course, at the lowest end of combat's spectrum—in the paddies, the plains, and the mountains of the Nam.

Saying that, I should mention that although the book embraces four diverse tours and times, its main theme centers on service with the First Air Cavalry in 1967–68. This was the time of Gen. Vo Nguyen Giap's Tet offensive and the apex of the American infantryman's involvement in the war. In short, it was the most exciting of the tours.

Similarly, although it spans an eleven-year period, the book is by no stretch of the imagination a history of our involvement in Indochina. This is a true story, based on my experiences as I recall them. Many of the names herein have been changed to protect the privacy of those concerned. In like manner, the book's quoted passages should not be looked upon as verbatim dialogue. Much of this dialogue is fictitious. Still, these or like conversations did take place, and the tone and tenor of what was said are as true to the spirit of those interchanges as memory will allow after a lapse of, in some cases, over twenty-five years.

Unit designations of friendly and enemy forces are, as best as retrospect and research permit, those of the actual units involved. Infrequently, however, there are minor discrepancies in the numerical designations of supporting forces. The most glaring example of this incongruity is the multiunit Binh Loc operation described in chapter one. In this instance, to facilitate clarity and continuity throughout the book, I have intentionally identified participating adjacent units as being those that were at the time assigned to my parent headquarters in the Fifth Cavalry Regiment.

Finally, radio call signs used throughout are, with few exceptions, those that were then in effect. However, there are some instances, again in the case of supporting forces, in which call signs are fictitious.

In sum, this is the story of America's soldiers in Vietnam. It is a story of victories and tribulations, fears and joys, laughter and tears. If in telling it I've offended any of those with whom I served, I apologize. Offense is certainly not my intent. You are the heroes of this work and of the nation that sent you forth to do battle on its behalf. You are, without question, far better men than those timid souls who refused to fight in that faraway place, so long ago.

Prologue

What time is it? Nighttime. Has to be nighttime 'cause it's still dark, right? Right. Who's mourning in the next cubicle? Very unmanly thing to do. Ah yes, it's the Huey pilot fresh from a tour of duty in the decidedly unfriendly skies of the Nam, and he's mourning because he has no legs! Well, welcome to the snake pit, my friend; you've done your full duty. "I wept because I had no shoes until I met a man who had no feet." Who said that? Who cares who said that, goddamn it, it's not important! Demerol's important.

Leg's on fire! Feels as if someone has pierced it with a white-hot poker, one that all the miracle healers of this exalted medical establishment are unable to dislodge. But they can quell the pain with a simple shot of Demerol. I'll call the nurse and tell her I need a shot. Yeah, I'll just politely say, "Nurse, nurse, I'm getting worse. Would you be so kind as to insert your magic needle into the attached IV and let that great destroyer of pain flow through my bruised and battered body, extinguishing the fire below?" But she'll say no! She'll say it's not time yet and then, smiling sweetly, tell me to just "hang tight" for another hour.

One hour, sixty minutes, three thousand and six hundred seconds. Don't count them. Remove your watch and put it under your pillow.

Good, now think of something else. Think of how fortunate you are; there's still a foot attached to your leg. And hey, that's a pretty unique occurrence in the "pit"! Think of the young lieutenant, so recently a whole and healthy warrior of the 173d Airborne, sleeping peacefully across the aisle from you. Between operations, he's relatively, momentarily free of the animal pain. However, the animal will return with the next operation. He'll lay with the animal pain again and again.

God, he's ugly! Blast must have hit him right at chest level, really messed up his face. But he's still got his sight, and they're building him a new nose. Got the makings of it transplanted on his forehead already. Looks kind of funny there with a nose hanging from his forehead to his stomach, sort of like an elephant with its trunk tucked into its belly button. Of course they know what they're doing here; they'll trim it up nice and neat when the time comes. Hope it takes, hope it works and never clogs, because, having no arms, he'll have no way of blowing it. On the other hand, they can do wonders in physical therapy. If they can teach you how to pick up marbles with your toes, I'm sure they can teach young Dave there how to pick his nose.

Unbearable! The goddamn pain's unbearable! Got to have a shot! Wonder where the old woman is with her Fourteenth Street go-go girls and bottle of Wild Turkey. What was her name? Sweet Mary? Gentle Mary? Now she knows how to treat America's wounded! Wish she'd come again tonight. Could leave her go-go girls behind, just bring the Wild Turkey. Yeah, that's what I need, same as the first night. When was that, last night? Night before? Whenever. No more morphine, makes me sick and the pain remains. No, same as that first night, a double dose of the big D, a sleeping pill, and a touch of the old woman's Wild Turkey . . . then just float away to never-never land.

She's coming! I can barely hear her soft-soled nurse's pumps on the darkened corridor's tiled floor, but my hearing is attuned to the sounds that signal the approach of she who bears the magic potion.

Smiling down at me like the merciful angel she, for a fleeting moment, truly is, she gives me the shot. The magic flows through me, bringing in its wake peace. I ask her for a sleeping pill, but she says no, no more barbiturates.

That's okay; it'll give me a few relatively painless, conscious minutes to think about the company, to wonder where they now are and what they're now doing. Rumor says they're about to sally forth to pull the

Marines' chestnuts out of the fire at Khe Sanh. Bet they do and wish I were with them. Wish I were there, CAR-15 in one hand, map in the other, sunburned, filthy and sweating, boarding a slick and flying into the unknown.

God, I wish I were with them tonight!

The Cav I

The Southern Airways Columbus-Atlanta connector departed on schedule. Like most other uniformed passengers aboard the early morning flight, I was on my way to the "pearl of the Orient"—Vietnam. Unlike most other uniformed passengers, I was on my way a third time.

As the two-engine turboprop gained altitude, I felt a sudden yet familiar uneasiness, an ominous fear of the unknown mingled with a fleeting longing for the security of yesterday's duties and the family that had just bid me farewell.

Why? I asked myself. Why go back again? Two times should be enough for any sane man. And don't tell yourself it's because of patriotic fever, that you're once again heeding the trumpet's call. You're not. Nor is it because America's infantry is now in the fray and you, as a captain of infantry, should be in it with them. That's not really it; you saw enough of that sort of thing last time around. Then why go again? You know the answer. It's because you like it! Yes, it's really that simple; you like the pace of combat, like that awareness of life that only it seems to induce. You like to feel that sudden surge of adrenaline when confronting the unexpected; you like the lack of routine, the opportunity to innovate, the hunting of animals who do indeed shoot back, the stark terror and brilliant splendor of a firefight . . . and you like

5

watching boys grow into men virtually overnight and in most cases being better off for having done so. You like the fear of the unknown, and for that matter you like these familiar feelings of apprehension and remorse you're now experiencing. It's all part of it, and you like it all, don't you? With a trace of a smile, I silently answered myself, yes, I really do.

A flight attendant interrupted these philosophical wanderings, asking if I'd prefer coffee or juice before landing in Atlanta. I ordered tomato juice and then on the spur of the moment corrected myself, saying, "On second thought, put a little vodka in that virgin Mary, please." *Might as well enjoy the service while it lasts; there's gonna be some long dry spells ahead.*

Reclining in my seat, drink in hand, my thoughts drifted back to that first trip to the Nam. Only five years ago? It seemed like a lifetime, and yet it seemed like only yesterday, but what a difference! There were no drinks served aboard that flight. In fact, there were few seats aboard those post–World War II, double-decker C-124 Globe Masters, three of which flew us in trail from Fort Bragg, North Carolina, to Saigon's Tan Son Nhut airport about as quickly as we could have swum the distance.

At the time I was a twenty-four-year-old buck sergeant in the Army's Special Forces en route to a war that had not yet become a war, or, as Sergeant Fallow was fond of saying, "It may not be much of a war, Jimbo, but it's the only one we got"; then winking, as if sharing a secret known only amongst those of us who wore the green beret, he would always add, "At least it's the only one the American people know about." Which was incorrect, of course, since in 1962 the American public didn't know or care about our "only war" in Vietnam, much less any of the smaller covert altercations he was alluding to.

M. Sgt. Al Fallow, my boss and mentor on that first tour . . . wonder whatever happened to him. Last I heard he was still somewhere in Southeast Asia doing his part for the CIA. I miss his endless philosophical quips and the way he related them to our "only war."

Although it was not much of a war as wars go, by 1962 it was taking its toll in Special Forces soldiers, many of them close friends. Yet death in combat was the exception, not the rule, in 1962. In fact, we saw more combat occur between different political and ethnic factions within South Vietnam than we experienced in our encounters with the Viet Cong (VC). We saw Montagnards we had trained to fight the VC turn instead on their South Vietnamese counterparts, we stood idly by as the country's Buddhists set out to topple a government, and finally, sitting in a sandbagged bunker on a chilly November night in 1963, we learned that a president—who, on reflection, was probably the best hope for stability in his young republic—had "accidentally" committed suicide.

It was in many respects a learning tour, as was the next; however, the differences between the two could hardly have been more profound. By 1965, our "only war" had literally exploded! Gone were the six-day work weeks and casual bus rides down to Cape Saint Jacques on Sundays; gone were greenback dollars, two-dollar whores, and ten-piaster beer La Rue. By 1965, prices had risen astronomically on everything except human life—it was still cheap, cheaper in fact.

I began that tour as a young, and very inexperienced, second lieutenant assigned to a remote Special Forces encampment on the Vietnamese-Laotian border. Its name was ARO, which translated could only mean "end of the earth." Located on an isolated mountaintop deep in triple-canopy, uninhabitable tropical rain forest, it sat on terrain that *could not* be defended, in an area that *could not* be resupplied or reinforced, astride a dirt airstrip upon which planes *could not* land. Actually, that's not completely true, now that I think of it. One airplane, an Australian Caribou as I recall, did in fact land . . . and I suppose it's still there, since no airplane ever took off from ARO. In the end, the most frustrating thing about ARO was our mission, a mission that *could not* be accomplished.

The flight attendant's announcement of our descent into Atlanta disrupted my thoughts. Good, I said to myself. Time to stop mulling over the past and start thinking about the future. After all, third time's the charm, right? Next stop San Fran for a good meal, a night on Broadway, and then off to the land that God created during a coffee break.

Early the next evening, along with 160 or so other soldiers and Marines, several Air Force personnel, and a single sailor, I boarded a chartered World Airways flight and followed the sun westward. It was a more comfortable and far quicker passage than the previous two had been. All of us were military, and all would be staying in the Nam. Most of us would return home whole in body twelve months hence, some sooner in pieces, and in the fall of '67 it was a statistical certainty that others would make the long flight back in flag-draped coffins.

The flight crew, of course, was civilian and would not be spending a single night in the Nam. After dropping us off and picking up a load of Stateside returnees, they would fly on to spend their night's crew rest in some four-star Tokyo hotel.

There were no four-star hotels in Cam Ranh. Upon landing, the trip-long horseplay, laughter, and joking ended abruptly, replaced by an eerie silence. Finally, a young flight stewardess, who had boosted morale throughout our Pacific crossing, announced our arrival over the plane's PA system.

"Good morning! We have now landed at Cam Ranh Bay International, where the temperature is 101 degrees and climbing. Welcome to sunny Vietnam! Please remain seated until the aircraft comes to a complete stop. On behalf of the captain and crew of World Airways, we hope you've enjoyed your flight and we hope we . . . we hope we can fly all of you back home again, safe and sound twelve months from . . ." Her voice broke, and she paused, apparently on the verge of tears. Then poignantly, almost bitterly, she said, "We hope you'll be all right—damn it."

As we were about to disembark, a young sergeant, who had befriended the stewardess during the long flight, remarked that the war had claimed a childhood friend of hers only weeks before. She was not at the aircraft's door as we deplaned.

Things happened quickly at Cam Ranh. Entering a screened inbound-outbound transit facility, we began filing past those who, having completed their year in the Nam, were about to embark on our plane for their flight back to the "world." In doing so, we suffered their caustic remarks and catcalls.

"Hey, cherry, Charlie's gonna get ya!"

"Raw meat, raw meat!"

"Hey, cherry, only 365 more days. You're getting short."

"Raw meat, raw meat!"

"Hey, cherry, might as well go and draw your body bag now, 'cause you ain't gonna make it."

And to the tune of Stephen Foster's "Camp Town Races," a couple of them sang, off key:

Oh . . . your son came home in a rubber bag, doo dah, doo dah.
Your son came home in a rubber bag, just the other day.

Oh . . . you take his watch and I'll take his coin, doo dah, doo dah.
You take his watch and . . .

Most of us shouldered these ungracious remarks in sheepish
silence as we self-consciously shuffled past our outbound brethren,
although a couple of my fellow passengers invited the returnees to go
fuck themselves. In the interest of good military order, a somewhat
hung-over major who had been aboard our flight pulled a young outbound captain aside and, not so very politely, asked that he exercise
whatever leadership influence he might possess in quieting the "ob-
noxious cluster of people in uniform" surrounding him.

A bit reluctantly, but dutifully, the captain did as he was told, and
Nam-bound and world-bound passengers then filed past each other in
relative silence.

As we did so, I could not help but notice the very perceptible difference between the two groups of soldiers. Those with me were in
most cases pale, soft, and obviously diffident. Many were overweight;
virtually all were sweating profusely in their rumpled, ill-fitted uniforms. Those moving in the other direction were lean, mean, tanned,
and toughened by a year of humping a rucksack through the jungles
of Vietnam. They *looked* like soldiers in their faded, starched, and
tailored khakis, and they exhibited a palpable air of confidence. And
why not? They had succeeded at man's ultimate competitive folly, that
of armed conflict. Who says the Nam is hazardous to one's health? It
certainly isn't for those who survive it—of course, surviving is the
catch.

Cam Ranh's replacement center was big, hot, sandy, and safe. So
safe that our commander and chief, President Johnson, had visited the
installation, barely a year before, and lunched with those he was sending
into battle. So big that I hardly recognized it as the same deserted stretch
of coastal sand onto which we had routinely parachuted back in '63,
when it was little more than a sleepy fishing village.

In-processing was quick, efficient, and confined largely to record
checks and administrative assignment procedures. If one arrived early
in the day, he would normally have his in-country assignment that evening
and depart Cam Ranh the following morning. I was no exception, and
within twenty-four hours of arriving in Vietnam, I was seated aboard
a C-130 Hercules, en route to An Khe, home of the First Air Cavalry
Division.

An Khe, Vietnam

If you were to deplane at An Khe in the early fall of 1967, the first thing you'd undoubtedly note would be the Goliath replica of the First Cavalry's black-and-gold patch painted on the side of Hon Cong Mountain, the predominant terrain feature overlooking the division's sprawling headquarters at Camp Radcliff. You might next be impressed by the division's "golf course," which was not a golf course at all but acres of cleared, rolling terrain upon which the First Cavalry parked its fleet of nearly 450 helicopters, five times as many helicopters as were found in most infantry divisions. The third thing noted, as would probably be the case if you descended on virtually any other U.S. encampment in the country's central highlands, would be the searing heat and suffocating, reddish clay dust that lay atop everything it couldn't penetrate.

However, the First Air Cav—the division's cutting edge—was not located at Camp Radcliff in the early fall of 1967. The division's fighting brigades were battling Charlie on the Bong Son plain in Binh Dinh Province, an area heavily infested by the Communists for over two decades, and reinforcing the U.S. Marines in I Corps, the northernmost of South Vietnam's corps tactical areas. With the exception of a single base security battalion, the division's forces at An Khe were composed of support troops responsible for sustaining the fighting force in Bong Son and I Corps.

An important part of this sustainment responsibility was shouldered by Lieutenant Colonel Know. He assigned incoming officers to the outlying brigades . . . sometimes.

"Please try to understand, Captain," Major Bork, Colonel Know's assistant, said, "we don't need rifle company commanders out *there*. We need good staff officers back *here* . . . and that's why you're being assigned to the G-5 section."

"Sir, I didn't come over here to pass out soap and toothpaste," I replied. "I mean . . . uh . . . 'course all jobs are important, but I'd really prefer a rifle company. So why don't you just go ahead and send me to one of the brigades and let the next captain who walks through that door do his bit to win 'hearts and minds' for you, okay? Mean he'll probably make a better staff officer, anyway."

"No can do, Captain. My charter is to fill officer vacancies where they exist, and right now they exist here in division headquarters. Besides, six months in the field and six months on staff is the norm for our captains. Makes little difference if you pull staff on the front end or rear end of your tour."

"Makes a difference to me, sir. See, this is my third . . ."

"Sorry, but the issue is nonnegotiable. Now you just finish up remount and report to the G-5. Do a good job there for six months, and we'll see to it that you get your fill of the boonies on the down end of your tour. End of conversation."

Remount school was a short finishing course for the Cav's newly assigned officers and NCOs (noncommissioned officers). Emphasizing aerial insertion techniques that in 1967 were still somewhat unique to an airmobile division (the First Air Cavalry then being the only such division in existence), its curriculum included helicopter rappeling and ladder drills, air-assault techniques, aerial fire support, air movement and logistical support planning, and so on. Upon its conclusion, I reluctantly reported to my new assignment in civil affairs. I couldn't take it. Three days later I returned to Major Bork's office, this time to plead my case with Lieutenant Colonel Know himself.

He was most understanding of my plight and talked to me like a father. "Son, I know how you feel. Hell, wish I were out there commanding one of those battalions. But we've both been in the Army long enough to know we go where we're told to go . . . go where we're most needed. And the simple truth is, right now we need good staff officers here at division."

"Yes, sir. It's just that . . . uh . . . I don't think I'm good G-5 material. I mean, I've had no training or experience in civil affairs. What I'd really like . . ."

"Well, hell, I can understand that, son," he chimed in, interrupting me. "I don't blame you for being reluctant to spend six months in G-5, what with all that entails."

He gazed at me in thought for a moment and then said, "Tell you what I'm gonna do. We really need good staff writers in the division historical section. You go down there and give them three months of hard work; then I'll reconsider your request for line duty. Fair?"

"Sir, I want to be part of the division's history, not write about it. What I really want, as I told Major Bork here, is a shot at . . ."

Smiling warmly, he interrupted me again, put a fatherly hand on my shoulder, and said, "Give it a try, son. Just give it a try."

I did. I tried it for the next two hours as an elderly officer, who really should have retired or resigned in lieu of coming to Vietnam, showed me around his little empire in the division's historical section.

"We really got it made here, Estep. Division pretty much leaves us alone. Hell, they're too busy fighting the fucking gooks to bother with us. Here you got hot showers, clean sheets, patio barbecues 'bout every night, plenty of cheap booze, always free to make a run on the ville or try your luck with one of the doughnut dollies when you feel a 'whiteout' coming on . . . and all we got to do is document the division's activities at our own pace. What do you think? Ready to go to work?"

"Sir, no offense, but I'm gonna do everything in my power to get out of this assignment."

For a brief moment, he stared at me as if unable to comprehend my response. Then, smiling, he said, "No offense taken, Captain. Want to be a hero? Well, you just go on out there and get your ass shot off. I'll write about it."

Colonel Know was about to leave his office for the evening when I returned and informed him that although my interviewer in the division's historical section found me acceptable, I found him and his job unacceptable. The colonel did not look upon my announcement in what I felt to be a fatherly fashion.

Colonel Know, I discovered, was a man with a short temper. "Unacceptable, my ass!" he exploded. "I'm sick and tired of your goddamn bellyaching, Captain! Just who in the hell do you think you are to *pick* where you're gonna work in this organization? Who? Goddamn it!"

"Sir, I . . ."

"Don't 'sir' me, you insubordinate little sonofa . . . whatever!" he screamed as his face turned a deeper shade of red.

This man is obviously pissed! I said to myself. There's simply too much stress on this staff for me to be a part of it. I must serve in a calmer work environment . . . someplace like the boonies. I remained silent, however, recalling another of Sergeant Fallow's ageless axioms: "Always remember, Jimbo, a good ass chewing is really a beautiful thing to behold. Enjoy it; it's a disappearing art form."

"Now listen, Captain, and I'll *tell* you what you're going to do," Colonel Know continued in a calmer, more constrained voice. "You will report to the division historical section at 0700 hours tomorrow. There you will write the history of this division until such time as *I* feel it appropriate to reassign you . . . which may be three months from now, or six, or twelve. And, Captain, if I see you in this office again *before* I feel it appropriate to reassign you, or if you *dare* go over my head on this, whether it's to the chief of staff, IG [inspector general], chaplain, your congressman, or whoever, I'll see to it that you're still here writing the history of this *magnificent* division when the war's over and the rest of us have redeployed to the continental United States, be that two, five, or ten years from now!" His voice had risen steadily throughout this brief discourse and was once again approaching the screaming stage. "Do you read me loud and clear, Captain?"

I replied, "Yes, sir!" It seemed the appropriate thing to say.

That evening, in celebration of my new duties with the division's "hysterical" section, I decided to go to the Cav's headquarters officers' club . . . and get smashed. Working on my fourth or fifth Jim Beam and branch, I was well on my way to never-never land when Major Bork came over and sat down beside me. He too was visibly into his cups.

"Bastard's gonna make you write history, huh?" he commented more than asked.

"Yes, sir, gonna write the history of this *magnificent* division."

"You know what you ought to do, Estep? You know Colonel Lich? Pronounces his name like . . ." Bork smiled faintly, " . . . like 'like.' Uh . . . commands the base security battalion."

"No, sir, I don't *know* Colonel Lich . . . and I don't *like* Colonel Know. (Heh, heh.)"

Ignoring what I felt to be a really funny remark, he continued, "Well, if I were you, and I'm not, and I wanted to go to the boonies, and I don't, I'd go see Colonel Lich."

"Who's Colonel Lich? Shit, I know he's not my congressman. Is he the chief, IG, chaplain, or what?"

"No, goddamn it! I just told you. He's got the base security battalion, Fifth Cavalry. They'll be rotating back to Bong Son—LZ English or thereabout—in a couple of weeks. Why don't you go ask him to take you along? I mean, shit, if he'll accept you in his battalion, my boss will roll over. Bastard's not gonna fuck with a field commander's request for a line officer."

I left the club immediately. Later that night, after a hot shower, coffee, and a change of uniforms, I met with the commander of the base security battalion in his quarters. Lieutenant Colonel Lich was a decorated veteran of the Korean war, had previously served with Special Forces, currently commanded in the Fifth Cavalry with distinction, and would eventually command a Special Forces group in like fashion. In short, he was a soldier's soldier, through and through.

After hearing my tale of woe, which he thought somewhat humorous, he welcomed me to the Fifth Cavalry, telling me to pack my gear and report to his headquarters the following morning.

"The good Colonel Know can just find someone else to write his damn history, Estep."

I was ecstatic. "Yes, sir! Thank you, sir! Uh . . . and good night, sir."

"Not good night, Jim," he corrected me, "not in Robert E. Lee's former command. Here, we part with the salute 'Ready'!"

"Ready, sir!"

And I was.

Unfortunately, when Colonel Lich so graciously accepted me into his command, he didn't need another rifle company commander. What he really needed was a "good staff officer." Hence, I was assigned duties as the battalion's adjutant (the S-1). But what the hell, at least I was serving in a line battalion instead of writing the history of what line battalions do.

As Major Bork mentioned during our hazy conversation in the O club, the battalion was at the time pulling duty as the division's base security force. Although often referred to as a "stand down," it was not. True, soldiers performing this mission had an opportunity to shower and change uniforms far more frequently than they would've had they been in the boonies. And, unlike with duty in the boonies, they had hot meals, clubs, and movies and could occasionally make a run on An Khe's ville. However, these soldiers were responsible for all facets of Camp Radcliff's defense, including manning its vast perimeter and patroling its "doughnut ring." (The doughnut ring was essentially a no-fire zone surrounding the entire camp several kilometers beyond its outer defensive perimeter. Within this ring base security forces could patrol and ambush freely, day and night, confident they would not become accidental casualties of friendly artillery fire. It was a good idea and, inasmuch as Camp Radcliff was never attacked in force, obviously worked. In addition to these defensive responsibilities, the base security battalion underwent an intense refit-retrain program during its short stay at Radcliff. In sum, the battalion's soldiers stayed busy.

Before they sallied forth to again battle the North Vietnamese in

Binh Dinh Province, I had an opportunity to meet most of the battalion's officers and key NCOs and many of their soldiers, or "snuffies," as they were then called. Collectively, they possessed a phenomenally upbeat, can't-lose attitude toward the war and the enemy they fought—and well they should. In the two years since so soundly defeating North Vietnam's finest in the Ia Drang Valley, barely two months after the division's arrival in country, the First Air Cav had kicked Charlie's ass whenever and wherever it found him. The problem now lay in finding him. North Vietnam's military chief, Gen. Vo Nguyen Giap, had made this task difficult since concluding, after assessing his losses in the Ia Drang campaign, that his forces couldn't shove the American Army around with quite the same impunity they had enjoyed while fighting the French. Hence, he had placed his army on the tactical defensive, directing his commanders to avoid combat with U.S. ground forces in general and, we snuffies supposed, the First Air Cav in particular.

This can-do winning outlook was so ingrained in the minds of the division's soldiers that it influenced virtually every facet of their daily existence. They quite simply believed they were better than their foe. And of course they were. The account of a young Cav trooper's first night in I Corps, after deploying there with his unit from Binh Dinh, is illustrative of this attitude. Supposedly, he sat down under a palm tree, in the black of night, on a defensive perimeter shared with the Marine Corps . . . and lit a long cigar. Seeing this abhorrent breach of light discipline, a Marine Corps officer ordered him to extinguish his cigar, quite naturally fearing it would draw enemy fire. In response, the young soldier, still sitting with the glowing cigar between his teeth, calmly replied, "Relax, Lieutenant, Charlie don't *fuck* with the Cav!"

Granted, his quote will never go down in the annals of history alongside "damn the torpedoes," but, apocryphal or otherwise, it certainly embraced the division's purview toward the enemy.

Sergeant Major Cooper, our command sergeant major, was one of the most colorful of the battalion's soldiers. I had the opportunity of becoming acquainted with him during the brief interval before the unit returned to Binh Dinh. A hard-charging, hard-drinking, totally professional NCO from the top of his head to the tips of his toes, he knew full well the importance of relaxing in a combat environment when one had the opportunity to do so. I liked him.

Booze, the hard stuff, was not permitted in the boonies, and rightfully not. Therefore, it flowed quite freely during a unit's so-called stand down at An Khe, the division's soldiers viewing Camp Radcliff, after months in the boonies, in much the same fashion as sailors look upon their home port after a long tour at sea. One of the hutches in which booze flowed most freely was that of the command sergeant major.

In the waning days of the battalion's stay at An Khe, Cooper invited a couple of the company commanders, several of their lieutenants, and some of us on the staff to his hutch for evening cocktails. Arriving late, I found that the sergeant major and my fellow officers had been "cocktailing" for quite some while.

"Yeah, and that's the last I ever heard of young Romeo," Cooper was saying, laughingly, as I walked in.

"Who's Romeo?" I asked offhandedly, pulling up a chair.

"Who's Romeo, indeed!" the sergeant major responded. "Well that was before your time, Captain. Matter of fact, it was before the old man's time." (A unit's commander, in this case Colonel Lich, is traditionally, and respectfully, referred to as the "old man.") "Well, Romeo—which is what we called him, for reasons that will soon be obvious—was a young seventeen-year-old from the farmlands of Indiana . . . or was it Illinois?"

He paused momentarily, as if this aspect of Romeo's earlier existence might have some bearing on the story, then, evidently deciding it did not, continued. "Oh, well, no matter where the fuck he was from, he was a young stud who ain't never been off the farm till he was drafted and found himself in the Nam . . . where he fell in love."

He started laughing, as did the others, who obviously enjoyed hearing the saga of Romeo again as much as the sergeant major relished telling it.

But then abruptly he stopped laughing and, in a serious vein, said, "Gentlemen, the unfunny part of this tale is that we lost, the Army lost, what might otherwise have been a good soldier to a goddamn Communist whore!"

After a brief pause, he continued. "But that's neither here nor there. Hell, story's old as the Army itself and ain't anything you can really do 'bout it. Young man leaves the farm, goes overseas, and falls in love with the first hooker he puts it to, which, likely as not, is also the first broad he ever put it to. Anyway, our Romeo falls in love with this sweet young thing from the ville last time the battalion pulled base security—shit, nearly a year ago now. Well, falling in love's okay, but when it comes time to go back to the boonies, Romeo decides he's gonna stay in the ville with his true love . . . uh . . . you know the story, first love, can't live without her, Charlie might get him if he goes back, so on and so forth. So the battalion returns to the boonies and reports young Romeo AWOL. And next day the MPs go down to the ville, police him up, and return him to the rear detachment [the battalion's residual force at An Khe], where he's restricted to quarters till his company can be informed of his apprehension.

"Meanwhile, his true love returns to her family in Qui Nhon with matrimony on her mind. Well, Romeo, knowing that, decides to 'unrestrict' himself. So he just walks out of camp, boards a gook bus, and goes to Qui Nhon. A week or so later, the MPs find him there, pick him up, and bring him back to An Khe a second time.

"Now the rear detachment commander—that's your predecessor, sir," he said, looking at me, "what with being just a bit embarrassed 'bout his first disappearance, puts a guard with a loaded forty-five on Romeo and initiates an Article 32." (Article 32 of the Uniformed Code of Military Justice provides for a pretrial investigation of serious allegations to determine whether or not the alleged offense should be referred for court-martial.) "That same evening, the guard, feeling he needs a short break for a beer at the Black Horse, handcuffs Romeo to his bunk and takes leave."

The sergeant major paused briefly to collect his thoughts and mix himself another drink. Several of us followed suit.

"Now, as you might guess," he continued, again looking at me, "when the guard returned, both Romeo and the bunk were gone! Damn, now I think of it, we never did find that cot. Well anyway, the MPs now know where to find young Romeo, so they quickly police him up in Qui Nhon and bring him back here a third time. Needless to say, the RDC is pissed!" (The RDC was the rear detachment commander.) "So he decides to send Romeo to LBJ." (Cooper was not, in this context, referring to our commander in chief, Lyndon Baines Johnson; he was referring to the U.S. Army's correctional facility in Vietnam located at Long Binh, which snuffies called Long Binh Jail or simply LBJ.)

"So the RDC calls Battalion Forward and starts to set the wheels in motion for pretrial confinement. Well, Romeo's company commander hears about this and says, 'No way! Ain't no goddamn AWOL of mine gonna sit on his lazy ass at LBJ, safe and sound eating three hots a day, while the rest of us suffer out here. You put young Romeo on the next log bird flying, and he can pull his pretrial here in the boonies!' Which, when you think of it, made a lot of sense."

"Guess so," I offered. "Mean, if he's in the field with his company, he can hardly wander off to Qui Nhon at will."

"Exactly!" Cooper responded. "Especially the area his company was then working, up there in the mountains west of Happy Valley. I mean it was Indian country, Charlie's playground, the fucking jungle miles from nobody and nothing!"

Again he paused briefly, much as a comedian might just before the punch line, and noting the smirks on the faces of my fellow officers, I sensed we were nearing that point in the sergeant major's tale.

"So," he said, starting to laugh, "young Romeo goes back to the boonies on the evening log bird out of LZ English. Goes back to his platoon and the lieutenant puts him in a two-man fighting position for the night—you know, one up, one down" (meaning one man awake while the other sleeps).

"Well, when the company stands to at first light, Romeo's gone! Weapon, rucksack, and Romeo—gone!"

This still is not the punch line. They're laughing, but with restraint. There's more to come.

"Now Romeo's commander has no choice but to report him as an MIA," Cooper continued. "You know, give the guy and his family the benefit of the doubt, 'cause he's probably dead now, and if he ain't, at best, he'll turn up as a returned POW when this thing's finally over."

After a brief pause, he smiled and said, "Next night the MPs stumble across Romeo at his girlfriend's hutch in Qui Nhon! 'Course they pick him up and return him to An Khe for a fourth and final time."

Punch line!

After the laughter died down, the sergeant major wrapped up his saga of Romeo in a quasi-serious tone.

"So like I say, last I heard Romeo was at LBJ pending court-martial. By now he's probably making little ones out of big ones at Leavenworth. But you know, the Army shouldn't have sent young Romeo off to jail. Should have sent him back to the States and had him set up an escape-and-evasion course—teach pilots and other high-risk wieners how to evade Charlie should they get caught in the 'badlands.' I mean, can you even imagine somebody just walking out of a company perimeter like that, in the middle of the night, in the middle of the jungle, and working his way through forty or fifty miles of Indian country to Qui Nhon! Shit, true love knows no bounds!"

"I don't know, Top," a somewhat aged but trim and deeply tanned first lieutenant from Bravo Company remarked. "I mean all a guy's gotta do is make it down to Highway Nineteen, go east to Highway One, and follow it on in to Qui Nhon. Hell, your Romeo probably hitched a ride with the first deuce-and-a-half traveling Nineteen the morning after he left the company, knowing the snuffie driving it ain't gonna say a word 'bout picking him up."

"Okay, Lieutenant Russell," Cooper responded, "if you think it's nothing more than a fucking walk in the woods, why don't you just try it next time Bravo's working Happy Valley? I'll clear it with the old man, see to it that you get your picture in *Stars and Stripes*, and then we'll send *you* back to Benning to teach E&E!"

Russell just smiled in return, apparently satisfied that he had, to some small degree, dampened the grandeur of the sergeant major's tale. I later learned there was nothing vindictive in this; Cooper and Russell, himself a senior NCO before acquiring a commission, had known each other "since Christ was a corporal" and merely enjoyed being in near-constant verbal discord. I was also told that if Cooper appeared to be winning one of their frequent altercations, Russell delighted in taking that opportunity to remind him, regardless of what they might have been arguing about, that first lieutenants outrank sergeant majors—which is something I couldn't conceive *any* lieutenant suggesting to *any* sergeant major! However, still later that evening, after the conversation had turned from the exploits of Romeo to the prerogatives of rank, and cocktailing had gone from social grace to competitive sport, I witnessed Lieutenant Russell do just that.

"Now don't get me wrong, Top," he said in a somewhat slurred yet subtly antagonizing voice. "Mean, you've done pretty good for yourself. Hell, battalion sergeant major's a pretty weighty position, pretty weighty indeed. Still, you ain't no officer and never will be, and 'course that means every officer in the battalion—whole fucking Army, matter of fact—outranks you. But . . . uh . . . you being a professional *NCO* and all, I'm sure you understand that."

The sergeant major, sitting across the table from Russell, was steaming. First of all, he obviously didn't like being referred to as "Top," a pseudonym normally reserved for a company's first sergeant, not the battalion's command sergeant major—and of course Russell knew that. Secondly, he wasn't too excited about the gist of Russell's comments concerning the Army's rank structure.

"Listen, asshole . . ."

"That's Lieutenant Asshole, *sir*, to you, Top," Russell interjected, smiling antagonistically, drunkenly.

"As you wish, Lieutenant Asshole, *sir!*" Cooper defiantly replied while getting, a bit uncertainly, to his feet. "I know goddamn well you're playing with my mind, *sir,* but the simple fucking truth is you couldn't make eight!" (Russell had been a sergeant first class E-7 before being commissioned. If he had remained in the ranks, his next promotion would have been to the grade of E-8.) "Couldn't hack it as a first sergeant of a line company, so you decided to play candidate at Benning's school for boys and by some miracle or administrative error got a 'butter bar' out of it . . ."

"And butter bars also outrank sergeant majors, Top," Russell said, trying with little success to stand so as to be on an even keel with Cooper.

"Well, Lieutenant, *sir!* I'll let you in on a little secret. I could've done the same thing; any NCO worth his goddamn salt could've. But you see, *we* prefer soldiering for a living! *We* like to think our next promotion is gonna be based on our ability to soldier, not how long and how *brown* our fucking noses are! Still, if I had wanted to, I could've been twice the officer you'll ever be!"

"Oh, yeah! Well, let me just challenge you then, Top. If you really think you'd make twice the officer I am, well, why don't you just put yourself in for a *direct* commission . . . hummmm?" Lieutenant Russell pushed himself from the sergeant major's table, at which he and several of us were sitting, in a final valiant attempt to get to his feet. He failed and fell backwards in his chair, his head striking the hutch's concrete floor with a dull thud.

Somewhat unsteadily but still firmly on his feet, Cooper worked his way around the table, looked down at Russell—who had apparently decided the floor was as good a place as any to spend the rest of the night—and said, "Well, Russ, I may do just that. Yes, sir, I may just do that very thing."

And he did.

It was not so very long after the sergeant major's cocktail party, while Bravo Company was on perimeter security at LZ English, that

First Lieutenant Russell got a message ordering him to report to *Captain* Cooper at battalion headquarters forthwith. Allegedly, Russell's only comment was, "Oh, shit. And I'm gonna have to salute him, too."

Captain Cooper, of course, did not long remain with the Fifth Cavalry. For reasons I've never been quite able to discern, the Army takes a dim view of its former NCOs serving as officers in the same unit from which they were commissioned. Soon after becoming a captain, ex–Sergeant Major Cooper was transferred to the division's only mechanized battalion, there to assume command of a mechanized rifle company. And one bright and sunny day shortly thereafter, while Captain Cooper was standing in the turret atop his M-113 armored personnel carrier, a north Vietnamese sniper got lucky and put an AK-47 round right through the center of our ex–sergeant major's chest.

The battalion rotated back to the boonies, relieved of its Camp Radcliff security mission by the unit next in line for a stand down. I remained behind at An Khe.

The S-1 is the unit's adjutant. He is responsible for those administrative functions associated with promotions and reductions, pay, awards and decorations, law, discipline and order, troop morale (in Vietnam, one of the more demanding of his duties), and troop safety (another somewhat taxing aspect of his responsibilities in combat). In short, his duties are many and varied—and boring. I was not terribly excited about my new job.

Fortunately, my PSNCO (personnel services NCO, the S-1's principal enlisted assistant) liked his job, did it well, and knew more about my job than I could ever hope to learn. Hence, we soon developed a great working relationship; I stayed out of his way, spending much of my time forward with our troops, while he minded the store.

During these staff visits with the battalion's line companies, I listened to our soldiers' various S-1-related problems, trying to resolve them. Rarely, however, did these complaints revolve around traditional military personnel issues such as pay, awards, or similar administrative shortcomings. More often, they centered on their *mail*. Mail, mail, mail! It was precious, and if it was not received regularly, snuffie was convinced the Army's postal services were at fault. Regrettably, this was seldom the case; it was usually the fault of the sender.

To understand something of the infantryman's war in Vietnam, one must first know of his extraordinary desire, his unparalleled need, for letters from home—letters that were, in many respects, his only tangible link with the sanity of his existence on this planet. Frequently kept in the top of his helmet liner, they were read and reread until memorized, folded and refolded until Vietnam's harsh climate reduced them to little more than confetti.

Of course mail from home has been important to all soldiers in all wars, but I believe it never before meant quite so much as it did to the American infantryman in Vietnam. The reason is that seldom before has an American soldier been asked to make such a profound change in his life—a condemned man's transition from freedom to incarceration pales in comparison.

Snuffie usually arrived in his unit via an early morning or late evening helicopter sortie as an eighteen- or nineteen-year-old replacement. At this juncture he probably realized his chances of dying in the Nam were, statistically, greater than those of any other man in the unit he had just joined because he would remain in harm's way longest—the others were all "shorter" and would rotate home before he would. From this point on, with the possible exception of a seven-day rest-and-recuperation (R&R) leave (probably spent somewhere else in Asia), he would live each day of the next year in the surreal, virtually indescribable existence of the "boonie rat."

He would dig a hole each night and, if he were lucky and things remained quiet, sleep half a night in it; he might dig three hundred or more such holes before completing his tour. He would stand to before dawn each morning because, centuries before his birth, great tacticians had concluded that this was the time he's most vulnerable to attack. With no attack forthcoming, he would eat his cold C rations; shave and wash out of his helmet, when water was available; and then clean his weapon—a daily ritual he could, and often did, perform in total darkness. Then he would walk the mountains, the jungles, the plains, and the paddies of Vietnam seeking Charlie. At night, after swallowing his nauseating daily malaria pill and digging a new hole in a different location, he would mark another day off his "short-timer's" calendar.

He would rarely bathe because bathing facilities were rarely available, would wear no underwear because underwear rotted, would reek of the unwashed but would be unaware of it because everyone around him smelled the same. When it rained, he would get chillingly soaked and pray for the drying rays of the sun, and when the sun appeared, he would sweat mightily and pray for the cooling comfort of a tropical shower.

During his twelve-month tour as a boonie rat, there would be no movies, no television, no radio, and no Bob Hope—these were reserved for those serving in rear-echelon assignments. He would read the *Stars and Stripes* when those of the rear echelon remembered to send it out on the evening log bird, on those evenings the log bird flew.

Human nature being what it is, he would try to make friends upon joining his unit but would often find others reluctant to befriend him, the reality of infantry combat being what it is. He would eventually find a close friend only to lose him through rotation, evacuation, or death. He would then be reluctant to befriend others.

He would live this day-in, day-out existence of denial and repetition, of heat, sweat, cold, mud, dust, boredom, and at times stark terror, until he was wounded, was killed, or completed his tour. Before that happened, he would very likely kill a fellow human being on at least one occasion. He would undergo all of this while his country was at peace and his more fortunate civilian counterpart was reaping the benefits of a prosperous nation ten thousand miles and another world away. His only anchor to his past, to the reality that that world still existed, was through those letters from home.

And too many of those letters were eventually stamped "Search."

"Sir, the reason they're on your desk is 'cause existing regulations dictate that an officer, normally the unit's S-1, review all Search mail before returning it to the division AG," my ever technically astute PSNCO explained.

"But why do we stamp them Search?" I replied. "Why not KIA, like you see in the movies? What the hell we searching for anyway?"

"Sir, we're not searching for anything. I mean Search doesn't mean *search*. It merely means the service member is dead, killed in action. You know, sort of a code word. Uh . . . guess it's kind of a morale thing; the Army just doesn't want a bunch of letters out there with KIA stamped all over them. Shit, somebody might think we're at war!"

"Okay. Understand. Now what happens to it after we verify the man is indeed dead . . . I mean 'searched'?"

"Beats me, sir. I don't know if they return it to the sender, forward it to the next of kin, shit-can it, or what. We just send it back to division AG stamped Search."

So, along with my other duties, I reviewed our Search mail, comparing the names of addressees with those listed on our rosters of battle losses. It was a depressing chore, especially with Christmas of '67 rapidly approaching, bringing in its wake holiday greeting cards marked Search.

Understandably, mail addressed to the most recent of our fallen was usually from the victim's immediate family—a father's or mother's letter to their son, a wife's letter to her husband. Of course, mail of this nature was nearly always postmarked before the soldier was killed, and by the time it crossed my desk, the father or mother knew they no longer had a son, or wife a husband. However, I was surprised at the number of letters addressed to soldiers who had died weeks or even months before. These were from friends (or I suppose other acquaintances) who were evidently disassociated from the victim's family and therefore not encompassed in the Army's casualty notification process—perhaps a fellow trainee during basic, an old school chum, a girl he might have met at Fort Benning, Jackson, Polk, or Dix. *Search!*

Fortunately, this disheartening task was soon someone else's responsibility. My short-lived tenure as a battalion S-1 ended abruptly late one night in early December when Colonel Lich sent word for me to report, "bag and baggage," to him at Battalion Forward, the following morning. Upon doing so, I learned he had relieved one of his company commanders the day before.

And I was that company's new "Comanche Six."

Bong Son Bridge, Binh Dinh Province: December 1967

At the time, Charlie Company was guarding Highway One's Bong Son bridge on the An Lao River in Binh Dinh Province. The evening log bird (logistics helicopter, normally a UH-1D [Huey]) deposited me, along with our evening meal, on the bridge at dusk. Within minutes of it having arrived, I made two observations: many of those who greeted me had been drinking, a couple excessively, and virtually all who greeted me held their previous company commander in high esteem, believing his relief to have been at best premature. With these truths in mind and recognizing discretion as being the better part of valor, I decided to retire to my bunker for the evening and start afresh with my new command the following morning.

Later that night, First Lieutenant Brightly, the company's attached artillery FO (forward observer), visited my sandbagged encampment and provided me his unsolicited evaluation of the company from A to Z, what was right with it (in his mind not an awful lot) and what was wrong with it (as he perceived it quite a bit). He was opinionated, somewhat intoxicated, and slightly disrespectful. He was also, I soon discovered, correct in much of what he said.

"Company's fucking shell shocked, sir. I mean they're goofy . . . uh . . . know what I mean?"

"No, I don't know what you mean by 'goofy.' Are you talking drugs?" I replied.

"Hell, no. And by the way, call me Slim, sir. Hell, I'm your Foxtrot Oscar, we're gonna be close. FO and CO gotta be close, 'cause you can save my fucking ass, and I for goddamn sure can save yours. 'Member, I'm the link between you and all the artillery in the fucking free world! FO and CO gotta be close, figuratively and literally. Me and the outgoing Six were close—yeah, close—and that's why I know what's wrong with this fucking outfit.

"Shit, it ain't drugs, and it *ain't* booze . . ." He paused momentarily, smiling, ". . . I mean regardless of what you've seen here tonight, hooch ain't a problem in the company; we see very damn little of that! And it's not snuffie either. Shit, company's got the best soldiers in the division, whole goddamn Army, matter of fact. It's Charlie. And the war. And luck, or the lack of it."

"Slim, you're gonna have to spell it out clearer than that," I said, unable to comprehend the drift of his rambling. "I mean I don't believe in luck or omens."

"Well, shit, neither do I!" he responded, almost indignantly. "But see, the company's had a bunch of folk killed in the last two, three months, more wounded. Snipers, booby traps, little piss-ant ambushes, you name it. And sir, we ain't even seen a fucking gook! Snuffie's saying he's in a hard-luck company. Fuck, every time we get into something, it's our guys who buy the farm or go out on dust off."

After a moment's silence, I asked, "Well, Slim, if that's the problem, what's the solution?"

"Solution! Shit, sir, the *solution* is to kill some fucking gooks! Solution is to get the body count going the other way. Company needs to see some dead dinks out there. That's the fucking solution!"

He was right. The company had suffered several costly "hits" with little to show in return. Largely because of this, many of our soldiers now perceived self-survival to be the predominate *unit* objective. Such a precept is dangerous since it weakens unit cohesiveness and, hence, combat effectiveness. And in infantry combat, as in all other facets of conflict, the strong destroy the weak.

Charlie Company was an airmobile rifle company that, at any given time, had a foxhole strength (the number of combat-deployable soldiers) of approximately 130 men. It was organized into three rifle platoons—the company's "cutting edge"—each carrying thirty to thirty-five men on its rolls; a weapons platoon of fifteen to twenty soldiers; and the command section composed of myself, the first sergeant, my two RTOs (radio telephone operators), a medic, and an attached artillery FO and his recon sergeant. Each of the platoons was commanded by a lieutenant and was normally referred to by that lieutenant's call sign on the company command (radio) net. Thus, 1st Platoon was called "One Six"; 2d, "Two Six"; and so on.

With the exception of vehicles, we were equipped basically the same as any other light-infantry rifle company. We had no need of vehicles, since we winged our way to war aboard helicopters.

Remaining on the bridge for another week, we trained, reequipped, suffered the constant red dust of endless military convoys traveling Highway One during the day, and slept on the damp floors of our sandbagged bunkers at night. In the meantime, I talked with our soldiers as opportunity availed itself, in doing so learning something of their frustrations. Not surprisingly, these centered on being away from home, in the Nam, in the infantry, in a hard-luck company that they felt too often came out on the losing end of the stick when confronting Charlie. Unlike the rest of the battalion—and certainly the division as a whole—which felt Charlie to be a second-rate opponent, in the minds of some of my soldiers the enemy had assumed an almost supernatural status. He was everywhere, behind every tree, beneath every rock, just waiting for an unsuspecting C Company to stumble across him. He was perceived by these soldiers to be a winner, a better and more competent warrior.

I knew, as did many others in the company, that this simply wasn't true. Charlie was good and should be so regarded; however, he was no superman, and he sure as hell could be beaten!

One of those who knew he could be beaten was my first sergeant, Sergeant Sullivan. Referred to by the troops as the "Bull," he was a tall, slim, wiry individual with a deeply tanned, weather-beaten face that sat under a closely cropped, grayish blond crew cut. He looked more like an aged SS storm trooper than like a bull. Or perhaps, more accurately, he looked like . . . a first sergeant.

Unfortunately, ours was not a case of love at first sight. Sergeant Sullivan was angry over the relief of his former commander and did little to hide his bitterness. And although he held me blameless for this turn of events, I was quite obviously the most visible reminder of his commander's impetuous departure. I, in turn, was angered by what I felt to be his misplaced loyalty and surly manner, and I briefly toyed with the idea of having him and my executive officer exchange places at company trains. (In the Nam, a rifle company's rear-echelon logistics base—normally collocated with battalion trains—was usually supervised by the company's executive officer or its first sergeant, the choice, of course, being left to the company commander concerned.) But Sergeant Sullivan would have none of that!

"Sir, don't even think it!" he said when I suggested the possibility of such a switch. "First sergeant's place is with the troops! Always!"

"Well, First Sergeant, I agree in theory; however, other first sergeants are in charge of trains, and they . . ."

"And they don't deserve to be called 'first sergeant,' sir!" he loudly interjected. "Good God, how can they look their soldiers in the eye when they conduct their so-called field visits or when the company stands down?"

He paused briefly and then in a calmer voice said, "Sir, I know you're upset 'cause I'm upset over your predecessor's relief, and I ain't doing an awful lot to hide my feelings. Well, rest assured, I know you're Comanche Six now, and you won't find a more loyal first soldier than me."

He smiled and added, "Shit, sir, I'm like an old wife now and then. Just gotta give me a couple days to work all this piss and vinegar out of my system."

I relented, thinking to myself, Would I think more of him had he embraced me with open arms upon my arrival and slandered my predecessor? Would he be a better first sergeant had he not possessed these lingering ties of loyalty to his former commander? Hardly.

My first sergeant and I avoided each other during our brief stay on the bridge, he going about his business—"working piss and vinegar out of his system"—and I going about mine. But that was okay.

The Bull and I would become close enough, soon enough. And I would soon discover that had I insisted on putting him in charge of our trains, I would have made the first and in all likelihood the biggest mistake of my tenure with the company. Because he was right; the first sergeant's place is with the troops—always. Moreover, I would find that there were many things I could discuss freely with my first sergeant that I would have felt uncomfortable talking about with my own officers—and would certainly have never mentioned to Colonel Lich or any of his minions. And there were many things I could learn from my first sergeant that these others could never teach me.

Looking back on it, company command would have been a lonely and dismal experience indeed had it not been for First Sergeant Sullivan.

PAYBACK TIME FOR CHARLIE COMPANY

"Battalion Three's on the horn, sir," Specialist Four Blair, my battalion RTO, said, passing me his radio handset.

"Comanche Six, this is Arizona Three, inbound your location in zero five with four, plus two, plus two. How copy? Over."

"This is Comanche Six," I replied. "Roger, that's a good . . . copy . . . uh . . . we'll be standing by. Out."

Our sort-of stand down on Bong Son's bridge had come to an end. Major Byson, the battalion's S-3 (Arizona Three), had radioed us a fragmentary order the night before, sending Charlie Company back to the boonies.

DTG 182145L DEC. FRAGO. TALL COMANCHE CONDUCTS AIR ASSAULT ON LZ DAISY, POINT OF ORIGIN RIGHT THREE TWO, UP ZERO FOUR, AT 190900 LOCAL DEC, VIA FOUR [UH-1D "Iroquois" troop-assault helicopters— "slicks"], PLUS TWO [CH-47 "Chinook" troop-transport helicopters— "hooks"], PLUS TWO [AH-1G "Cobra" attack helicopters], TO SEEK AND DESTROY ENEMY IN AO TIGER THREE. BLUE MAX [radio call sign for the division's aerial rocket artillery, or ARA] SUPPORTS INITIAL ASSAULT. DS ARTY PROVIDES TWO-MINUTE LZ PREP AND SUBSEQUENT FIRES ON CALL. CURRENT CEOI IN EFFECT. ACKNOWLDEGE.

After receiving Byson's message, I had spent nearly two hours preparing the company's air-assault order, relying heavily on a pound or more of laminated doctrinal material I'd "liberated" from the Infantry School's air-operations department before departing Fort Benning. My efforts, I thought, had not been in vain. It was a model air-assault order, written strictly in accordance with the doctrinal requirements of those who teach others how to do such things. It had everything—assembly procedures, load plans, stick orders, helicopter ACLs (allowable cargo loads), contingency considerations en route, and, at the objective, LZ consolidation plans, fires, and on and on.

Having issued this work of art to my platoon leaders late the night before, I'd gone over it with them a second time after the morning log bird departed. Now, with our helicopters only five minutes out, we were once again assembled as I tried for the third time to explain my order to them—and they still couldn't quite grasp it.

"Sir, I take the slicks, right?"

I turned to Lieutenant MacCarty, 2d Platoon, and somewhat impatiently replied, "Yes, Lieutenant, *you* take the slicks. I've stated that as clearly as I know how under paragraph three, 'execution,' subparagraph b, 'subordinate unit tasks,' and I quote, '2d Platoon conducts initial assault, via four UH-1D helicopters, to secure LZ Daisy. Is that clear?"

"Uh . . . yes, sir, that's clear, but somewhere else in there you mentioned something 'bout the ACL and cross-loading . . ."

"Right," I quickly responded, "that's under paragraph three c, 'coordinating instructions.' As I see it, based on what we know of the LZ's air density and altitude, coupled with the info Three sent us, the approximate ACL per Huey is eight men. You have a foxhole strength of twenty-eight soldiers; there's five of us in the command section. That's a total of thirty-three, which means we exceed our ACL by one person. So you coordinate with Lieutenant Norwalk aboard the first Chinook and . . ."

Suddenly, I heard the familiar *whump, whump, whump* sound of inbound helicopters. All heads turned to see four dots on the southern horizon, closing fast.

Oh shit!

"Slicks on final, sir! Two minutes!" Blair yelled from where he stood atop the bridge's command bunker, his AN/PRC-25 radio at his feet.

Oh, double shit!

I turned to my leaders, who as one looked back at me in total bewilderment.

Sergeant Marvel, Weapons Platoon leader (the platoon had no officer assigned), broke an uneasy silence by somewhat meekly asking, "Sir, where do you want my people to go? I still don't really understand . . ."

Fuck! I can't believe this!

"Sergeant," I replied as calmly as possible, "you take the second Chinook . . . or is it the first? No, I think you have to divide your people between . . . wait a sec, goddamn it, I have the numbers right here under paragraph . . ."

The *whump, whump* of the inbound Hueys was noticeably louder when 1st Sgt. Bull Sullivan decided to intervene and save his new commander's ass.

"Sir, why don't you let me try to clarify your order?"

"First Sergeant, please be my guest," I hastily responded, hoping for some small miracle on his part.

"Okay, you want Two Six to conduct the assault and the rest of the company to follow in the hooks, right?"

"You got it, First Sergeant. That's the order in a nutshell."

He turned to Lieutenant MacCarty and said, "Sir, you take the slicks and go in hot. Make room for headquarters on number four."

MacCarty gave a thumbs up and replied, "Right, Top."

Turning back to me momentarily, Sergeant Sullivan asked, "You *did* want to go in with the assault, didn't you, sir?"

"Of course I go in with the assault. See, it's right here under paragraph five, 'command and signal,' 'Company headquarters initially accompanies' . . . oh, to hell with it."

He had already turned to Lieutenant Norwalk, 1st Platoon. "Sir, you take the first hook, okay?"

"Right, Top."

Then, speaking to Lieutenant Halloway, 3d Platoon, he said, "Three Six, you've got the second hook."

"Right, Top."

Finally, turning to Sergeant Marvel, "Haden, split your people between the two hooks and consolidate on the LZ."

"Right, Top."

"Any questions?"

In unison, "No, Top."

And they assembled and loaded, quickly and efficiently. The lift-off went like clockwork, letter perfect, smooth as Thai silk.

On the way to our helicopter, just before taking off, Sergeant Sullivan mentioned that he had normally handled the company's air movements under the previous commander, and, if I so desired, he would continue to do so during my tenure.

"Gives me something to do, sir, and takes another little piss-ant admin burden off your back. I mean you ain't got time for this small shit."

I couldn't have agreed more and assured him, with perhaps more enthusiasm than I intended to show as his new commander, that henceforth he was the company's "air-movement officer."

Before boarding the Huey, I threw my pound or so of laminated air-assault doctrine in the nearest fifty-gallon trash drum, recalling as I did so another of Sergeant Fallow's military axioms, "There's the way it's taught, and the way it's done, and in combat, any similarity between the two is usually a matter of pure coincidence."

AO Tiger was located in western central Binh Dinh, encompassing portions of the province's Bong Son plain and the mountains beyond. The plain was sparsely populated, composed mainly of rice paddies and lightly vegetated, gently rolling terrain. The mountains were generally uninhabited—except for the enemy—steep and densely vegetated under double- and triple-canopy rain forest. LZ Daisy lay at the base of the mountains.

Shortly after lifting off from the bridge, the number-four Huey's crew chief had handed me a headset, enabling me to monitor Major Byson on the battalion command net. As the S-3, he controlled the assault until such time as we were on the ground and the LZ was secured.

Now, at two minutes and seconds before touchdown, I overheard him working our artillery preparation. "Roger, I have rounds on the way, wait . . ."

Leaning out of the helicopter's door, into its ninety-knot slipstream, I saw our distant LZ suddenly explode in an orange-white-and-gray fury, as the artillery rounds threw foliage, dirt, dust, and debris high into the calm morning air.

Beautiful! I thought to myself. Sure as hell beats those nonprepped, door-gunner-only-supported inserts we used to make around and about ARO.

In the First Cavalry, as in most U.S. divisions in Vietnam, it was pretty much standard procedure to fire a short artillery preparation on any LZ that could conceivably be occupied by the enemy, which, of course, was virtually any LZ *not* occupied by friendly forces. Due to the number of air assaults made daily in the division and the ensuing expenditure of artillery ammunition, the cost-effectiveness of such a policy was sometimes questioned by those who involve themselves in such trivia. Obviously, it was only "cost-effective" if Charlie was indeed waiting in ambush on the landing zone. Having once seen the consequences of such an ambush, I quickly became an avid supporter of preassault artillery preps.

We were on fifteen-second final, coming in fast and low, skimming the treetops twenty or thirty feet below, when the last artillery round (white smoke) impacted. As our helicopters flared tails down, preparing to land, the two accompanying Cobra gunships roared past us on our flanks, pouring 2.75-inch rocket and 7.62-mm minigun fire on the LZ's perimeter. Finally, as the Hueys' skids were about to graze the landing zone's protruding foliage, our door gunners opened up with their M-60 machine guns. We were off the helicopters in a split second. They were gone just as quickly, clearing the trees on the far side of the LZ, gaining altitude and airspeed as they did so.

Within a matter of another very few seconds, Two Six had secured the LZ. They accomplished this by establishing defensive positions around its perimeter using a clock system to appropriate sectors of responsibility. In other words, an imaginary face of a clock was superimposed over the LZ, twelve o'clock being the direction of inbound flight—that is, the nose of the lead helicopter was pointing at twelve o'clock. Upon disembarking, each of the platoon's three rifle squads was responsible for securing and defending a twenty-minute portion of this circle, or one-third of the LZ. After the remainder of the company landed, the perimeter would be extended outward, a twenty-minute portion of it being allocated to each of the company's three line platoons. This system of assigning initial defensive responsibilities was standard practice in securing a night defensive position (NDP), LZ, and other perimeter-oriented defenses. And inasmuch as there were few linear fronts in the Nam, the perimeter—circle the wagons—was virtually the only defense used.

"Arizona Three, this is Comanche Six. Lima Zulu is green. I say again, LZ green. Over," I said, radioing Major Byson and informing him that the landing zone was secure.

Orbiting above us in the battalion C&C ship (command-and-control helicopter—a Huey outfitted with extensive communications assets), he replied, almost nonchalantly, "Okay, Comanche, I'll be out of here soon as I get your hooks in. Good luck and good hunting in the high country. Out."

The Chinooks landed in trail, discharging the rest of the company. As they descended, and again when they ascended, we turned our backs to them, bracing ourselves against the violent downdraft created by their rotary blades spinning at near full pitch. In the meantime, the Cobra gunships continued to circle the LZ, protecting the Chinooks until they had lifted off and were out of harm's way. Our eight helicopters quickly became but mere specks on the eastern horizon—and Charlie Company was on its own.

If our elusive foe was to be found on this bright December day, we assumed we would find him in the mountains west of Daisy. With this in mind, I had initially toyed with the idea of sending the company's three rifle platoons into the mountains on separate routes in order to cover as much of our opponent's lair as possible. However, this suggestion, when offered the night before, was not met with wild enthusiasm by some of the company's more cautious men, who felt it to be too risky. Others of us thought this was but manifestation of the "Charlie's-everywhere" syndrome. However, I did feel that our first operation, a "shakedown," so to speak, should risk little while hopefully building confidence among our rank and file. Therefore, we had decided to work the mountains with two platoons on a single route while the remainder of the company, Weapons and 3d Platoon, searched the valley floor, seeking both Charlie and a good location for an NDP.

Leaving Lieutenant Halloway in charge below, we began our foray into Byson's high country ten minutes or so after our helicopters departed. Movement was difficult from the start. Barely nine-thirty in the morning, the heat and humidity were already unbearable, and within a matter of minutes, our sweat-soaked jungle fatigues had transformed themselves to a darker shade of green.

Following one of several narrow trails leading from the valley's low-lying rice paddies into the lightly vegetated foothills and then, the ascent becoming decidedly steeper, up the eastern side of the mountain, we climbed . . . hour after exhausting hour. Finally, nearing the mountain's crest, we paused, noting that our trail had leveled off somewhat and now seemed to run generally parallel to the mountain's face in a north-south direction. We also noted it was well, and recently, traveled.

"Fresh hoofprints, sir," Lieutenant MacCarty whispered, pointing at the telltale footprints in a portion of the trail wetted by the mountain's runoff. "These aren't VC; they're NVA, and a lot of 'em!"

"Yeah," I whispered in return, "and most of them seem to be moving the same way, north to south."

Cautiously, we continued moving north along the narrow trail. And, I observed with satisfaction, we were moving as men ought to move in such a situation. Proper distances were maintained, there was no talking or horseplay, and weapons were kept at the ready, trained on both sides of the trail. These soldiers of Charlie Company were quite obviously professionals who knew what they were doing and were deadly serious about doing it. I was impressed.

Twenty meters or so to our front, a single point man led the column, followed by his squad leader and a two-man M-60 machine-gun team. Lieutenant MacCarty and his RTO were behind the machine-gun team, with me and my two RTOs trailing him. Lieutenant Norwalk and his 1st Platoon trailed Two Six.

Not at all the way we taught it at Benning, I thought to myself. But, like Al Fallow says, There's the way it's taught and the way it's done.

Yet it made sense in this kind of war, in this kind of terrain. We knew that if we found Charlie it would in all likelihood be by means of a frontal meeting engagement; in other words, the two of us would just run into each other. If that should happen, it was important that we have two assets well forward: firepower and leadership. Few things are more frustrating to a commander than finding himself midway in a column moving through dense vegetation when a firefight suddenly erupts a hundred meters and two platoons to his front.

Bam! Bam! Bam!

Three ear-shattering rifle shots from the point man's M-16 abruptly interrupted my philosophical wanderings concerning small-unit tactics in a jungle environment.

Everyone dived to the ground, training their weapons on the thick foliage flanking the trail but holding their fire.

Simultaneously the point man yelled, "I got that dink sonofabitch, know I got him!"

MacCarty and I ran forward to find our point man grinning excitedly, and perhaps a bit nervously. In his hand he held a Chinese SKS carbine, now legally his as a war trophy.

"I got him, LT! You ain't believing it! Fucker's just bopping along like he ain't got a care in the world. Had his weapon shoulder slung, fucking sloppy. But I got him, got him dead in the chest, sir, I mean blew him *away!* The mother ain't gonna go far."

Sure enough, we had a good blood trail. Leaving the rest of the column in a hasty trail-watch defense, we cautiously followed the blood markings north, accompanied by MacCarty's leading rifle squad. Within a matter of minutes we found our quarry wedged between two fallen trees about fifteen feet off the trail. Although it was obviously a painful task, he was busily trying to conceal himself with whatever vegetation he could grasp.

Our point man was right. He had hit his foe dead center in the chest, collapsing a lung and producing a hole in his back the size of a baseball. Gazing up at us, the wounded soldier's eyes reflected a dead certainty that regardless of how lucky he might have been in surviving his initial encounter with Charlie Company, the coup de grace was to be administered momentarily.

Taking the extended handset from Specialist Anderson, my company RTO, I told Lieutenant Norwalk to bring the rest of the column forward. Upon its arrival moments later, "Doc" Heard, our company medic, went to work doing what he could to patch up our wounded captive. As he did so, I reported our contact to battalion, requesting a dust off (aerial medical evacuation) for our prisoner. Overhearing me, Heard yelled out that the man could not survive the trip down the mountain and would have to be picked up in place.

This meant the dust-off helicopter would have to hover over us, using a jungle penetrator to retrieve the wounded soldier. This procedure would in turn reveal our location on the mountain to anyone who might be watching. And some of Charlie Company's rank and file looked upon this with disfavor.

Pulling me aside, Lieutenant MacCarty said, "Sir, you can't do this, not to save one fucking gook. Hell, leave him here for his own to find, or if he's gotta be evac'd, let's take him back down the mountain. He buys the farm en route, to hell with it; we did what we could."

"Perhaps, but higher ain't gonna get much intel out of a dead man, right? Besides, hooking him to that penetrator won't take but a matter of minutes, and we'll be long gone before anyone watching has a chance to react."

Seeing that he was unsatisfied with my response, I added, "Hey,

Mac, it'll be all right. And anyway, we don't have any choice. I mean we just don't leave enemy wounded to die. It's not the way the game is played."

He looked at me a moment and then, a bit cuttingly, said, "This is not a *game*, Captain!"

"I know that, Mac. Poor choice of words. Now let's just get the guy out of here. We'll talk about all of this later."

But we never did.

The medevac was uneventful. We moved our wounded prisoner fifty meters or so back down the trail to a point where we felt the jungle penetrator (basically a steel shaft with retractable arms upon which an evacuee was seated and secured) could most easily access the forest's thick canopy. Hearing the helicopter overhead, we marked our position with colored smoke and minutes later had our captive tied to the penetrator, which had been lowered to us by means of a retrievable steel cable.

As the prisoner was being hoisted upward, one of our soldiers gave a thumbs up to the crew chief aboard the helicopter. Our wounded prisoner, evidently believing the gesture was meant for him, weakly returned the thumbs up and briefly smiled at us below.

Mac's wrong, I thought silently. In many ways it is a game, a competitive sport, the ultimate of man's competitive follies.

Later that night we learned our captive had died en route to an ARVN (Army of the Republic of Vietnam) hospital in Qui Nhon. Perhaps it was just as well; he wouldn't have lasted long in an ARVN hospital.

Working our way down the mountain on a different route of regress, we ended up on the valley floor about a half a mile from where we'd started our climb that morning. With the company again consolidated, we set up our NDP a short distance from Daisy, which was where 3d and Weapons Platoons had waited out most of their day uneventfully.

In the Nam there were generally two schools of thought on the establishment of NDPs. The first, and I suppose most prevalent, embraced a policy of getting into the NDP as early as possible so as to have sufficient daylight for optimal defensive preparations—in other words, plenty of time to clear fields of fire, dig fortifications, set up claymores and trip flares, send out listening posts and ambush patrols, and so on and so forth. In my mind, the drawback to this line of thinking was twofold: first, time spent preparing an NDP was time *not* spent looking for Charlie, and finding and destroying Charlie was the only reason the American infantryman had for being in Vietnam. Second, the longer a unit spent organizing its defenses, the longer the enemy had to ready himself for an attack.

We of Charlie Company were proponents of the second school, believing it best to enter our NDP late in the day, thereby reducing the enemy's ability to react to our choice of site. Charlie was good, but he was slow and needed time to prepare his attacks. However, to further confuse our enemy, we would sometimes enter our NDP early in the evening, set up a hasty defense, bring in the log bird, and then after dark move a kilometer or so to a second NDP at a previously selected location.

On my first evening with the company in the boonies, we established our defenses in generally the same manner we would throughout my tenure. Each of the three rifle platoons assumed responsibility for a third of the perimeter's periphery. Within their assigned sectors, the platoon's soldiers prepared two- or three-man fighting positions, to the front—or enemy side—of which they cleared fields of fire, set out trip flares, and, between the trip flares and fighting positions, emplaced command-detonated claymore mines. In addition to manning this defensive trace encompassing one-third of the company's perimeter, each of the platoons normally established a listening post (LP) on the enemy's side of the trip flares and a squad or fire-team ambush astride a likely enemy avenue of approach at some greater distance. In the Cav these ambushes were traditionally, and quasi officially, referred to as "trick-or-treat" sites.

Weapons Platoon located itself centrally within our defensive circle, manning their guns (one or two 81-mm mortars) when we opted to bring them forward on the evening log bird, acting as the company's reserve when we did not.

We in the headquarters section would usually collocate ourselves with Weapons Platoon or one of the line platoon's command posts (CPs).

Viewing the company's perimeter from above, it rarely depicted a circle; more commonly it looked like an irregular, deflated football. The nature of the terrain we defended, of course, mainly determined the perimeter's outline.

After we established our defensive positions for the night and while we waited for the log bird to bring in our rucks (rucksacks) and a "hot" (meal), the talk turned to the day's action on the mountain. Two Six's point man related his "kill" to anyone willing to listen, and, as killing the enemy was a somewhat unique experience in Charlie Company, virtually everyone was willing to listen.

"Yeah, man, oughta seen 'em rounds hit the dink. Ping! Ping! Ping! I mean blew him *away!* See, he's just bopping along like he owns the fucking mountain, and 'bam!' I put a hole in his chest what you can see daylight through. Dink looks at me, sorta surprised like, and . . ."

"Shit, we know you waxed him, Lean Man," one of the point man's onlooking listeners said, interrupting him, "but if you hit him all that good, why the fuck you have to chase him a mile or so up the trail 'fore you found him 'bout to bury himself, huh?"

The point man, smiling, responded by comparing his kill to a species of snake indigenous to his native Georgia mountains. "Well, see, these dinks, they different from us. They sorta like them timber rattlers back home. You can cut the heads off of 'em, but they keep on wiggling and crawling 'cause they don't die till the sun sets. These dinks here, they the same way. Fuck, they so used to doing things at night, they ain't never learned how to die 'cept in the dark."

"Bullshit!"

"Ain't no bullshit, man! No matter how many caps you pop, gotta chase Chuck till sundown. 'Cause they night people. Why you think their eyes look like . . ."

But it was no joking matter. I was concerned about our enemy's ability to elude us after suffering such a serious, indeed, mortal, gunshot wound—a wound that would have stopped most of us dead in our tracks. And this man was not atypical. Recalling previous experiences with our foe and countless accounts from other combat participants, it seemed to me you had to literally shoot his legs out from under him to stop him in place. After thinking about this for a while, I decided that the claymore mine was perhaps the weapon to do just that.

But I was also concerned about the manner in which we had initiated the engagement, in effect by just running into our enemy. Moving up and down such a well-traveled trail seeking Charlie seemed to make little sense, and it could be dangerous. Inasmuch as we could access the main north-south trail from any of several ascending routes on the valley floor, it seemed wiser to interdict it in ambush at different points and wait for our enemy to come to us.

With these thoughts in mind, I assembled Charlie Company's platoon leaders to discuss the next day's operation. The offshoot of this parley was that Two Six, having had its moment of glory, would man the company's base, conducting screening patrols around its perimeter, while Three Six worked the valley floor in a broad sweep looking for signs of enemy movement between the sparsely populated plain and supposedly uninhabited mountains to the west. One Six would return to the mountain and test our daylight trick-or-treat concept.

Shortly after breaking up our little war conference, the evening log bird arrived and off-loaded ammunition and water.

Tactical situation and weather permitting, deployed Cav units were resupplied nightly, ammunition being the first priority of resupply, water the second, rations the third, and comfort items (our rucks) the last. Normally the evening log bird flew two sorties, carrying ammo and water on the first and next day's C rations, a hot meal (A or B rations), and sling-loaded rucksacks on the second. The rucks were backhauled to battalion trains each morning, relieving us of the requirement of carrying them during the day, which in turn put us pretty much on an even par with our lightly encumbered and highly mobile enemy. Lacking the airmobile assets organic to the Cav, other U.S. infantry divisions could ill afford to embrace this policy; hence, their soldiers were normally burdened with forty- to sixty-pound rucksacks, day and night. Such loads restricted foot mobility, frequently produced heat casualties, and could limit fighting effectiveness in a fast-moving tactical encounter.

However, there were many nights in the Cav that the log bird didn't fly because of adverse weather or other higher priority airmobile contingencies. On these occasions we usually spent a cold and hungry night in our NDP.

As darkness approached, Sergeant Sullivan moseyed over to where I sat nursing a final cup of battalion's fresh coffee, a brew that was ever so much better than the standard C-ration instant issue. Pulling up a discarded mermite can (a small field food container) and sitting upon it, he said, "Let's parley, sir."

"Good idea, First Sergeant. We really didn't have a chance to do a lot of talking on the bridge. Uh . . . my fault. I apologize."

"No problem, sir. Hell, we were both busy back there, but . . . me and the outgoing Six, we always tried to find a few minutes each evening to sorta rehash what happened that day and what's on tap for the next."

"Sounds like a solid policy to me, Top . . . uh . . . First Sergeant. Let's continue it."

"Okay. And you can call me Top, sir. That's what snuffie calls me, 'less I'm on his ass, then it's First Sergeant. Behind my back, he calls me the Bull, or worse."

The Bull spoke briefly of what he perceived to be his responsibilities in the boonies, which in the main related to the company's administrative and logistical requirements. He also saw himself as the final enlisted authority on recommendations for awards, promotions, and disciplinary actions and, since he was the company's senior NCO, felt that any NCO-related problem should go through him before it was brought to my attention. Finally, he monitored troop morale and oversaw the distribution of our mail. In sum, he was the unit's field XO (executive officer) and, as I was soon to discover, a damn good one.

Agreeing with everything he said, I reminded him that he was also, as of that morning, the company air-movement officer.

He gazed at me with a perplexed look for a moment, then smiled and said, "Oh, yeah, air-movement officer. And, sir . . ." he continued, a wily look in his eyes, "as you'll probably soon learn, *that's* the very least taxing of my many company chores."

There was a brief lull in our conversation as I tried to discern some hidden meaning behind his remark. I was unable to do so.

Changing the subject, he commented, "That was a good hit on the mountain today. Company needed it."

"Yeah, talked to Lieutenant Brightly first night on the bridge—or to be more accurate, he talked to me—and he said you've had some rotten luck lately."

"Sir, I don't believe in luck, but yeah, we've had some rotten luck lately! It ain't snuffie's fault, and I don't give a simple fuck what the old man might think—it wasn't the outgoing Six's fault neither. Just seems we were always in the wrong place at the right time or right place at the—shit, you know."

He paused briefly, then added, "But even though I don't believe in luck, the hit today was a good omen. Maybe it's payback time for Charlie Company."

"Hope so, Top, but like I told Brightly, I don't believe in luck or omens."

But perhaps I should have. I would later find my first sergeant possessed an uncanny ability to predict the company's future based upon the outcome of events such as our encounter on the mountain that day.

"Understand you're a mustang . . . uh . . . used to wear stripes," he said, again redirecting the conversation's course.

I nodded.

"That's good. Ex-NCO usually makes a better officer, least ways better line officer. 'Course we can't 'ford to lose our NCOs to any source right now; war's killing 'em off too fast. Know that, sir? Fucking backbone of the Army, and we're killing 'em off, or running 'em out, faster than we can produce them! Army don't realize it yet, but it will, and then it'll be too goddamn late 'cause it won't no longer have a *professional* NCO corps to man its fighting units. Mark my words."

"Hey, Top," I replied, "we've fought bigger wars than this without destroying our NCO corps."

"Yes, sir, but never by ourselves! Before we've always had the Reserves 'long side of us, had our citizen soldiers taking up the slack. Shit, even in Korea we had 'em sharing the . . . uh . . ."

He paused introspectively, then continued. "I tell you, sir, if you're an NCO, grade E-5, -6, or -7, and carrying an eleven prefix [infantryman's military occupational specialty], there ain't no end to this war for you. I mean this is where our infantry is, so you're either gonna be here or getting ready to come back here till this thing's over—and who the hell knows when that's gonna be? Shit, it's just simple mathematics; there's only so many of us folk. Fact is, you're gonna find yourself coming here more often, 'cause your peers—what with them and their families understanding these mathematics—are retiring or just plain getting out 'bout as fast as they can sign the papers.

"So, sooner or later, odds are . . . Well you know what snuffie says."

"No, Top. What does snuffie say?"

"Says you can lead a horse to water, but if you do it too many times, Charlie's gonna shoot his nuts off!"

I laughed. What my first sergeant foresaw as the demise of our infantry's NCO corps in Indochina was a sore point with him, one he would return to time and again. With the passage of time, much of what he prophesied would come to pass.

"Also understand this is your third tour over here," he continued, in another vein.

Again I nodded.

"Then we have something in common."

"This your third tour, Top?"

"No, sir, my third *war*. And, by God, it's my last one, too! Ain't gonna make war no more; gonna go back to the States, get me some ROTC duty, and teach others how to do it."

It was now dark, and we were carrying on our conversation in whispers just loud enough to be heard above the low rushing sound—a paltry constant static—emitted by the company's radios. After talking a bit longer, mostly about the war, previous assignments, the Army in general—what was right and wrong about it—families, and snuffie, we made our way to our separate holes and tried to find a few short hours of comfort in a parcel of Vietnam's freshly dug soil.

Later, wrapped in my poncho liner, I realized we had spent far more time philosophizing and simply shooting the bull than discussing company specifics. Our nightly ritual would continue in that vein, first reviewing the "state of the command" and then touching on virtually every subject under the stars. There was plenty of time for talking in the Nam.

With the exception of radio checks between us and battalion and between the platoons and their trick-or-treat sites and LPs, the night's passage was uneventful.

At before morning nautical twilight (BMNT) the company stood to, LPs were pulled back into our perimeter, and just before first light we fired our "mad minute," an exercise in which everyone on the NDP's perimeter fired their weapons simultaneously at the highest sustained rate of fire, covering defensive sectors to their front. The primary purpose of this morning tactic was to dissuade an enemy force that might have penetrated our outer defenses during the night from initiating an attack at first light. As such, it was most appropriately used in densely vegetated areas where Charlie had the least difficulty positioning himself around the NDP under cover of darkness. In addition to this tactical practicality, the mad minute provided us an opportunity to test-fire our weapons.

As the sun rose over Bong Son's plain, we repacked our rucks, stacking them on cargo nets left behind by the log bird, and washed and shaved. In the Cav, you were always expected to shave even if there wasn't enough water to wash.

Around eight o'clock the morning log bird arrived. After quickly dropping off our morning "C&D" (coffee and doughnuts, although the fare normally included other portable breakfast items such as fresh fruit, hard-boiled eggs, toast, milk or juice, and so on), the helicopter took on water cans and food containers from the previous night's meal and then, hovering six to eight feet above the ground, had the cargo nets containing our rucks hooked beneath its underside. Once these were in place, the log bird lifted off en route back to the battalion's trains area. Another day in sunny South Vietnam was under way.

Shortly thereafter, Three Six departed our NDP, traveling in a northerly direction. At approximately three klicks (kilometers) out, they would turn to the east, move in that direction for two or three klicks, and then, turning south, move another six klicks before changing direction again, this time moving due west toward the mountains. In this fashion, they would sweep our outer perimeter at a distance of about three kilometers to the north, east, and south. In the meantime, One Six, as planned the night before, would test our claymore concept in the mountains on our NDP's western flank. I, along with the rest of the command section, accompanied One Six as they departed the NDP.

Quickly discovering another, shorter access route up the mountain's eastern slope, we reached our well-traveled north-south trail within an hour or so of departing the valley floor. There we set up what was to become a pretty standard two-point, north-south claymore ambush—an ambush in which one man armed with a claymore mine (the "hit" man), accompanied by a two-man M-60 machine-gun team, established a killing position on the trail to the north, while an identical three-man team did the same to the south. The remainder of the platoon went into a tight perimeter defense across the trail midway between the two ambushes, thus prepared to reinforce either of the committed positions.

At each killing position, the hit man emplaced his claymore to the side of the trail, often securing it to the trunk of a large tree. After covering the claymore with loose vegetation, the hit man moved down the trail, on the "friendly" side of the mine, a distance of fifteen or twenty meters and then concealed himself in a position from which he could electrically detonate the claymore upon observing an approaching enemy. The machine-gun team concealed themselves similarly, usually on the hit man's uphill flank. Upon detonation of the claymore, they engaged the enemy with machine-gun fire, fixing him (denying him the ability to maneuver) until the rest of the platoon moved forward to reinforce the killing position.

Our weapon of choice was the M18A1 claymore mine. Weighing 3.5 pounds, it contained 700 hardened steel balls of 10.5 grams each, embedded in a horizontally convex face, behind which was a 1.5-pound layer of composition C-4 plastic explosive. When detonated, this plastic explosive hurled the steel pellets outward in a 60-degree arc, usually killing everything therein up to a distance of 100 meters. In other words, it produced a killing zone roughly equivalent to the area encompassed by an entire football field.

Ambushing an enemy is a lot like fishing: 98 percent waiting and 2 percent executing. Moreover, for every successful ambush, there are many others where the enemy never shows up. On this occasion, however, the gods of war were with us. Forty-five minutes or so after setting up our ambushes, two North Vietnamese regulars walked unsuspectingly into the north killing zone.

Whoom! The claymore exploded.

Rat-tat-tat-tat-tat-tat! The M-60 opened up as the claymore's detonation echoed through the mountain's draws.

Lieutenant Norwalk and I had been carrying on a lazy, whispered, somewhat disjointed conversation about families, kids, careers, women, or some such when the mine's explosion shattered the noonday silence. Accompanied by our RTOs and one of the lieutenant's rifle squads, we moved rapidly to the ambush site.

"Lookie here, lookie here . . . holy shit!"

"Goddamn!"

"My man, this here is a fucking *mess!*"

"Sweet mother of God, that claymore's *bad!*"

In unison, everyone uttered some comment of surprise, shock, or incredulity regarding the two *very* dead men at our feet—everyone except the hit man, a seventeen- or eighteen-year-old Pfc. Apparently in shock, he just stood staring fixedly at the mess he had created. On activating the claymore's electrical detonator, he had instantly solved our problem of wounded runaways—you cannot run when you have no legs.

Our hit man had obviously waited until the last possible moment before detonating the mine. The remains of the two enemy soldiers were less than ten feet from the base of the tree on which the claymore had been placed, a range at which the seven hundred steel pellets were concentrated horizontally in a pattern little greater than the width of the human body. This force had struck the lead man at midwaist, literally cutting him in half. Since the two men had been walking in file up a slight incline when hit, the mine's force had slammed into the second man at a greater height, virtually decapitating him. It was not a pretty sight. Moving them off the trail, piece by piece, was like working with rag dolls inasmuch as the hundreds of steel pellets had essentially pulverized their bodies.

After cleaning up our mess, we moved the north killing position thirty or forty meters farther up the trail, leaving the south position in place. We waited, in vain, for another couple of hours, hoping that Charlie might once more fall victim to our devastating claymore ambush.

We used this ambush technique, with great success, on many occasions. One might view this method of killing as excessively cruel or ugly, but there are several factors to consider: dead is dead, and it makes little difference to the deceased whether his demise is caused by a machine-gun bullet, napalm, or a claymore mine. Moreover, the ambush is one of war's oldest tactics and in Vietnam was executed far more frequently by the enemy than by U.S. or South Vietnamese forces. Thirdly, the North Vietnamese soldiers who perished in our December '67 and January '68 claymore ambushes were then in the process of staging for their infamous Tet offensive, an operation in which the enemy committed monumental atrocities against a defenseless civilian populace, at times murdering entire families. Finally, the nature of war *is* excessively cruel and ugly.

Returning to our NDP later in the afternoon, we learned that Three Six, although discovering many enemy footprints, was still scoreless after completing its long trek on the valley's floor. Because of this, and because of the flak they were catching from the rest of the company for being the only line platoon without a kill to its credit, Three Six's soldiers were anxious to work the mountain the next day. But so were One Six and Two Six—success does indeed breed confidence.

Unfortunately, or perhaps fortunately as things turned out, the operation was not to be. While waiting for the evening log bird, we received a warning order from battalion telling us to prepare for an airmobile extraction at 0900 hours the following morning to conduct an air assault approximately twelve klicks north of our present location. The warning order was not greeted with wild fervor by the men of Charlie Company.

"Goddamn, isn't that just like battalion. First time we're in a locale where we're getting good kills, and they move us," MacCarty commented.

"Yeah, it's that fucking S-2. He keeps his head up his ass," someone else added, while others expressed themselves in a similar vein.

I assumed that battalion had a good reason for moving us, and I told Sergeant Sullivan, our "air-movement officer," to organize the company for an airmobile extraction. Then I had an idea!

Turning to my assembled platoon leaders, I said, "Hey, we know Charlie's around here, probably watching us right now. Seems to me a false extraction might be in order." (In essence, a false extraction was a deceptive ploy in which only a portion of the unit actually got on the helicopters. Those remaining hid in ambush around the pickup zone, waiting for Charlie, who, seeing the helicopters take off, might very well visit the supposedly vacant pickup zone to scavenge anything usable or of an intelligence interest.)

The others looked at me for a few moments in uneasy silence before MacCarty and Bull Sullivan tactfully explained that such an operation wouldn't work. "Naw . . . sir, false extractions worked back in '65, and maybe early '66, when the Cav first got over here. Don't work now 'cause it's an old trick and Chuck knows all our old tricks," MacCarty commented.

"Yeah, LT's right, sir. Charlie's always watching for a false extraction, and counting. If the numbers don't add up when we get on the helicopters, he ain't gonna go near our PZ," Sergeant Sullivan added.

Made sense to me.

Putting the idea aside, we talked briefly about the next day's air assault and subsequent search-and-destroy mission in our newly assigned operational area astride Binh Dinh's Route 506. At the conclusion of this brief planning session, Bull Sullivan issued a clear, concise, and *very* condensed air-movement order, and I was confident the lift-off would be flawless. At this point, having completed company business, the conversation drifted to R&R and what the married men were going to inflict upon their wives when they met in Honolulu—"and the *second* thing I'm gonna do is kiss her and say, 'Hello'"—and what our single soldiers were going to do to every sweet young thing they could lay their hands on in Bangkok, Sydney, Manila, or wherever. In the midst of these mutually shared fantasies, Blair received a change to the next day's mission.

"Sir, helicopters've been scratched. Battalion says rest of the order stands; we walk in." Mutually shared fantasies quickly turned to mutually shared groans.

Radioing battalion, I spoke with Major Byson, who confirmed that we had indeed lost our birds. He still wanted us to conduct the operation, pointing out that our new AO was less than twelve kilometers' walking distance in fairly open terrain and therefore shouldn't pose any great problem. He was right. And Slim Brightly had an idea.

"*Now* is the time to try a false extraction, sir," he blurted out.

Lieutenant MacCarty, as usual, was the first to speak, "Slim, you can't do a false extract without helicopters. See, you gotta have a platform upon which to be extracted 'fore you can be *falsely* extracted! I mean, honestly, I've never heard it worked any other way."

"No, Mac, and maybe Charlie hasn't either," Brightly replied. "I mean, like you say, he's probably looking for false extracts with helicopters. Maybe, just maybe, he's not expecting a stay-behind if we move out of here on foot!"

MacCarty, Sullivan, and the other platoon leaders stood in silence for a moment, obviously mulling over the feasibility of such a proposal. Then they all started talking at once.

"Yeah, might work. Must've been tried before, but not on my watch."

"False extraction *without* helicopters! Shit, let's do it."

"Can't hurt to try it, might get lucky."

"Sure, couple squads could pull it off. Set up an L-shaped ambush from there to there. Cover the whole fucking NDP."

"Right, and put a couple claymores over there, covering the open end of your L."

Ideas, good ideas, were coming faster than we could assimilate them. Within a very few minutes, however, we had jointly developed our basic plan.

As the Bull had suggested, two of our rifle squads would position themselves in an L-shaped ambush along the densely vegetated eastern and southern sides of the NDP, thirty to forty meters outside its perimeter. Machine-gun teams would anchor each of the ambush's flanks, while claymore mines covered the site's killing zone and dead space on the NDP's western side, where the ground fell sharply into a rice paddy. The ambush force, manned by Two Six, would be in position before dawn, remaining there until Charlie took the bait or until 1000 hours.

Meanwhile, the rest of the company would go through its normal morning routine, limiting its mad-minute fires to the northern and western sides of the perimeter and then casually leaving the NDP after the C&D

bird had departed. Lieutenant MacCarty and I would remain with the ambush party.

"What time's first light?" I asked no one in particular.

Blair, referring to his CEOI (communications electronics operating instructions), responded, "BMNT at 0532, sir."

"Okay, Mac," I said, "let's have our ambush force in position by 0500. Don't want to take a chance on Charlie seeing us moving around after first light."

"Can do easy, sir."

"And make sure your squad leaders do a good daylight recon of their slice of the site. Gonna have to put their people in position, in the dark, without making any noise. Not much light left, so you better get on that right away."

"Can't do no recon, sir," Sullivan interjected. "Charlie sees anybody messing around the bushes outside our perimeter, he's gonna know something's up—and you gotta assume he's watching us right now."

The Bull had a point, but I hated the thought of our squad leaders trying to noiselessly put eighteen or twenty soldiers into concealed positions at night without first having had the opportunity of seeing those positions in daylight. What to do? Suddenly, Blair spoke out, and in doing so solved the problem.

"Have 'em take a shit, sir."

"What?" I asked.

"Just have your squad leaders act like they're taking a shit. Charlie pays no attention whatsoever to a grunt leaving the perimeter, weapon in one hand and E tool in the other." (An E [entrenching] tool is a small, collapsible shovel.)

Brilliant! I thought.

So our early morning ambush positions were thoroughly surveyed in daylight by leaders who did so from a squatting position.

Continuing our preparations, I mentioned to MacCarty that I wanted faces camouflaged and helmets "tree topped," that is, covered with foliage. MacCarty balked at this.

"Aw, hell, that's pussy, sir. Basic training stuff. 'Sides, we don't have any cami sticks."

"Mac, do it! It's not pussy, it's professional, and it might just mean the difference between a good kill and a wait in the weeds." Then, turning to Blair, I said, "Call trains. See if they can get some cami sticks on the log bird."

Winding up our ad hoc planning session, I asked if there were any questions, comments, or other ideas. There being none, I briefly turned my attention to the other platoon leaders, emphasizing the importance of playing the game the following morning. Although their men would know we were in ambush positions thirty meters or so from where they were drinking their morning coffee, they must in no manner indicate this to Charlie. Everything must appear completely normal—just another day in the Nam.

As we were about to break up, Slim Brightly made another perspicacious suggestion. "Have 'em carry their hutch poles, sir."

"What?" I asked, then immediately said, "No way."

In much of Vietnam, hutch poles (usually a bamboo pole six to ten feet long, used with the soldier's poncho to construct a makeshift tent) were difficult to find. Because of this, some units allowed their soldiers to carry hutch poles from site to site, a practice especially favored by ARVN forces. If I had anything to say about it, and of course I did, Charlie Company would never do this; a soldier simply isn't ready to fight carrying a weapon in one hand and a hutch pole in the other.

Slim, however, would not take no for an answer. "I tell you, sir, have the company carry their hutch poles, just this once. Charlie sees you leaving an area with hutch pole in hand, he knows you're leaving for good. It . . . uh . . . enhances deception."

I thought about it for a moment, then changed my mind. "You're right, let's do it."

Blair woke me at 0445 hours the following morning. With no moon, it was dark as hell—and quiet. Too quiet. Turning to Anderson, the company's RTO, I said, "Goddamn it, we're supposed to be in position in fifteen minutes, and they're not even up yet. Get Two Six on the horn."

"They're up and ready to move, sir," Anderson whispered in response. "Lieutenant says he'll be over here to guide us into position in zero five. You want some of this makeup, sir?"

"Huh . . . uh . . . yeah, thanks," I said, accepting his offered camouflage stick.

Up and ready to move without making a sound. Super! Hell, these people know what they're doing, I thought to myself as I applied the greasy green-black camouflage compound to my face and hands.

Slim silently approached and whispered, "Good luck," as Blair, Anderson, and I donned radios and gear. Although attached to our command section, we had decided it best that he and his recon sergeant depart the NDP along with the rest of the company. This would allow both elements to retain direct communications with battalion, us through the command net and Slim through the fire-control net. More to the point, we simply didn't need any additional people at the ambush site; indeed, there was no real reason for me to be there.

MacCarty and I, our RTOs trailing us, followed at the rear of the platoon's file as it soundlessly left the NDP's eastern perimeter. After moving a distance of thirty meters or so, the ambush force split into three different factions, a prepositioned guide leading the first squad to the right to its site covering the southern side of the NDP, another guide leading a second squad to the left on the eastern side, and a third leading Mac and me to a concealed position behind and generally between the two squads. Not a word was whispered as we ensconced ourselves for the more difficult part of the operation—the waiting.

As the first subtle light of dawn began to show in the east, and after sitting out a somewhat frightening mad minute, I saw we had a clear view of our NDP. Before long, I could see, and *hear*, our soldiers beginning to move about.

"Up, goddamn it! Boom Boom, get your fucking ass out of the sack. *Now*, goddamn it!"

"Who swiped my fucking heat tabs? Shit, just want a fucking cup of coffee and somebody stole my fucking heat . . ."

"Jesus H. Christ, who did this? Short Round, you shit next to my hole last night?"

"Just another day in the Nam. Beautiful, fucking beautiful!"

Damn, their noise discipline is atrocious! Then it suddenly dawned on me. They were merely playing the game, purposely being a bit louder and more obvious than usual to attract the enemy's attention. This, of course, was unnecessary. Charlie knew where our NDP was.

The morning log bird arrived, then departed. Shortly after eight, Charlie Company saddled up and began moving, casually, almost aimlessly, in a northeasterly direction, its soldiers carrying their hutch poles.

And we waited: thirty minutes, an hour, an hour and a half. By nine forty-five, Mac and I had concluded that Charlie wasn't going to visit us on this occasion. I wasn't surprised. I knew there would be countless other days in which we would sit and wait in vain, hoping our enemy would take the bait. Nor was I that disappointed. Our ploy had been well planned and, if Charlie had cooperated, would have been well executed. It had been a good rehearsal.

Just as we were about to terminate our wait in the weeds, Mac touched my arm, pointing toward the NDP. A North Vietnamese soldier was scurrying across it, stopping here and there to pick up discarded C rations—our bait. Through a break in the foliage, Mac pointed toward two more NVA standing on the periphery of the NDP, just outside our killing zone. I knew, at that moment, we were all thinking the same silent prayer: please, let them step into the killing zone. Come on, Chuck, don't let your selfish friend get all those goodies. Join him, please, just step . . .

Suddenly, the machine gun on the short southern side of the L opened up! Simultaneously, the claymores exploded, and everyone began firing into their assigned sectors of the ambush's killing zone and, those who were postured to do so, in the direction of the two NVA outside of it—but they were no longer there.

Within a matter of seconds all firing ceased, and an eerie silence settled over our smoldering NDP. Lieutenant MacCarty looked at me, smiling broadly.

"Good show, Mac, let's sweep it," I said.

He and I trailed the squad composing the broad side of the L as its soldiers began sweeping across the killing zone, while the other squad remained in position as a covering force. Midway through this maneuver, I happened to look at the soldiers on my right and left; in a certain respect it was as if I were seeing them for the first time. Faces blackened, green foliage covering their helmets and protruding from their webbed gear, weapons at the ready, they moved across the killing zone, cautiously, silently, with the cold and sure confidence of men who knew they were good at what they had been called upon to do. These men are professionals! I thought. These eighteen- and nineteen-year-old draftees are professional soldiers who can outfight and outfox the North Vietnamese regulars! The image of those soldiers at that moment remains as clear in my mind today as it was then, nearly a quarter of a century ago. I was very proud of them at that moment, proud to be one of them.

Our kill was an NVA lieutenant in his early twenties who, having been shot several times in the mouth, was without much of his skull.

Searching him, we found some documents and a photograph of him in an austere NVA dress uniform standing next to a rather plain young woman holding a small child. We laid him out neatly, compassionately, on a paddy dike and folded his arms across his chest. Then one of our soldiers placed a black-and-gold Cavalry patch in the center of the NVA's chest.

Meanwhile, one of MacCarty's squads was pursuing the two more fortunate enemy soldiers, at least one of whom had been wounded. Regrettably, the blood trail soon petered out, and the squad returned empty handed.

I queried our machine gunner as to why he had opened fire before the claymores were detonated, as their detonation was to initiate the ambush, and learned he had had little choice in the matter. Having located himself in dense shrubbery on the southern left flank of the ambush, he was little more than five feet from where the NVA lieutenant met his maker. While our man waited, hoping that the other two enemy soldiers would step into the killing zone, the NVA lieutenant stooped to pick a pack of C-ration cigarettes up and, in doing so, just happened to look directly into the muzzle of the machine gunner's M-60. The instant the doomed man opened his mouth to shout a warning, or scream in terror, snuffie squeezed the machine gun's trigger.

Later that day we rejoined the company in our new area of operations astride Route 506. The following morning, after an uneventful night, we were airlifted from this location and inserted into yet another AO known throughout the division as "Happy Valley."

That evening, our first in Happy Valley, I reflected back on our four days in the boonies, trying in the process to evaluate the company's performance. With four confirmed "hard" kills to our credit and suffering not as much as a scratch in return, we had done rather well, I concluded. Of course, the demise of four NVA soldiers would have little impact on the war's outcome; however, it was the method by which these soldiers had been dispatched that counted right now. For these were not red-leg (artillery) or air-strike body counts; these were good, clean, warrior-to-warrior infantry kills. Even the company's most doubtful soldier now knew he was every bit as good as the enemy he opposed. In little more than seventy-two hours, we had all gained enormous confidence.

Shortly after dusk, as I sat pondering all of this, the Bull strolled over for his nightly parley.

"Hell of a good score today, sir. First time I ever saw a false extract work without helicopters."

He paused momentarily, introspectively, and then added, "First time I ever saw a false extract work, period. Snuffie loves the shit out of it. Morale soars tonight, boss!"

"That's my sounding, Top," I replied. "And, Top, you ought to have seen 'em! I've never seen a better ambush laid in. Never seen soldiers do things more right than ours did today."

"Well, shit, sir, I could've told you that. Like I said, we've just had some bad luck lately. But today was a good omen."

"And like *I* said, Top," I responded, smiling, "I don't believe in luck or omens."

He smiled in return, and after a short lull, I asked him why Happy Valley was called Happy Valley.

"Beats the shit out of me, sir. There sure as hell ain't anything happy about it!"

HAPPY VALLEY TO BINH LOC 4

No, Happy Valley wasn't a very happy place at all. In fact, its few inhabitants seemed to be some of the unhappiest people on earth. In every village, there was always a faint but discernible fright in the eyes of those we met, as if at any moment they expected the next ax to fall, the next unfortunate turn in their lives to occur. This wariness on their part was well founded, for the people of Happy Valley were "twilight people."

Most areas of Vietnam were actually relatively stable: the daily routine of living, of nurturing families, and so forth was rarely interrupted by the war. For example, in and around the larger cities and provincial capitals, as well as throughout much of the country's coastal plain and, by 1967, most of the Mekong Delta, the people were only sporadically disturbed by enemy intrusions. And in much of the country's hinterland—previously the Viet Minh's and now the Viet Cong's stronghold—life was interrupted only infrequently by aerial bombings or, at times, by allied incursions. Happy Valley and much of Binh Dinh

Province, in contrast, rested in a twilight area between these two extremes, with neither the republic nor the Viet Cong able to fully and consistently exercise control over the population therein. The area's strategic location, midway between the demilitarized zone (DMZ) and the southern tip of the Cau Mau Peninsula, meant that both sides continued to fight over it.

This back-and-forth battle for the hearts and minds—and taxes, recruits, porters, laborers, rice, cattle, and so forth—of the valley's people had been going on since 1946, twenty years before. As we worked the valley, we could imagine what it must be like to live in such a life-threatening political milieu. Currently, the republic, thanks to U.S. intervention in the form of the First Air Cavalry, had the upper hand. But when the First Cav departed, as of course we did following the Tet offensive, the Viet Cong would return. And there would be reprisals against the people of Happy Valley.

We had been working the valley for about a week with little to show for our efforts. We were therefore anxious to return to the mountains above Daisy, where we felt the hunting was better. One late afternoon, as we were somewhat lethargically searching for an NDP, Blair passed me his handset.

"Three's on the horn, sir."

"Hey, Tall Comanche," Major Byson said, a touch of excitement in his voice, "we got a big fight going on farther up the valley. I'm inbound for pickup and short hop insert in one zero with four, plus two, plus two. Will brief you en route. How copy? Over."

"This is Comanche Six, solid copy," I replied. "We'll be standing by with smoke."

Passing the handset back to Blair, I asked Anderson to give the platoon leaders a call-up and, once they were assembled, quickly relayed to them the gist of Byson's message. Then I turned the whole affair over to the Bull, telling him only that One Six was to conduct the assault.

Donning one of the Huey's headsets as we lifted off, I listened to Major Byson's description of what we were getting into: "Gotta be brief, Comanche, touchdown in zero five. LZ green, no prep. Got a large enemy force bottled up in Binh Loc four . . . uh . . . least a company, might be a battalion. Red leg, Blue Max, and the fast movers been working the area for thirty minutes or so. Got 'little people' to the north of the village and just inserted Ridge Runner [Bravo Company] on the west side. They'll tie . . . hey, are you copying this? I mean really *copying* it, 'cause it gets sort of detailed. Over."

"This is Comanche Six. Roger, taking notes. Over." And I was, while sitting in the door of a Huey traveling at ninety knots!

"This is Arizona Three. Okay . . . Ridge Runner will tie in with the little people on the north. I'll be putting you in to the south. Want you to tie into Ridge Runner on your left and then string your men as far east as you can, all the way to the river that runs along the east side of the village, if possible. How copy so far? Over."

"This is Comanche Six. Good copy . . . little people to the north, Ridge Runner to the west, we're on the south. I tie in with Ridge Runner on my left and the river on my right. Over."

"Roger, solid copy, Comanche. Now I know that's a lot of territory to cover, but I may not be able to get Lean Apache [Alpha Company] in before dark, and we want to seal the damn village before then . . ."

Byson signed off, and Anderson passed word to One Six that we were going in green.

Once on the ground, and after the Chinooks had off-loaded the rest of the company, I contacted Bravo Company's commander and, in doing so, discovered we had nearly four hundred meters of frontage between his right flank and the river on the village's eastern side. Far too much terrain to cover at night, and day's light was quickly fading.

The platoon leaders and I hurriedly discussed the task Major Byson had set out for us, in the end deciding that each of the three line platoons would take approximately a hundred meters of coverage, putting us within fifty meters of Bravo on the left and the river on the right. In the center of their assigned sectors, the platoons would establish an elongated perimeter defense, stationing listening posts on their flanks, thus maintaining loose contact with each other and with Bravo Company. Hence, from left to right (west to east) the company would defend with One Six on the left, tying in with Bravo Company, Two Six in the center, and Three Six on the right, hopefully tying in with the river. We in the command section and Four Six would collocate ourselves with Two Six.

Taking advantage of what little twilight remained, we cleared fields of fire, set out our claymores and trip flares, and dug the holes in which we hoped to awaken the following morning. Meanwhile, we periodically gazed at the village to the north of us, watching as it and the surrounding area were worked over by a combination of artillery, air, and ARA.

Slim Brightly was kind enough to explain this manner of madness to anyone willing to listen. And I was willing to listen.

"What we have here, sir, is a classical air-and-artillery pile-on wherein every deliverable form of ordnance is placed on a single target simultaneously—without shooting your own aircraft down in the process."

I nodded, then asked him to elaborate.

"See the gunships over there from the 20th ARA? You know, Blue Max? Well, if you notice, they're coming in on their firing runs from the east and then breaking sharply before retracing their route and then doing it all over again, always staying on the east side of the river. That keeps 'em out of the fast movers' flight path and off the gun target line."

"Yeah," I replied, "well, keeping one's helicopter off the gun target line *would* seem to be a wise thing to do. Mean I'd hate to be winging along and suddenly find a 105 round in my lap."

"Sure, just fucking common sense, right? But you'd be surprised at the number of times something like that happened earlier in the war. Shit, sir, I could tell you some real horror stories coming back to Fort Sill in '65 and early '66. I mean, you talk 'bout how fucking important this war is in fielding another generation of combat-experienced *infantry* officers. Well, sir, what you're watching right now is just as important to us in producing the next generation of experienced *artillery* officers!"

"Well, guess so, Slim, but . . . uh . . . I never really thought 'bout the whole thing in that context. I mean . . ."

"Shit, sir, we cannon cockers just don't get many opportunities to mass fires from multiple sources on a single target in peacetime."

"Well, guess not, Slim, but . . ."

"Now watch the fast movers," he said, obviously excited and again interrupting me. "See how they've divided the village between them and division artillery? They're dropping on the eastern side, while divarty's working the western side. And look, look up there . . ." He paused, diverting my attention to a light observation aircraft, an O-1E "bird-dog"—the military's version of a Cessna Piper Cub—lazily orbiting high above the village. "That's the guy controlling it all, the forward air controller. He's got all the players on his push and can shift fires any fucking way he wants. Mean, if the fast movers have to leave to rearm, he just starts putting red leg on their side of the ville."

Slim continued to watch the village's bombardment through his binoculars, obviously enthralled by its devastating splendor.

"Beautiful, fucking beautiful," he mumbled to himself, as I turned to other things.

Oh, well, whatever turns you on.

Actually, his artilleryman's spectacle was impressive, in a macabre sort of way. Although most of the village was obscured by dust and smoke, we could still see proximity-fused rounds airburst above it in brilliant red-and-white flashes and seconds later, as the sound of their detonation reached us, hear the sharp *crack* of their explosion. At the same time, we heard the more constant deep, nearly muffled explosions of those rounds armed with point-detonating or delayed fuses, rounds that exploded upon contact with, or after burying themselves in, the ground.

And even from this distance, the destructive power of these fires was awesome, throwing dirt, foliage, bits of rock, and thatched roofing high into the air. Before long it was mostly divarty's show. The F-4 Phantoms, evidently having expended their heavy ordnance, had begun making firing passes using only their multibarrel 20-mm cannon. Blue Max, in the meantime, had departed.

Well, if red leg was the name of the game, we might as well play too. I told Blair to contact trains and have them put both our 81-mm mortars on the log bird along with a healthy mix of illumination and HE (high-explosive) ammunition. Although the fires of our two 81-mm tubes would contribute little to the destruction of Binh Loc 4, this seemed a good opportunity to get Four Six's crews some time on their guns. They needed the firing practice. Vietnam simply wasn't a very good war in which to enhance the technical proficiency of those assigned to a rifle company's weapons platoon.

Looking back on it now, it wasn't a very good war in many respects.

And where is the damn log bird? I thought to myself. Shit, it's almost dark.

"No can do on the eighty-ones, sir," Blair said, moments later. "No log birds tonight unless we need ammunition. Trains says all birds are committed to troop lift."

Those within hearing distance of Blair collectively moaned at this bit of information.

"Well, here we go again—'nother cold and hungry night in the

NDP. Thank God, it ain't raining," Four Six's RTO, a young soldier nicknamed "Smiley," muttered.

"Thank God, my rosy red ass," another bystander somewhat irately responded. "Here we are in the middle of a fucking rice paddy, in the fucking Nam, at night, with nothing but dinks 'round us, all of 'em wanting nothing better than to feed us our balls for breakfast, and then, on top of all this shit, battalion says they ain't gonna get chow to us and we're gonna freeze our nuts off 'cause they ain't gonna send us our rucks. And you say, 'Thank God it ain't raining'! Smiley, you are a hopeless, brainless, fucking incurable optimist! I mean, fuck me . . ."

Smiley just smiled.

Shortly after dark, Lieutenant Halloway radioed that his platoon and its LPs were in position. He was the last of the platoon leaders to do so. Minutes later, Blair, radio in hand, walked over to where I sat talking to Sergeant Sullivan.

"Three's on the wire, sir."

"Arizona Three, this is Comanche Six," I said softly into the handset.

"Roger, Comanche." (In the night's stillness, Byson's voice sounded louder than usual.) "I'm inbound vicinity your location in two zero with Lean Apache. Gonna insert between you and the river and want you to mark your right flank."

Insertion? Now? It's darker than the bottom of a well.

"This is Comanche Six. Uh . . . Roger Arizona, but be advised I've got men within fifty meters of the river. Over."

"This is Arizona Three. Too close. Want to give Lean Apache 'bout two hundred meters of frontage. Can you move your flank to accommodate? Over."

Well, shit, I wonder if you happen to recall it was you who told me to tie in with the fucking river.

"This is Comanche Six. Can do but may need more than two zero . . ."

"Roger, Comanche, but make it quick as you can. Probably be putting in a light prep and don't want any of your folks on the wrong side of your marker . . . break. How do you plan on marking your Romeo? Over."

"Comanche Six. Prefer to identify marker on your zero one final . . ."

Shit, our radio procedure is at best horrible, and if Charlie has ears, I don't want to give him twenty minutes to duplicate our marking signal all over these fucking rice paddies. And besides, at the moment I have no earthly idea how we're going to mark our flank at night.

"Roger that, Comanche. Good idea. ID your flank on one-minute final . . . break. Be advised that after Lean Apache is in position, we'll be putting artillery fire and intermittent illumination on the village the rest of the night."

"This is Comanche Six. Solid copy. Any further? Over."

"Negative further, Comanche. Get your people moving, 'cause I'm going light on the skids with Apache inbound, now. Out."

Hurriedly telling Anderson to call up Norwalk and Halloway, I sent Blair to find Lieutenant MacCarty, his CP being located only twenty meters or so from ours. I needed to quickly discuss the company's reorientation with the three of them.

My plan was to pull Three Six out of their position adjacent to the river, on our right, have them pass through us, and then assume a new defensive posture between us and One Six. Thus, the company's new orientation, from left to right, would be One Six, Three Six, Two Six, with MacCarty's platoon responsible for marking our right flank during Byson's insertion.

Upon his arrival, I asked Mac, and anyone else within hearing distance, if he had any idea how we should go about marking our flank. Everyone had an idea.

Mac's RTO, perhaps after referring to his bible, the CEOI, suggested we use a red-filtered flashlight to flash a predetermined letter in Morse code.

"See, we call Byson and tell him the code letter marking our flank is, say, S, you know, Sierra. Then, when he tells us to mark on one-minute final, we just point the flashlight at the helicopters and flash 'dar-dar-dar' . . . or is it 'dit-dit-dit'? Anyway, whatever it is, that way he'll know it's us and not Charlie, right?"

"Shit, Farmer, what do you mean, he'll know it's us and not Chuck?" the Bull replied. "What in the hell's secret 'bout the Morse code? Why the hell you think it's called the *international* Morse code?"

"Well . . . uh . . . it's just a thought, Top."

"Sure. I know that, Farmer," Sergeant Sullivan replied, almost apologetically, "and a damn good one too, but, see, Byson's gonna be coming in here hot and heavy at ninety knots. He ain't gonna have time to be looking for any red-filtered flashlight." Then, turning to me, he said, "No, sir. Best thing to do is just dig a little hole out there on our flank, and when he asks us to mark, have someone pop a trip flare in it."

Made sense to me.

Understandably, inasmuch as they were not required to move, neither MacCarty nor Norwalk saw any great problem in relocating Three Six between their two platoons. Mac would furnish guides to escort Three Six through his platoon sector, while Norwalk agreed to leave his right flank LP in position as a contact point.

In contrast, and just as understandably, Lieutenant Halloway saw many problems with the move and was not at all enthusiastic about taking part in it.

"This is Comanche Three Six. Strongly recommend against moving. It's not that we just got our holes dug and have settled in here. I just feel it's too dangerous, might get some of our men shot. Might shoot each other. Over."

"This is Comanche Six. Sorry, but the issue is not negotiable. If you stay where you are, you *will* get shot 'cause that area's gonna be prepped in about one five. So pack it up and start moving now! Over."

"This is Three Six. Well, I copy that! We'll be moving in zero five . . ."

"This is Six. Okay, know and use current challenge and password. Inform me when your last man closes Two Six's . . ."

By the time we heard the faint *whump, whump, whump* of distant helicopters, Bob Halloway's last soldier had safely passed through our perimeter. Byson came up on the battalion command net moments later.

"Comanche Six, this is Arizona Three inbound with Lean Apache. You prepared to mark your Romeo, over?"

"This is Comanche Six. Roger, standing by."

"Okay, Comanche, coming up on one-minute final. Mark now! I say again, mark your Romeo flank now! Over."

I repeated "mark" three times into Anderson's handset, signaling Mac, who was monitoring the company net, to activate the trip flare. Concurrently, I informed Byson of our marking technique via Blair's handset.

Night suddenly turned to day on our right flank. Damn, that flare is putting out a lot of light. If they dug a hole, it's sure as hell a shallow one.

"Uh . . . Roger, Comanche," Byson said. "Got your flare, nothing subtle about *that!* We'll be coming in hot in minus one minute. Keep your heads down. Out."

The helicopters, Cobras leading, were now clearly visible against the darkened southeasterly sky. For a moment they looked as if they were heading straight for us. Careful, Blue Max. No-fire line is to the left of the flare, not the right. Abruptly, the gunships veered right, corrected, and then started their firing run. It was beautiful! So much more impressive at night.

"Wow!" someone said. "Fourth of July in the Nam! Look at the fucking fireworks!"

"Them Cobras are *bad* mothers," someone else commented.

Blue Max had a section of four gunships working the LZ, first with rockets and 40-mm grenades, then 7.62-mm miniguns. The rate of fire of this multibarreled gun was so fast, its bullets with their tracer tips were spaced so close together, that when fired the weapon appeared to produce an unbroken, brilliantly illuminated red line stretching from its muzzle to the ground. The deadly red line sometimes ran straight and true, at other times weaved lazily back and forth. And while the machine guns echoed their familiar *rat-tat-tat-tat-tat* sound, the minigun produced an eerie, constant *bruppppppppppp.*

"Here comes Alpha Company, sir," the Bull commented, obviously impressed with the show. None of us had seen a night air assault before. If not a rarity, they certainly weren't commonplace in the Nam, even in the Cav.

"Damn, look at that," he continued, "ain't putting no hooks in here at night. All Hueys. I count twelve of 'em."

The Cobras were now working the LZ's periphery, their uninterrupted streams of red tracers striking the ground and then aimlessly, crazily, ricocheting off and into the night.

"Looks like a four-ship LZ," I commented as the first four troop-laden Hueys set down and then hurriedly took off again, making way for the next four.

It was all over in a matter of minutes. Then Alpha Company was on the ground to our right, and, except for the fading sound of the departing helicopters, silence returned to the valley—a silence occasionally interrupted by artillery H&I (harassment-and-interdiction) fires landing in Binh Loc 4.

An hour or so later, Byson's voice again pierced the night air. "Arizona, Arizona, this is Arizona Three. Over."

He was making a net call, requiring all the battalion's line companies to answer him. We did.

"This is Lean Apache, over."

"This is Ridge Runner, over."

"This is Tall Comanche, over," I chimed in.

"This is [garbled] Running Navaho, over."

"This is Arizona Three. Running Navaho disregard. Break. For the rest of you, this constitutes a frag order. At first light, or as soon thereafter as visibility will allow, we go into the ville. Intend to hold little people and Ridge Runner in their present positions and then sweep north with Lean Apache on the right and Tall Comanche on the left . . . . uh . . . a touch of the old hammer and anvil.

"Fires and time of attack to be announced. Lean Apache and Tall Comanche, you two choose a mutually agreed-upon line of departure and let us know what it is in the A.M. Boundary between the two of you is the main north-south red line." (Red line was a road or highway, so called because that's the way it appears on a map; rivers appeared as blue lines.)

"If you need ammo, get your wants in tonight. Arizona Six will be airborne at the objective. And I hope you fellows got all that."

We had and, in sequence, signed off.

After thinking briefly about next day's operation, I made a net call to the platoons, informing them of the gist of Byson's FRAGO and telling them we would attack with Two Six on the right, Three Six on the left, and One Six trailing in reserve. Then perhaps belatedly, I asked my first sergeant if he agreed with all of this.

"Sure, best way to do it, considering our disposition right now," he replied. "Two Six and Three Six can just pick it up and move forward, while One Six falls in behind. But shit, tell you the truth, Six . . ." Sergeant Sullivan had recently begun calling me "Six" when others of the company were not privy to our conversations. "I just wouldn't worry 'bout it too much. I mean, I'll bet you diamonds to doughnuts that the ville over there, you know, Benny Lock 4 or whatever, will just be another walk-through. Ain't gonna be no fight 'cause Charlie's gone!

"Shit, sir, I've been through this before, and I'm telling you, no matter what you do to seal a village at night, Charlie's gonna be long gone at dawn. Don't care if you put snuffie 'round it arm to arm, Charlie will find a way out 'fore first light."

He paused a moment and then said, "I stand corrected. I saw it . . . uh . . . heard 'bout it working once. Alpha Company, six, seven months ago, when I first got here. 'Course that was on the beach, easier to trap Chuck on the beach. I mean, where the fuck can he go? Can't hardly swim back to Hanoi!"

"Hardly," I offered, trying to catch the drift of what he was talking about.

"Yeah, see, Alpha was just doing another walk in the weeds, well, in this case, a walk in the sand and rocks 'long Binh Dinh's coast. Where, unknown to them, the NVA—think it was part of the 22d Regiment—had a battalion hiding in these rocks, you know, in caves and all, and Alpha Company nearly walks right over 'em, probably like a bunch of the rest of us had done a number of times before.

"Well, way I heard it, this last little snuffie stopped for a minute to fill his canteen from some water what had settled in the rocks. You believe that, Six? I mean he just happens to stop so as to fill his canteen, and this gook raises his head—you know, maybe he just wanted to see what an American 'round eye' looks like—and snuffie nails him right between the eyes.

"So, Alpha set up 'round this rock pile and in the next week or so kill a hundred or more of Charlie without losing any of their own. Great fucking hit!"

"Super," I commented, as he paused briefly, before changing our conversation's direction.

"But to hell with these war stories, sir. What I'm worried about right now is taking care of the troops. You know we ain't had a hot since last night, and it's pretty obvious, what with Three's plans for an attack tomorrow, we ain't gonna get a hot before tomorrow night. That means forty-eight hours without chow!"

"Well, not really without chow, Top," I responded. "We did have C&D this morning and a charlie rat today, right?"

"Yeah, but that's just one meal, sir. You know, C&D is nice, but it ain't no meal. We need charlie rats in the morning. I mean shit, sir, to hell with battalion and their 'class V only' message; troops need class I! They're getting hungry!"

Although I did not at the time recognize the signs—I would later— my first sergeant was starting to bristle over what he perceived as something less than unconstrained dedication on the part of our higher headquarters toward "taking care of the troops." This is a somewhat common, and I've always thought healthy, perception among rifle company first sergeants.

"I mean fuck it, sir!" he continued, his self-induced anger intensifying. "Sometimes battalion's philosophy 'pears to be, 'Fuck the troops; just feed 'em beans and mark 'em for duty'!"

"Well, Top, no one said we wouldn't get a bird in the morning. You know, they just said they're committed to troop lift tonight. But if you feel that strongly about it, why don't I just call . . ."

"Shit, there ain't no goddamn soldier in any fucking war ever suffered no more than snuffie here," he went on as if not hearing me, his voice becoming perceptibly louder, "and all he asks in return is his mail and a hot meal now and then! And these goddamn chairborne, barbecue-eating, cot-sleeping, maid-fucking, beer-drinking, sonofabitching rear-echelon *wimps* put out that 'class V only' bullshit! I mean I'm *pissed,* sir!"

And he was.

"Hey, Top, I'll call the colonel and ask him to rescind that ammo only bullshit. I mean seriously, if we need C rations, I'm sure battalion will get 'em to us at first . . ."

"No, sir," he interrupted, now visibly upset. "Taking care of the troops is my job! That's first sergeant business! I'm gonna get trains on the horn right now and tell them, not ask, *tell* them to get us charlie rats out here in the morning! And if they mention one fucking word 'bout 'class V only,' *I'm* gonna call the colonel. I'm getting sick and goddamn tired of this bullshit!"

Resignedly, I replied, "Okay, Top," as he angrily stomped off into the night.

He returned within ten minutes or so, looking a little disheartened.

"What say, Top? Time for me to get involved one on one with Colonel Lich?"

"Naw . . . uh . . . everything's worked out," he responded a bit timidly. "Called trains, and they said they'd already planned to get us charlie rats and water at first light, just waiting for our head count . . . uh . . . I forgot to send it in, what with everything else going on."

He paused momentarily, then added, "Said they're gonna do everything possible to get us a hot breakfast out too—you know, if they can figure a way to backhaul the mermites."

We looked at each other in silence a moment and then started laughing.

"You know, sir," he said, smiling shyly, "you and me, we're lucky as hell to be in the Fifth Cav! 'Cause those *other* outfits, well I can tell you right now, *their* philosophy is, 'Fuck the troops; just feed 'em beans and mark 'em for duty.' Right, Six?"

"Right, Top."

"Comanche, this is Arizona Six. Give me some smoke on your right flank, okay? Over." It was Colonel Lich, orbiting above us in his C&C.

"This is Comanche Six. Roger, wait," I replied, then told Lieutenant MacCarty, via the company net, to pop smoke.

In a matter of seconds, Colonel Lich was back on the air. "This is Six. Okay, I've got your yellow smoke. Now listen up; you're moving too far ahead of Lean Apache. They've got something in some caves along the river slowing them down. I don't want the two of you shooting each other, so ease it up a bit till I give you word to throttle forward again. Over."

"This is Comanche Six. Wilco."

It had been an uncomfortable and, for the most part, sleepless night. Although Vietnam's days can be sweltering throughout the year, its January nights are often quite cool. And trying to sleep wrapped in only a thin poncho, lying in the middle of a rice paddy, with artillery rounds exploding half a mile away in a village that may be occupied by a battalion of armed enemy who will probably have an opportunity to shoot you when you attack them in the morning—well, all in all, these conditions simply aren't conducive to a good night's sleep. On the bright side, however, it didn't rain.

But things looked better as dawn broke in the east, bringing in its wake a clear sunny morning devoid of fog. Things looked better still when the log bird arrived a short time later with C&D and our charlie rats—and 7.62-mm linked ammunition for One Six. Why the ammo? I asked myself. To the best of my knowledge we haven't fired a round since last being resupplied a couple nights ago.

I asked the Bull about it, and he said he and Lieutenant Norwalk had jointly decided that since we were facing what might be an enemy battalion, it seemed neither illogical nor imprudent for the company's reserve to carry along a little extra machine-gun ammo.

Well, I couldn't argue with that.

"Besides, Six," he added, a wily look in his eyes, "it was good insurance. Mean, if trains sent us out the bullets, they'd have little damn excuse for not putting some beans on the same bird, now, would they?"

And I couldn't argue with that either.

Shortly after the log bird's departure, we began moving toward the village. We were at its outskirts when Colonel Lich slowed us down so as to allow Alpha Company time to investigate their caves. So far the exercise had been an uneventful walk in the weeds.

"Lean Apache is sending to the old man, sir. You want to listen in?" Blair said, extending his handset.

Nodding my head, I took his extended handset and monitored Alpha Company's transmission to Colonel Lich.

"Roger, got caves or shelters dug in the side of the riverbank. Must be most of the ville's population in 'em. They're reluctant to come out, which I guess is understandable under the circumstances. Over."

"This is Six. Any enemy intermingled with them?"

"This is Apache Six. Not sure, but I would guess not."

"Okay, Apache, see if you can talk any of 'em out. If not, leave 'em alone, let's get on with the op. Comanche's ready to enter the village now . . . break. You got a Kit Carson with you? Over."

"This is Apache Six. Affirmative."

"This is Six. Well, put him on those villagers and see what he can find out . . . uh . . . then get back to me. Out."

A "Kit Carson" was a VC or NVA defector who usually spoke some broken English. In talking to the villagers, he would try to find out if the enemy was still in their midst while concurrently soliciting information on the unit's designation and order of battle, the number of casualties it might have suffered, how it was armed, whether morale was good or bad, and so on.

We entered Binh Loc 4 around 1000 hours; it was an anticlimactic event. As the Bull had predicted, Charlie was gone before dawn. However, he had left many a dead comrade behind when he departed—red leg and the fast movers had done their jobs well. Surprisingly, and happily, for it was something that worried many of us the night before, there were few civilian casualties. That was perhaps not so surprising. Having obviously been through all of this before, the villagers had their caves and bunkers dug deep and knew how to get to them in a hurry. One simply doesn't survive in places like Binh Loc 4 without knowing such things.

So we counted enemy kills reaped by death from the heavens instead of at our own hands. It was not a happy task—many of the bodies were horribly mutilated by the artillery and air strikes. Most, perhaps all, had died the night before and now, rigor mortis having set in, lay in the grotesque, distorted positions of those who suffer death suddenly and violently. They lay on their backs with arms extended, as if reaching for something, someone. They lay on their sides, glazed eyes open, stiffened in a fetal position. One clutched his weapon, an RPG (rocket-propelled grenade) launcher, as if his punishment would indeed be severe if he surrendered it, even in death. But surrender it he did, as did several others who had evidently been overlooked by their surviving comrades as they departed the village, evading us in the darkness of the night before.

After spending the rest of the morning and most of the early afternoon in these joyless duties, we departed Binh Loc 4 and later established an NDP to the north of it in the same general area ARVN had previously occupied.

Our log birds flew early, bringing with them our rucks (containing those comforting poncho liners), steaks and mashed potatoes, and one can of beer and one of coke per company head count. Such a small offering, as I think back on it, but that evening, north of Binh Loc 4, it was like Christmas. You could actually feel the company's morale soar.

Sharing a beer with me, the Bull summed it up. "Like I say, Six, we're lucky as hell to be in the Fifth Cav, 'cause those other outfits' attitude, most likely as not, is 'fuck the troops; just feed 'em beans.'"

LZ DAISY AND POINTS BEYOND: JANUARY 1968

For the next week or so, we worked the area northwest of Binh Loc 4, discovering nary a trace of the elusive NVA battalion. Of course the question that those in Saigon, Honolulu, and Washington would have liked answered was not where the remnants of a single and now combat-ineffective battalion were, but why these forces were massing just days before Tet, the Chinese lunar new year. Where were they coming from, and why were they assembling in the populated coastal and piedmont areas, when the real threat was supposedly poised against the country's hinterland, primarily against a remote Marine Corps outpost and its six thousand occupants at a place called Khe Sanh? In a matter of days, the questions would be answered. In Saigon, and throughout much of Vietnam, the answers would be punctuated in blood. And within a month, we would win the war's greatest battle—and the war would be lost.

But tonight we settled into our NDP in the mountains surrounding Happy Valley. Major Byson radioed us a very informal warning order for the following day's operation.

"Comanche Six, this is Arizona Three. I'll be picking you up in the A.M. soon as the ground fog clears with four, plus two, plus two. Gonna put you in on LZ Daisy again. Uh . . . you seem to have pretty good hunting in that area. Conduct operations at your discretion and see what you can come up with . . . break. Higher is screaming for intel. Anything you come up with might be significant. You know, maps, documents, rumors amongst the villagers, POWs—anything we can pass to higher. Over."

"This is Comanche Six. Roger that, but be advised there's not many villagers vicinity Daisy, over."

"Understand. Just keep your eyes open and give your kills a good going-over."

Our extraction from Happy Valley and air assault on LZ Daisy the following morning might well have been a company airmobile test conducted by the 11th Air Assault Division (the forerunner of the First Air Cav) at Fort Benning four years before—unopposed, uneventful, LZ green.

We had decided the night before that One Six and Three Six—Three Six with the command section in tow—would establish separate two-point claymore ambushes on the mountain west of Daisy, while Two Six would work the valley floor. As we prepared to depart the LZ in different directions, I pulled Lieutenant MacCarty aside, giving him an additional task to perform during his sweep of the valley.

"Hey, Mac, while you're working the floor, I'd like you to find us a new NDP within a klick or so of the LZ. I just don't feel comfortable setting up here so soon after our stay-behind."

"Roger that, sir. I agree."

"Think what we'll do," I continued, "is go ahead and set up here this evening, bring in chow and our rucks, and then, 'bout time it starts to get dark, move to whatever site you select. That means you ought to be thinking 'bout guides, okay?"

"Okay, and I'll try to find something fairly close, since it'll mean carrying our rucks, mermites, eighty-ones and their ammo . . ."

"No problem on the eighty-ones, Mac. We won't bring 'em in tonight."

"Good idea," he said, then commented, "hey, sir, you see our dead lieutenant over there?"

"What?" I said a bit frantically, momentarily not knowing to whom he was referring, then quickly realizing he was talking about the luckless NVA lieutenant we had killed in our "helicopterless" false extraction. Smiling, I recalled a similar incident on the bridge when the Bull, during the course of one of Colonel Lich's inspections, whispered in my ear, "Sir, we're in trouble. The old man found a dead soldier in one of our bunkers." I nearly went into shock! The Bull thought it absolutely hilarious that, having been in the Army ten years, I didn't yet know that a "dead soldier," in a soldier's vernacular, was an empty liquor bottle.

Turning in the direction Mac was pointing, I noted the neatly packed mound of raw earth where someone, most likely his more fortunate comrades, had buried our lieutenant.

I wonder what happened to our Cav patch.

Climbing the mountain's eastern slope via the same trail we had used in setting up our first claymore ambush, we reached the main north-south juncture within an hour or so of departing the LZ. One Six turned left to the south, while we began following the trail to the north. Within minutes, we were overwhelmed by the stench of rotting flesh—the haunting odor of our first claymore victims.

"Whew! They sure did ripen, didn't they?" Anderson said, covering his nose with the sweat towel that RTOs, and many of the rest of us, wore about our necks like scarves.

"Yeah, isn't it great, Andy!" Blair responded, gleefully. "Just another unique but integral part of our daily nature walks through this tropical paradise. But one of many memorable ingredients that will make up your 'Vietnam experience' as the years unfold. Savor it, my friend. For though many were called, few were . . ."

"Okay, let's hold it down and keep moving," I said. Then, turning to Blair and winking, I added, "And you better watch it, Blair; your college is showing again."

My battalion RTO was one of those rare animals who had gone to college and *still* got drafted, and *still* ended up in the infantry, in the Nam.

After moving thirty minutes or so, our trail intersected with yet another well-traveled trail running generally southwest toward the mountain's crest. We climbed upward astride this new route for perhaps another half hour before Lieutenant Halloway, finally, thankfully, found what he felt to be a good ambush site. He sent his claymore hit teams up and down the trail, and then we waited.

We waited and munched on charlie rats and napped, waited and whispered of or daydreamed about home, women, the Army, the war, families, and R&R. Combat, at least combat in the Nam, is mostly waiting, I thought to myself. Waiting in ambush, waiting for mail, for chow, for dawn, for insertion or extraction helicopters, for R&R—and most of all, waiting for that magic end-of-tour date when we'd put Vietnam and all the waiting behind us.

My thoughts were interrupted by a distant but loud explosion, followed immediately by the rhythmic *rat-tat-tat-tat-tat-tat* of an M-60 machine gun.

"One Six got 'em!" Blair whispered, gleaming.

Anderson, sitting on my right, quietly asked, "Want me to give 'em a call, sir?"

"No, not yet," I responded. "They're busy. Let 'em sort it out."

And again, I waited. Two minutes, three minutes, five minutes. Anxious, then annoyed, and finally a little angry. Yeah, waiting really is the name of the game. But goddamn it, Norwalk should give me some indication of what's happened.

We had talked of this before, and it was a problem at every level of command, because the Nam was a different kind of war. In previous wars, lines were drawn with platoons forward of companies, companies forward of battalions, and battalions forward of regiments. And commanders at each intervening level would anxiously, but usually tolerantly, await the results of any ongoing engagement, influencing its outcome with the resources they could bring to bear but relying on their subordinates to fight the battle at hand. In Vietnam, in contrast, a platoon leader frequently had every commander in the world directly over top of him in his C&C ship within moments of a single round having been fired in anger. From that vantage point, colonels and general officers too often tried to become squad leaders. Thankfully, that was rarely the case in the Cav. General Tolson, the division's commander, believed firmly in letting his subordinates fight their own battles while ensuring that they had the entire division and all its resources behind them. Colonel Lich, a decorated veteran of our little Korean ado, who knew what it was like to fight the fight on the ground, adhered to the same philosophy.

However, commanders at all levels had one thing in common: when their soldiers got themselves into a fight, they wanted to know what was going on as soon as possible. Or as Colonel Lich had told me on the bridge, "If you get into something, *tell me*. I can't help you or prepare others to help you if you don't. And don't wait until you can consolidate an Infantry School–formatted situation report. Just give me what you got at the time and 'more to follow.'" Charlie Company's platoon leaders had been told the same.

"Six, this is One Six," Norwalk said, his voice emanating from Anderson's handset. "At one four two five hours local, engaged NVA at point of origin right two eight, up zero six. Three, say again three, NVA killed in action. One AK-47 and two SKS assault rifles captured in action. No friendly casualties. How copy?"

Good report. Clear, concise, and complete. Provides the who, what, where, when, and results. And the results were good, the claymore having proved once again to be the weapon of choice. Three dead, three weapons taken, none of us hurt. Good show! Bill Norwalk is a solid officer. Hell, they all are.

"This is Six," I replied. "Good job. Pass along a 'well done' to your hit man . . . break. You've done a day's work. Go ahead and pack it up and start moving toward Daisy. We'll be an hour or so behind you. Don't forget to give Two Six a call before closing the LZ; they may be occupying it!"

After waiting in ambush another thirty to forty minutes, we too started down the mountain. Shortly after passing the point at which our new descending trail bisected the main north-south route, we got lucky.

Rat-tat-tat-tat-tat! The sound of Three Six's point man's M-16, firing on automatic, pierced the air!

As on that first day on the mountain, everyone dived to the ground, pointing their weapons outward, doing things right. Within moments Lieutenant Halloway and I, our RTOs in tow, were running forward, quickly closing the twenty meters or so between us and his point man.

The point man was in a crouch, his weapon at the ready, looking left, right, and down the trail as he should have been. At his feet were what appeared to be two long socks, a string connecting them, filled with dry uncooked rice. These straddled the neck of a dead NVA soldier. Three Six's point man had evidently elevated his weapon while firing on automatic. His foe had been "zippered" through his groin, stomach, chest, neck, and skull.

Recalling Byson's guidance, we searched the bloodied khaki-clad body thoroughly but other than personal effects found nothing. Clearing the trail, a couple of Three Six's soldiers then heaved the body, in a one-two-three count, off the path's embankment. It tumbled two or three meters before lodging itself against a tree. We retrieved the dead soldier's weapon and then continued our downward movement toward Daisy.

While waiting—always waiting—for the evening log bird, I strolled over to One Six's piece of our perimeter and congratulated their hit man on his kill. After doing so, I continued on to Three-Six's position, arriving in time to overhear Bob Halloway's point man describing his kill.

"It was just like Lean Man said, LT! See, I'm moving 'long real cautious like, and all of a sudden this dink comes strutting 'round a curve in the trail, carrying this double sock of rice over his shoulders, you know, like saddlebags. And I swear to God, sir, the fucker had his weapon slung 'cross his back!

"I mean, this dude's doing everything what they told us not to do in basic. Shit, he wasn't even looking where the fuck he was going! Just looking at the ground, at his feet, you know, like them Ho Chi Minh sandals was the biggest thing he had going for him today. I swear, sir, I don't think he ever saw me. I mean he's just staring at his fucking feet when I blew him away."

After congratulating our young point man, Bob and I talked briefly about the incident.

"What do you make of it, Bob?" I asked. "Why are they so fucking sloppy up there? Hell, these are regulars, the People's Army of North Vietnam, supposedly one of the world's most professional infantries."

"Yes, sir, and they probably are when they come down here to play, you know, on our turf. But up there, well, it's pretty obvious they think they own the mountain, regard it as their own private sanctuary, and can therefore traverse its trails with impunity. You know, just like walking the streets of Hanoi."

"Well, they by God don't own it no more, Robert!" I retorted, arrogantly, cockily.

"Uh . . . right, sir, and that's what surprises me—I mean that they haven't concluded their little haven of security is no longer secure. You'd think, seeing the dead bodies we've been leaving around, they'd take some precautionary measures."

After mulling this over, I responded, "I don't know, Bob; maybe that's not so surprising—I mean their reaction to our kills. Hell, there's dead bodies all over this country; it's almost the norm. Way I figure it, these people are regulars in transit, you know, just moving from point A to point B. They see some of their own laid out 'long the way, they just chalk it up to H&I fire, aerial-delivered mines, and a stray bomb—in short, the fortunes of war."

"Maybe so," he replied, "but it's funny they're not using their VC brethren as guides. And why are they moving in singles, pairs, or groups of only three or four per? And where are they moving to?"

Good questions, but ones that neither Bob Halloway nor I were able to answer on that January day in 1968.

As dusk fell, Two Six departed Daisy en route to our new NDP, leaving behind a guide with each of the remaining platoons. An hour or so later, in darkness, the rest of us followed. Upon arriving at our new position, Lieutenant MacCarty quickly emplaced the company in an elongated perimeter. LPs were sent out, and we settled in for the night, each of us seeking what cover and concealment our immediate surroundings afforded. We dug no holes in this instance: security was dependent on stealth, on silence.

After C&D the following morning, we again assaulted the mountain, going about what had now become business as usual. Three Six worked the main north-south trail, and One Six the valley floor. Two Six, accompanied by the command section, followed our newly discovered trail of the day before up and over the mountain's crest. We wanted to see what was on the other side.

I tagged along with Two Six. Although we found little of consequence on the mountain's western slope, I had the opportunity to observe the best of the company's point men at work. And the company had no bad point men in the Nam. They were the best and bravest of a unit's soldiers because the laws of jungle warfare permitted nothing less. The point man was a twentieth-century gladiator, a man who fought the war at its most personal level. And, like the gladiator, he could lose the game but once. If the pilot of a B-52 bomber was on one end of the war's spectrum, the point man was at the other end. Unlike the B-52 pilot, who would push the buttons on his onboard computer to release his fury on an unseen enemy below, the point man was nose to nose with the enemy—man against man, with weapon in hand.

Passing Three Six's previous day's ambush site, we continued to climb upward toward the mountain's summit, the trail becoming abruptly steeper, nearly perpendicular to the valley floor below. Ladderlike footsteps had been carved into the mountain's face, and, straddling these, woven vines conveniently hung down from the heights above. Movement was tedious, difficult, and exhausting, but the flow of adrenaline dulled the effects of exhaustion and kept us going.

"Hey, sir," Mac whispered, momentarily turning and looking down at me. "We're *really* in Indian country now."

"Looks like it, doesn't it, Mac. They say there's always good hunting in the high country."

"Damn right we're in Indian country," Anderson said, behind and below me, not bothering to look up. "These ain't wait-a-minute vines we're hanging onto. These vines been woven by some zipperhead. Shit, sir, we're in Charlie's backyard!"

Looking up, I saw the mountain's top looming before us. Concurrently, the trail leveled off slightly, still steep but no longer straight up.

Two Six's point man was within perhaps ten meters of the mountain's razorback crest when, suddenly, two NVA soldiers appeared on the summit and began their descent toward us. If they saw our point man before they died, it was only for a fleeting second. Because he saw them first.

Bam! Bam! Bam! Bam!

The exploding twelve-gauge shotgun shells were louder than an M-16 round, yet our point man fired the rounds so quickly that the shots sounded like an automatic weapon. He hit the first of the two enemy soldiers dead center in the chest, lifting him up and backwards for a fraction of a second before he fell, face forward, tumbling past us. The second man, struck in the chest and face, fell back across the mountain's crest.

We searched the bodies, retrieved the weapons, and reported the contact to battalion. Then we continued on over the top of the mountain and down its other side, arriving back on the valley floor in midafternoon.

The mountain's western slope produced no startling discoveries, just heavily traveled trails, indicating that our enemy was constantly moving across the mountain's face, usually in a southerly direction. Our disappointment was lessened somewhat when a loud explosion occurred to the northeast: two unwitting NVA soldiers had fallen victim to Three Six's claymore ambush.

That afternoon, in yet another NDP, I wandered over to Two Six's slice of the perimeter and congratulated MacCarty's point man on his kills.

He was a big, black street tough named Wester and, as I would later learn while lying helpless in a rice paddy, a man of great personal courage. On this occasion he was noncommittal and rather reserved, merely thanking me.

Later that evening, after the log bird had departed and the company had messed, Lieutenant MacCarty dropped by my CP for a little after-dinner conversation.

"Well, what do you think of my man Wester, sir?" he asked.

"Hell of a good shot," I responded.

"Yeah, best point man in the company, maybe the division. Cool under fire, like ice. Kind of guy you want around in a firefight."

"Well, Mac, why is he still a Pfc? Sounds like NCO material to me."

"Yes, sir, and his spec-four stripe should be coming down any day now. Uh . . . sergeant may be a bit more difficult. See, fortunately, I have the best point man *and* the best platoon sergeant in the company. Unfortunately, the two of them don't always see eye to eye. Know what I mean?"

"No."

"Well, Wester's the new breed—here to do a job, great combat soldier, but not all that enthused 'bout some of the other more . . . uh . . . subtle aspects of soldiering. Sergeant Naple, on the other hand, is the typical hard-core infantry platoon sergeant. You know—right way, wrong way, and the Army way. And, 'course, the Army way is always the right way."

"Okay, understand."

"But they're both super soldiers," he continued, "and I think both realize the other is good at what he's responsible for doing."

"Well, in any event, Wester is deadly with that shotgun," I remarked. "I mean, goddamn, it sounded like an automatic weapon."

"You bet it did, sir! Hey, every time the platoon gets a cherry in, Wester bets him he can empty that pump action faster than the cherry can fire a twenty-round magazine on full automatic. He hasn't lost a bet yet!" He paused, smiling, and added, "See that bronze Cav patch he has embedded in the stock?"

I nodded. Changing the subject, I asked, "What about you, Mac? You're 'bout ready to leave us, aren't you?"

"One more week, mon capitan! Seven more days and I start migrating toward *my* freedom bird, back to the land of the living." Then, a bit despondently, almost angrily, he said, "I'll miss the men. I won't miss another fucking thing about this whole stinking, chaotic, fucked-up mess, but I'll miss my men."

"Sure you will, only natural. And they'll miss you. Uh . . . what's your plan, Mac? Staying in?"

"No! I'm not sure what I'm gonna do, but the Army won't be a part of it. I figure I've paid my dues, and now it's time to get on with my life. And quite frankly, sir, I don't see the profession of arms as being part of that life. I mean, I'm not having that much fun right now, and if I stayed in, I'd be right back over here in, what? A year? Two years? Mean, shit, sir, you're career, and this is your third trip, right?"

"Right on both counts," I answered. "Yeah, you'd probably be back over here in a year or so. I mean, you're infantry and, like our first sergeant says, till this thing's over, you're either gonna be in Vietnam, preparing to go to Vietnam, or recuperating from having been in Vietnam. Infantry officers can just forget about touring Europe for a while."

Recalling the gist of an Infantry Branch orientation at Fort Benning shortly before my departure, I added, "In fact, Branch told us they'd assigned only *two* infantry captains to all of Seventh Army! Think about it, Mac. Our nation's commitment to NATO and traditionally our largest field army, and only *two* infantry captains assigned! And get this, Mac, one of 'em is an *amputee!*"

Laughing, he replied, "Well, we heard that infantry lieutenants were getting a lot of company command time in Germany. Guess it's true."

After a moment's silence, MacCarty continued in a more serious vein. "But you see, sir, I really don't care how many infantry captains we have in Seventh Army—you do. You do 'cause you're career, and it's all part of this military profession you and others like you hold so dear. And please don't misunderstand me, sir; I respect you all for it. But I'm not career, and I'm not part of it and don't want to be.

"I guess we're just different in that respect. I've often wondered why.

"You know what I think, sir?" he asked rhetorically. "And I've thought about this from time to time, watching and working with you and Byson and other careerists. I think it's World War II. I think it's the environment you all grew up in."

"What?" I asked, wondering what the hell he was talking about.

"What I mean, sir . . . well how old are you?"

"I'm twenty-nine, no, thirty now, and tonight I feel it, but what the hell's my age got to do with careers—yours or mine? Or the war? Or World War II? I mean I sure as hell wasn't involved in that one! Shit, I was only three, four years old when we got into it."

"Yeah, but I'll bet you remember it, the war years and all. You know—the rationing, paper and scrap-metal drives, and so forth."

"Well, yeah, I do," I said, smiling as I recalled those long-ago "good war" years. "And I remember the milkweed pod drives."

"What?" Mac asked. "Milkweed pods? What the hell did the Army need milkweed pods for?"

"Beats the shit out of me, Mac. But my second-grade class must've picked a ton of 'em. I think they used them in life vests on troopships or something."

"Bet you remember the day it was all over, too, don't you?"

I nodded. "Sure do. V-J day. Big parade down Main Street; everybody went a little crazy. My dad, just back from the Big Red One in Europe, set me up on a fire truck so as I could ring its bell. Big kick for a seven- or eight-year-old. But I still don't see what you're getting at, Mac. What's any of this got to do with the price of rice in China?"

"Well, you see, sir, while you and Byson and the old man were doing those paper drives and ringing those fire-engine bells, the rest of us in the company here weren't even lecherous gleams in our fathers' eyes. I mean, these were your formative years, and it was all good against evil, right against wrong, God's on the side of the pure of heart, and so forth.

"And it was the country's military that made the world 'safe for democracy.' Hell, it's only natural that you see the profession of arms as a higher calling. And, for the same reasons, it's only natural you all can't conceive of losing this, or for that matter, any other war.

"But you see, sir, the rest of us didn't grow up in that environment. Hell, I can't even remember Korea, and we really didn't win that one."

I didn't like the direction our conversation was taking, and I *still* didn't know what the fuck Mac was talking about. What the hell's environment or the "goodness" of World War II got to do with the Nam? Suddenly, suspecting I might know the genesis of his remarks, I asked, "Hey, Mac, what was your major in college?"

"Philosophy, with a minor in international relations."

Bingo!

"What about you, sir?"

"Never went to college," I answered. "Came out of the Appalachian Mountains of Virginia, with a clean set of underwear and ten dollars in my pocket, and joined the 'regular' Army. And the regular Army, by the way, tells me I'd better be getting some education pretty damn soon if I want to remain part of the regular Army.

"But that's neither here nor there. Mac, career aspirations aside, you can't seriously question whether or not we're gonna win this thing? Shit, look at the record. How long have we been here? I mean our ground forces, the infantry, 'queen of battle.' Two years? And in that two years, we've done nothing but kick ass! From Ia Drang in '65 till right now while we're talking, we've beaten Charlie every single time he's come out to play! It's just a question of time till he's gonna have to throw in the towel. Hell, we're bleeding him white, Mac. You can't question that."

"No, sir, I don't. But they're still fighting; they're still in there kicking. I mean if they weren't, we wouldn't be here, right?"

"Well, yeah, but . . ."

"And I'm afraid they may continue kicking longer than we, and I mean the folks back home, can put up with it."

This was heresy! One of us was out of touch with reality, and I figured it had to be Mac. I couldn't even fathom what he, somewhat less than subtly, was alluding to—losing!

"Uh . . . don't get me wrong, sir," he quickly added, perhaps noting the bewildered, agitated look on my face. "I hope and pray we do win; we've already paid a hell of a price. And I know we have the wherewithal to do it. I just question whether or not we have the guts to continue the fight at this pace. You know, sir, there's a very vocal minority back in the States right now that would like to see us out of here; and daily they're becoming more vocal and less of a minority.

"Sir, all I'm saying is I think we're in a race against time on the thing, and I don't believe our leadership, from LBJ on down, realizes it."

"Well, Mac, you're wrong. We're gonna win this sucker, even at this pace, and ten years from now South Vietnam will be another Korea, an up-and-coming economic power in the Pacific. And twenty years from now, it'll be competing with Japan. It never fails: wherever we go and whenever we win—and, Mac, we always win—good times follow."

He nodded, but without conviction. So I continued. "Well, economics aside, you can't actually conceive of North Vietnam simply overrunning the country, can you, Mac?"

"No, sir, I can't really envision that. I see the whole thing just kind of petering out, just dying a slow and uneventful death. You know, sort of like Britain's experience with the CTs in Malaysia, well, Malaya at the time. Hey!" he said, suddenly brightening. "Maybe that's what we should do, sir! Know what the Brits did in Malaysia?"

I shook my head. As far as I could recall, they pretty well whipped the CTs (Communist terrorists—Malaysia's Viet Cong).

"Well," he continued, "after fighting the CTs for years and finally concluding they were at a Mexican standoff—you know, with neither side able to defeat the other—the Brits suddenly announced to the world that they had won, period. Said they had won the war, the emergency was over, the colony was to be granted independence, and they were going home. And they did! It was that simple. When they discovered they couldn't beat the CTs, they just said they already had and then packed their rucks and left!"

The two of us started laughing.

"Yes, sir, LBJ ought to read more British history. Hell, he could solve this thing the same way, right? Hey, sir, couldn't you just see him there on TV, you know, 'Ma fellow 'Mericans, we've won! We've arrived at the end of the tunnel, turned off the light, and now ah'm gonna bring our 'Merican boys home, so them little Asian boys can continue' . . . huh?"

Our laughter set a poor example in after-dark noise discipline. But no matter how hard we tried to suppress it, neither of us could.

"Of course, there'd still be a lot of VC in Vietnam," Mac added, "same as there's still a lot of CTs in Malaysia, right?"

"Guess so," I replied, wiping my eyes. "But tell me, Mac, how the hell did we get around to LBJ and Malaysian history?"

"Think it started when you asked if I planned to stay in, and I guess I took the long way 'round the hutch in saying no," he said, still laughing.

"Well," I responded, soberly, seriously, "you may change your mind, and I really hope you do, Mac. 'Cause you're one hell of a combat leader. And, by the way, whether you stay in or not, I mean regardless of what you might do in the future, that's something no one can ever take from you."

"Thanks, sir," he said, then got up and strolled into the night, back to his place of rest in Vietnam's sod. Only six more such holes to dig.

One Six and Two Six, working the mountain the next day, surprisingly came up dry, no contact whatsoever. But Three Six, while walking the valley floor, unexpectedly came upon three NVA napping in a grove of palms. One of the three was quick enough to get away with his life; the other two became part of the war's body count.

We moved our NDP again that night and then continued our operational routine the following day with One Six and Three Six on the mountain and Two Six in the valley. The command section accompanied One Six.

It was nearly three o'clock in the afternoon when a single unsuspecting NVA soldier walked into our ambush.

"Thank God," I said to Sergeant Sullivan, who was sitting beside me when we heard the familiar *whoom!* of the claymore's detonation. "Thought we were gonna go two days in a row without a hit in the high country."

"Yeah, and you know what snuffie's beginning to say," he replied, smiling. "A day without a hit is like a day without sunshine."

"Goddamn, he's a mess, ain't he?" the Bull observed as we surveyed the ambush site. The hit man, perhaps because there was only one enemy soldier to contend with, had waited until the last possible moment before detonating his claymore, thus ensuring a kill. The mine's force had virtually severed its victim at the waist, with only the spinal column and shreds of flesh connecting his upper and lower torsos. It was a quick, merciful death.

After reporting our kill to battalion, we began our descent down the mountain. As we did so, I radioed Halloway, telling him to remain in position for another twenty to thirty minutes and then follow us.

Within minutes after we joined Two Six in our NDP, Major Byson called.

"Comanche, this is Arizona Three. Are you in posture to move within one zero? Over."

"Uh . . . negative. Still have my Three Six on the hump. They should close my location within two zero or so. Over."

"This is Arizona Three. Okay, tell 'em to hustle it up. I'm inbound with four, plus two, plus two in two zero. Arclight opened up a large bunker complex on the side of a mountain to the northeast of you, and you're the closest and fastest thing we can get on top of it. How copy?"

"This is Comanche Six. Roger, solid copy. We'll be ready."

En route to our objective, Major Byson informed us we would have to work our way into the bunker complex from the valley below since he simply couldn't find a suitable LZ atop the mountain. This was an atypical method of air-assaulting a target inasmuch as one of the division's tactical strengths lies in its ability to land a force above the enemy and then attack downward. It never ceased to amaze us that, regardless of how many times we so conducted our assaults, the NVA, I suppose being set in their ways, continued to defend downward, in the opposite direction from which we were attacking.

Overflying the B-52 (Arclight) strike before landing, we saw it had made an ugly mess of the untouched tropical rain forest. The double- and triple-forested canopy had been torn asunder, revealing a maze of giant teak trees and other jungle vegetation lying in disarray. Yet in another, somewhat morbid sense, the strike was beautiful! Beautiful in its manifestation of destructive power, in the near-perfect symmetrical pattern its bomb craters formed upon the face of the mountain below.

"Comanche, this is Arizona Three. We've seen some movement in the strike area, so I'd like you to get up there as quickly as possible. You've got Blue Max and red leg on call, but don't think you're gonna need 'em. Charlie's probably still in a post-arclight daze . . . you know, walking around with his head on backwards, mumbling to himself. So the sooner you get up there, the less time he'll have to recock his brains."

I rogered his transmission and, noting that we were speedily approaching the LZ, quickly passed the headset back to the crew chief. Then I mounted the skids of the Huey (located approximately three feet below each of the aircraft's doorless door frames). The rest of those on board followed suit. We grasped the aircraft's door frame or floor attachments with our inboard hands while holding our weapons in our outboard hands.

We were now just seconds from touchdown, coming in low and fast, the Huey's fifty- to sixty-knot backwash creating a comical pattern of moving wrinkles on even the youngest of our faces.

Suddenly the Huey slowed and flared, tail down, preparing to land. When it was within three feet or so of the ground, we jumped. Simultaneously, the helicopter flared again, this time in a nose-down attitude, immediately picking up forward airspeed. In seconds it was gone, having never touched the earth. If one learns little else in the Cav, he quickly becomes adept at swiftly off-loading a UH-ID Iroquois slick.

One Six, having conducted the assault, speedily secured the LZ, permitting me to signal Byson that we were green. Moments later the Chinooks landed with the rest of the company. It takes longer for thirty or forty armed cavalrymen to disembark these huge troop-transport helicopters—perhaps five or six seconds.

The platoon leaders and I hurriedly planned our incursion into the strike area, wanting to get in and out as quickly as possible since darkness would be upon us within a couple of hours. Having noted during our flyover several trails that seemed to lead from the valley floor up the mountain, we decided to approach the strike area from two directions. Two Six would attempt to access it on the left, while Three Six did the same on the right. We would accompany Three Six. One Six, already in position around the LZ, was to remain in place, securing the landing zone as our NDP. They would, of course, be augmented in this task by Four Six.

We had been climbing for thirty to forty minutes when our trail fizzled out, and we had to start chopping our way through the dense foliage. I was the fourth or fifth man in the file. Suddenly, a dazed NVA soldier plunged at us from the thick uphill vegetation, less than ten feet to our right!

Our reaction was simply a matter of reflex. I habitually carried my CAR-15 (a shortened version of the M-16) in my right hand, its muzzle pointed forward, my finger in the trigger guard and thumb on the safety selector, the weapon's weight supported by a carrying strap across my right shoulder. Spinning to the right, I fired at the charging blur before me! The soldier in front of me did the same. The dead man's forward momentum carried him crashing through us, throwing me to the ground. Quickly, but a bit tremulously, I got to my feet.

"You okay, sir?" Sergeant Buckley, the man who had been in front of me, calmly asked.

"Uh . . . yeah, sure. No problem," I replied, hopefully with more conviction than I felt.

"Must've been a crazy whose brains were scrambled by one of those five-hundred-pounders," someone commented.

Sergeant Buckley had turned his attention to our lifeless intruder, an officer of the People's Army of North Vietnam, in whose outstretched hand was a tightly gripped P-38 Walthers pistol. Buckley looked at the weapon, then at me.

"Hey, Sergeant," I said unhesitatingly, "it's yours. No doubt in my military mind that you were the one who got him, and God bless you for it."

We began moving again and within a few minutes were in the strike area. Our progress then became far more difficult, for no jungle is quite so impenetrable as one that has been rearranged by an Arclight strike. Trees and foliage that had been growing as nature intended them to, vertically, were now a chaotic *horizontal* entanglement.

As we slowly worked our way through this wooded clutter, we were suddenly confronted by three unarmed NVA soldiers just standing there as if in a daze, staring at us. Momentarily, we stared back.

Three Six's point man yelled, "*Chu Hoi!*" (surrender). They didn't respond. Seconds passed. Then, as if in slow motion, one of the three enemy soldiers raised his arm, which he had held behind him, and in a wide overhand sweep threw a grenade into our midst! He was dead before he hit the ground, but his two companions, miraculously and instantaneously recovering from their post-Arclight trance, made good their escape.

As was often the case, the hand grenade was a dud. The luck of Charlie Company was holding.

After marrying up with Two Six, we jointly worked the bunker area for another half hour or so, counting the dead and occasionally recovering a weapon. It was dark by the time we rejoined One Six in our NDP. We were ready to drop, too tired to even talk.

But Major Byson wasn't. "This is Arizona Three. Good show, Comanche . . . break. Be advised there's gonna be another Arclight flown in your vicinity tonight. You're well out of range, but it might spoil your sack time . . . break. Unless we find something on first-light recon in that area, I'll probably be moving you again in the Alpha Mike. How's your copy?"

An hour or so later, the world to the northeast of us exploded! We could only imagine the stark terror felt by those who found themselves on the business end of an Arclight mission. You could not hear or see the B-52s: they flew too high. With no warning the earth simply turned itself upside down.

That night's target, the reverse slope of the mountain on which we had worked earlier in the day, was at least a mile from us and it was still a frightening experience—frightening but fascinating. The sky suddenly lit up in multiple brilliant-vermilion flashes, silhouetting the mountain to our front. Moments later, the crashing sound of these 500- and 750-pound bombs reached us in an awesome, earth-shattering shock wave.

We had been told that the U.S. Air Force considered the Arclight mission to be "demoralizing to an enemy force caught within its periphery." This had to be the understatement of the year.

AREA 506

The following morning we were picked up and inserted into area 506, so called because Route 506, an unpaved secondary road running east-west from Highway One into Binh Dinh's mountains toward Kontum, was the only distinguishable cultural feature therein. In reality, however, it was distinguishable only as a thin red line on our 1:50,000 tactical maps; like much of the country's secondary-road network, it was a communicable roadway in name only. Its surface was marred by artillery and bomb craters, its bridges had long since collapsed, and much of it had been overgrown with vegetation by the surrounding jungle as it went about reclaiming the land, inch by inch.

After an uneventful insertion on a green LZ, we established a company base astride Route 506 and began conducting "cloverleaf" operations. This maneuver was generally regarded as defensive, not offensive, in nature, its primary objective being not to find and attack the enemy but to make sure the enemy was not about to find and attack us. It was a good technique to employ in a circumstance, such as this one, in which we didn't know where to concentrate our offensive efforts—where the hunting in one direction looked no better or worse than in any other. The operation derived its name from the diagram that depicts it, the company base being the clover's stem, and the three platoons' large circular sweeps outward from the base the clover's leaves.

Our first day in area 506 was obviously going to be a day without sunshine. The last of the platoons returned from its cloverleaf maneuver in the early afternoon having found, like the two earlier returning platoons, no trace of our elusive foe. We were surprised as this point on Route 506, where it enters Binh Dinh's mountain passes, was only six to eight kilometers northwest of "our" mountain where we had been consistently successful with our claymores.

The afternoon heat was blistering, and the previous day's B-52 postmission assessment coupled with our cloverleaf walk in the weeds had nearly exhausted us. Since we seemed to be in no imminent danger, we decided to convert our cloverleaf base to an NDP, call the log bird in early, and get some rest. The decision was popular and, as events would unfold, auspicious. We would need the rest.

Most of the company napped away the afternoon. Shortly before dusk, the log bird dropped off a smattering of ammo, water, a hot, our rucks, and one can of beer and one of coke per company head count. All was once again right with our little piece of the republic.

But the First Air Cavalry was a large organization, and while we were at peace with the world astride Route 506, other cavalrymen were still at work. As we sat sipping our warm beer, an OH-6A Cayuse helicopter pilot was flying last-light recon. He was becoming increasingly interested in the side of a mountain only six to eight kilometers from where we sat.

Whoom! Whoom!

"Red leg going in. Not too far from us," Sergeant Sullivan offhandedly commented.

Minutes passed as the Bull, Slim Brightly, and I chitchatted about unimportant things.

Whoom! Whoom! Whoom! Whoom!

"Sounds like one five five," the Bull said. "Sounds like it's going in on our mountain."

"Maybe H&I, huh, Slim?" I asked.

"Naw, too much of it for H&I," Slim replied, and he should know.

"Well, then, how about seeing if you can find out what's going on, Lieutenant Brightly!" I said jokingly. "You know, get on the horn and talk some of your cannon-cocker lingo to your red-leg connections."

"Roger that, Six," he responded. Smiling, he got to his feet, muttering as if to himself, "And putting his precious three-point-two elixir aside, the company's attached forward observer hurried off to do his master's bidding. For an artilleryman's duties amongst infantrymen are many and varied. He must, for example, count for them when the numbers surpass that of single digits; must read their mail and comic books to them and apprise them of the difference between a right and left piece of footwear. He must teach them to tell time . . ."

The Bull and I were laughing as he turned to leave.

"And when Mickey's big hand is on the . . ."

"Hey, Slim, see if you can get a grid, okay?"

"But of course, sir, and I shall even spell it for you . . ."

Whoom! Whoom! Whoom! Whoom!

The artillery fires continued to increase in tempo and were producing a fairly steady rumble to the southeast of us when Lieutenant Brightly, now all business, returned from his radio set.

"Got a grid, sir," he said, "and it looks like our mountain." He paused, flashlight in hand, as he plotted the grid coordinates on his map. Then he replotted them. "Shit! If this grid is correct, I'll bet we were within twenty fucking meters of this bunker complex on nearly that many fucking occasions."

"That's what it is?" I asked. "A bunker complex?"

"Yes, sir. Seems one of the Cav squadron's birds was doing a routine last light, thought he saw some smoke or something, so he called in a couple rounds. Well, that opened the canopy up a bit, so he called for effect, and, hey, that really opened it up! Says he saw all kinds of bunkers with a bunch of gooks scrambling about 'em."

"Sonofabitch!" I said, looking at the plot on his map. "Target's no more than a klick from Daisy!"

"Damn right, it's not!" Slim retorted. "And that's where we should be tonight, sir. Right at the base of that fucking mountain! It beats the shit out of me why battalion put us out here 'stead of back there where we were killing gooks 'bout every fucking day."

"Well, you're sure as hell right on that, sir!" the Bull interjected. "We ain't *never* had any luck in the 506. Sometimes I really question the operational thinking of some of those shits in the three section. I mean who sets their head space and timing? Ho Chi Minh?"

Someone else echoed the first sergeant's sentiments. "Yeah, Top. It's the fucking S-2! He keeps his head up his ass."

As word of the discovery on "our" mountain spread throughout the company, it became apparent that the consensus sided with Slim and the Bull. And it *was* a shame we weren't located at the base of the mountain as we had been on so many uneventful nights in the recent past. But what to do about it?

I decided to call Major Byson and ask if he was aware of the artillery strike and, if so, to tactfully suggest that we were poorly postured to influence its outcome.

"Listen, Comanche," Byson somewhat irritably and indignantly responded, "we know about the strike, we're working on it, and if we need your help, *I'll* call *you*, okay? Out!"

Oh, well, tact never was my forte.

Thirty minutes later, Blair passed me his handset with his familiar, "Three's on the horn, sir."

"Okay, listen up, Comanche," Byson said in a calm, business-as-usual voice. "We know you want to get back up on that hill of yours, and I'm gonna put you in there just as soon as I can make a pickup in the A.M. If it looks like the weather won't allow an early extract, it may be best for you to go in overland—it's only eight klicks or so. What do you think?"

"This is Comanche Six. Sounds fine to me. Just give us your weather decision as early as possible."

"This is Arizona Three. You'll be making it, not me, Comanche. Weather at your end will be the deciding factor . . . break. Prepare for a pickup with four, plus two, plus two."

Passing the handset back to Blair, I recalled the Bull's tactical dictum: "They're long gone at dawn, Six. Always!"

"Andy, get the platoon leaders over here, please. It's time to talk."

"They'll be gone at dawn, sir," Sergeant Sullivan predicted, after he, Slim, the platoon leaders, and I had assembled for a council of war.

"Top's right, sir," Mac said. "And the 506 sets right in a valley here, so it'll be socked in till eight, nine o'clock in the morning. Right, Top?" he asked, turning to Sergeant Sullivan, who nodded his head in agreement.

"Yes, sir," the Bull said. "We've been in this area more times than I want to count, and it's always like sitting in a fucking cloud in the morning. Shit, if we wait for an extract, we'll be lucky if we're on the mountain by ten."

"Kind of ironic, isn't it? I mean, we're undoubtedly the unit closest to the objective. Yet, because of the morning fog, I'll bet any other, and I really mean *every* other, company in the battalion is in a better posture for an early extract. See what I mean? We're both the closest to, and farthest from, the target," Lieutenant Norwalk commented, philosophically.

Mac gazed at Norwalk incredulously for a moment, then said, "Well, Bill, that's really an interesting observation, and if you should ever write a book on the role weather plays in combat's decision-making process, I suggest you include it. In the meantime, could you please tell us just what the fuck that has to do with solving our predicament? Huh?"

Norwalk just smiled.

"Why not move out at first light, sir?" Bob Halloway proposed. "I mean start moving right at BMNT. Shouldn't take us more than an hour plus, two at the most."

"Too late," the Bull replied. "They'll be gone at dawn. Never fails."

"Why not start moving now, tonight?" Brightly suggested.

"Think that's the answer, Slim," I said. "If you look at our options, that's the only one that'll get us into the area at first light."

Silence.

"Uh . . . you mean overland, sir?" Sullivan asked. "There's no light tonight. That shit's just too thick to navigate with no moon, sir. It'd take us the rest of the night and most of tomorrow."

"Naw, not overland, Top. Right down the red line, straight down Route 506. It'll take us within a klick of the mountain, two at the most."

Again, silence.

"Sir," Mac said, "you just don't move on a red line at night. I mean, honestly, sir, it just isn't done. We'd only be asking for trouble. 'Sides," he added, smiling, "I've only got four more days. Don't want to become a fucking ambush statistic with only four days to go!"

"Come on, Mac," I responded. "No one's gonna become a statistic 'cause no one's gonna get ambushed. Who the hell's gonna ambush us? This is our AO, there's no other friendly folk in the area, and we'll confirm that with battalion before we depart. That leaves only Charlie and . . ."

"Right!" Mac interrupted. "And he, sir, is our concern." Then, turning to the others, "Hey, fellows, when you all start getting old mail on me next week, I want it marked PCS, not Search!"

"Mac, Charlie ain't gonna be lying in ambush on 506 tonight," I argued. "I mean, why the hell should he? He knows that our units don't move around at night; he sure as hell knows we don't move bold ass down a red line! Hey, Mac, you said it yourself; it just isn't done. So why the fuck would he waste time setting up in ambush on a remote secondary road, waiting for an enemy that, by doctrine, never travels those roads at night?"

I paused briefly, allowing the "council" time to recognize the logic of my argument. I'd already pretty much decided we were going to go along with Slim's proposal, but I wanted the willing support of the others.

And, with the assistance of my first sergeant, I got it.

"CO's right, gentlemen," he said. "Charlie's good, but he ain't behind every rock, and he sure as shit can't ambush the whole country. He only goes into ambush when he knows target A is gonna travel route B on date C, and then he spends a hell of a lot of time planning, preparing, rehearsing, moving, and so forth. And none of that's applicable here."

"Well, shit, Top, we know all of that," Mac said, a bit tauntingly, smiling. "And we're ready to move. We just wanted to see if you knew what the captain and Slim there were talking about."

While they remained assembled, I got on the radio to Major Byson. Gotta be careful here, I thought to myself. Don't want to piss him off again. I'll just state the facts as we see them, make our proposal, and if he says no, we'll all go to bed. Company needs the rest anyway.

The battalion TOC's night watch replied that Major Byson wasn't in the area but relayed that they would try to locate him. Oh, shit, hope I'm not getting him out of the sack! Majors don't look kindly on captains interrupting what little cot time they get while assigned duties as a battalion S-3.

Moments later, Byson came on the air.

"Comanche, this is Arizona Three. What have you got? Over."

"This is Comanche Six. In regard to tomorrow's op . . . well, what with the fog on this end in the Alpha Mike, feel we're gonna miss the boat if we wait for an extract." I paused for a second and then continued, a bit more confidently. "Really think we ought to move out on foot tonight. That way we'd be in position to hit the objective at first light. I'm confident we can make the move without problem. Over."

"Hey, sounds good to me, Comanche. What're your proposed route and start point time? Check that, I'll extend your AO. You choose the route and get back to me ASAP."

"This is Comanche Six. Roger. Need to confirm absence of any other friendlies in our extended AO and ensure red leg isn't active anywhere between us and the objective after start time. My FO is working this through his channels . . . uh . . . just want to advise you of my concern."

"Roger, Comanche. Good copy, and there are no other friendly folk in your area. I'll double-check the red-leg issue also . . . break. Now listen, I think it's a good idea, but before I give you a green light, want to pass it by the Six. So stand by a moment . . ."

And so I stood by. Within a matter of minutes, Colonel Lich was on the radio.

"Comanche Six, this is Arizona Six. Understand what you want to do. Now listen up. It's your AO. You're the man on the ground, and if you think it's a sound move, do it! Any questions?"

I liked Colonel Lich.

Passing the handset back to Blair, I gave the council a thumbs up. "It's a go! Let's get ready to move."

"One thing, sir," Mac said. "I don't think it's a good idea to move too early. Mean, it's only gonna take us a couple hours to get down there, and we don't want to go into that bunker complex in the dark. Recommend we start moving around 0300 hours. That should put us in position to hit the complex at first light."

"Good idea, Mac," I said. "Let's plan on it. That'll also give our troops some more sack time before we move—God knows they need it; we all do."

I paused, collecting my thoughts, then continued. "Okay, we want to move light, silent, and fast. That means leaving our rucks, mortars, and starlight scopes behind. And that's too much for Four Six to handle by themselves. They just don't have the bodies."

Turning to Lieutenant Halloway, I said, "So I'm sorry, Bob, know you want to be on this, but you're staying with Four Six. You'll be in charge, of course; coordinate with Mac and Bill on how you're gonna fill in their portions of the perimeter."

Then, looking back at the others, I said, "Okay, order of march is Two Six, followed by One Six." Winking at Mac, I added, "This probably being your last one, Mac, think you should have the honor of leading it."

He grinned and, replied, somewhat sarcastically, "Thanks, sir, and I want you to know I appreciate it."

"Thought you would. Start point time is 0300 hours. Start point is . . . any suggestions?"

"Why don't we make it the 506 at the point it crosses our perimeter on the east?" Mac offered.

"Great!" I replied. "Okay, I'll be accompanying Two Six. Anything we missed?"

"Yes, sir," the Bull said, turning his attention to the others. "When you gentlemen return to your platoons—and this is just a reminder, *sirs*—make sure your people tape and tie weapons and LBE for silent movement. Don't want any clang, clang on the 506 in the morning."

"What about immediate action in an ambush . . . uh . . . I mean if we should get hit from the flank, sir?" Bill Norwalk asked. "'Course, like you all say, that's not gonna happen. But just in case something *like that* should happen, what's the procedure? Same as in daylight? Mean, charge it if it's near, go for cover if it's far?"

"Uh . . . right," I said, mentally kicking myself for not thinking of so obvious a contingency. Bill Norwalk has his head screwed on tighter than I do tonight.

"Good point, Bill," MacCarty said, "but I wouldn't worry too much about it. I think a greater concern is a meeting engagement, you know, just running into Charlie going the other way. 'Cause, like the Six says, it's his road at night."

"And *that's* a good point, Mac," I said, rebounding. "Which reminds me—and 'course it's your platoon—who's gonna be our point?"

He smiled and said, "Shit, sir, you know damn well who—Wester."

As planned, we left the NDP's perimeter at three o'clock in the morning, Wester and his bronze plate–embedded twelve-gauge shotgun leading the formation, followed by his squad leader and a two-man M-60 machine-gun team, Mac and his RTO, and me and mine. It was pleasantly cool and very dark.

The column moved east along Route 506 for an hour or so—silently, speedily, professionally. There was no cussing, clanging, banging, jingling, or needless whispering. They're good, I thought to myself, moving as infantrymen are supposed to move in the still of night in Indian country.

Abruptly we halted. Mac moved forward, passing his machine-gun team as he did so. I waited in place for a few moments, then, telling Blair and Andy to stand fast, followed after him. I found him twenty-five to thirty meters forward of the column, huddled with Wester and Sergeant Baker, the lead squad's squad leader.

"Problems?" I whispered.

"Uh . . . no, sir," Mac whispered in return. "Just checking to see if this is 'bout the right place to leave the 506 and cut south toward the mountain."

Recalling our previous night's map reconnaissance, I was about to say I thought we had another couple hundred meters to go when Wester whispered, "Shhhh! Think I hear something."

The four of us stood in silence, looking down the road, which inclined gently upward and over a small hill before falling off again toward the east. For a moment we heard nothing. Then, faintly, we could hear the rhythmic, crunching sound of footsteps on the sparsely graveled surface of Route 506. We stared at the top of the hill, twenty meters or so to our front.

Suddenly, silhouetted against the murky night sky, a man's head appeared, rising over the hill's summit. Then another. And another. They seemed to wear helmets of a sort and looked to be carrying weapons, but who were they? The enemy? And now, behind them, as they started down the hill toward us, two more heads appeared on the hilltop's skyline. Were there others behind them?

We continued to stand and stare as if frozen in place, Wester in front—closest to the approaching figures—Sergeant Baker to his rear, and Mac and myself behind Sergeant Baker. Five of them, four of us. Within seconds, they'd have to see us, either that or run straight into us. It was one of those electrifying, exhilarating moments that make soldiering a more memorable endeavor than other walks of life.

The first three figures, evidently seeing us, stopped abruptly less than ten meters to our front. One of them yelled, "*Dung lai!*"

It was the biggest mistake of his life, and the last one he'd ever make. Americans don't yell "*dung lai*" when they want someone to stand in place, and Wester knew that.

Bam! Bam! Bam! Bam!

Each time Wester fired, the muzzle flash from his shotgun momentarily and brilliantly illuminated another blood-splattered, khaki-clad figure caught photolike in a grotesque dance of death.

In not more than two seconds, his chamber was empty, and he yelled,

"Grenade!" We fell to the ground, thinking he was warning us of an incoming grenade. We quickly saw that was not the case as he threw one of his own grenades across the bodies to our front and into the ditch on the left side of the road. Then he hit the dirt.

Whoom!

The four of us got up and slowly, cautiously moved forward. In the center of the road, spaced within five feet of each other, lay three dead NVA soldiers. On the ground next to them lay two AK-47 assault rifles. In the ditch adjoining Route 506 we found two more enemy soldiers, both of whom were superficially wounded; and neither one could surrender quite fast enough to suit the other.

Mac wisely and hurriedly called his lead squad forward, sending them on down the road another twenty to thirty meters in case those who lay dead at our feet had friends following. Doc Heard had also charged forward and, after ensuring none of us were injured, began examining our wounded POWs.

"Lucky, both of them," he said. "Lot of blood, shrapnel, but don't think either one's hurting that much. Vital organs appear to be untouched." Then he added, "'Course, who can see a fucking thing in this light."

I heard him mumbling and said offhandedly, "Go 'head and use your flashlight, Doc. It's okay."

With the rest of the column now moving forward, I thought it best to go into a hasty perimeter defense where we stood, Two Six on the right of the road, One Six on the left. Having so decided, I radioed battalion.

"Arizona Three, this is Comanche Six. We're in contact, over."

"This is Arizona Three. Send your traffic."

Damn, it's Byson! Four-thirty in the fucking morning, and he's on the horn in a flash! Doesn't the man ever sleep?

"This is Comanche, Roger. Ran into five NVA on 506 at . . . uh . . . zero four ten hours." That's got to be close. "Got three NVA killed in action, two POWs, both lightly wounded. Also got two AK-47s and one SKS. No friendly casualties. Over."

"Understand you've got two prisoners, two live ones. Is that correct?"

"That's affirmative." I replied, beaming.

"This is Arizona Three. Okay! Super! We'll want to get them out as quickly as possible. I'm gonna pass this on to the Six, then get back to you. Stand by."

The two platoons, having moved forward, were hurriedly and noiselessly establishing their perimeter, though there was little real need for noise discipline at this juncture. Doc Heard, meanwhile, was performing some quick patchwork on our prisoners, while Sergeant Baker, assisted by one of his men, was binding their hands behind their backs with WD-1 (communications wire).

"Comanche, this is Arizona Six. Over." It was Colonel Lich on the battalion command net.

"This is Comanche Six."

"This is Arizona Six. Good job, Comanche. Now I want to get your prisoners out of there and interrogated right away. They may know something 'bout the area you're going into. The Three's gonna have a bird inbound in—wait—fifteen minutes. Any problem? Over."

"Negative, no problem. We'll be ready, over."

"Okay, pass on a 'well done' to your soldiers. They've already done a good night's work. Out."

Mac, having just positioned his platoon in a half circle on the right of 506, walked to our center-of-the-road CP and, gesturing toward the prisoners, asked, "What about our newfound friends here, sir? It's gonna slow us down if they have to tag along."

"Colonel says he'll have a bird here in fifteen minutes to evac 'em," I replied. "How 'bout bringing it in on the paddy over there on the right, Mac."

Sergeant Baker, completing his task of binding the two unfortunates, turned to MacCarty and said, "My squad will set up the LZ, sir. It's all part of a POW package deal we're offering tonight, and these two runts belong to us!"

"Uh . . . how do you want me to mark it?"

I looked at Mac. Mac looked at me.

Before either of us could think of how best to bring in the helicopters, Sergeant Baker continued, "Why don't I just give 'em a three-flashlight triangle and bring the bird down in the middle of it?"

Mac and I again looked at each other, then nodded our heads. We might do better in this war if we simply turned it over to our sergeants, I thought to myself.

"Battalion wants to know our location for the POW extract, sir," Blair announced, his handset to his ear.

"Tell 'em to just fly the red line," I replied. "We'll mark when they're overhead."

Ten minutes later, on schedule, we heard the familiar *whump, whump, whump* of a Huey pounding toward us from the east.

"Comanche, this is Arizona Two inbound on the red line. Ready for you to light up."

"This is Comanche Six. Roger. Marking with a three-flashlight delta in paddy on the south side of the red line. No obstacles other than some eight- to twelve-foot minipalms right against the road. LZ green. How copy?" I responded, concurrently signaling Mac to light up the landing zone.

After a brief pause, Arizona Two came back. "Roger, Comanche. Got your Lima Zulu. We'll be coming straight in, east to west, and probably turning our lights on just before touchdown. Might want to warn your men."

"This is Comanche Six. Roger . . . break. Listen I don't want to lose foxhole strength guarding prisoners. Want to make the handoff right here. They're secured with WD-1 and shouldn't cause any problem. Over."

"This is Arizona Two. Understand and no sweat. We'll take 'em from here. See you on the ground."

But he didn't. Baker and his men literally threw our two prisoners through the helicopter's open doors the moment its skids touched the ground—and the Huey was gone. And moments later, so were we.

The sun was high in the eastern sky when we finally entered the bunker complex. We had been delayed by the meeting engagement and subsequent difficulties in negotiating the terrain between Route 506 and the mountain. As the Bull had predicted, Charlie was gone. However, he left behind several small arms and some of his dead. We recovered the former, counted the latter, and having done so were preparing to move back down the mountain, when Lieutenant Norwalk yelled, "Hey, sir, look what we found over here!"

I strolled over to where he was standing, chest deep in a caved-in bunker.

"You believe this, sir?" he asked, smiling broadly. "It's a .50-caliber machine gun, whole receiver group, everything but the barrel. In great condition, too."

The words were no sooner out of his mouth than one of his men, who had been probing the ground behind him, announced, "Got the barrel, LT! Shit, it's good as new, still in Cosmoline." Then, moments later, "And here's the tripod! We got us a whole fucking gun, LT. Lookie here!"

Colonel Lich, after we had reported our find, extended his congratulations and promised to pass the good news on to our supporting aviators. There was a reason for this. In early 1968, the enemy had not yet widely introduced his heat-seeking missiles in the south; the greatest threat to helicopters flying Binh Dinh's plain was still the .50-caliber machine gun. And although the Cav's aviators were the bravest, most courageous, devil-may-care of all the pilots who flew in Vietnam—and all the pilots who flew in Vietnam were brave—even they were somewhat intimidated about being shot at by a .50-caliber machine gun. As they often said, "It's so darn difficult to be *wounded* by .50-caliber." Regardless of where they were hit by one of these sizable rounds, they'd very likely "buy the farm" before landing their helicopter, if it was still flyable.

Therefore, an infantry company's quality of life in the boonies was enhanced by finding and neutralizing one of these weapons. Life in the boonies was in large part dependent on Army aviators and their willingness to fly rucks, hot meals, beer, and coke when the weather or tactical situation was iffy. And these aviators were more apt to risk their lives for soldiers who had recently captured one of the enemy's more frightening antiaircraft weapons.

Before moving off the mountain, Bill Norwalk and his platoon rigged the area for an organic ambush. This was a little trick of the trade we employed in situations where it was almost a given that Charlie would be back, in this case looking for his .50-caliber. Setting up the ambush was relatively simple. First, Norwalk and his platoon emplaced trip flares, lots of them, throughout the bunker complex. If Charlie revisited his ravaged lair that night and tripped a single, virtually invisible wire on just one flare, the whole area would light up like a Christmas tree. Then we retired from the mountain and established our NDP on the valley floor below.

That evening, after the log bird had delivered our two 81-mm mortars, the gun crews adjusted fire on the mountain's bunker complex by "direct lay," meaning they could see their target from the guns. After so doing, the lay of the gun was not disturbed. High-explosive ammunition was then readied for firing, that is, charges were cut and the rounds placed beside the guns. And the vigil began.

From that point on until a trip flare was activated or dawn broke, one of the gun's crew would remain on each of the weapons, a round at his side and his eyes glued to the mountain. The instant either saw a flare pop, the two of them would drop their six or eight rounds down the gun's tube as fast as it would accept them.

On this occasion, around nine o'clock, Charlie turned on his flashlight before encountering one of our trip flares. And our gunners mercurially loosed their rounds on the bunker complex.

As was the case in most of our organic ambushes, it was difficult to ascertain whether or not we hurt Charlie that night. We rarely revisited these sites because we knew our enemy would either haul his dead and wounded off before dawn or, anticipating our return, leave them there as bait while he set up a counterambush. But if we didn't hurt him, I'll bet we scared the living hell out of him! I'll bet in the future he thought twice before using a flashlight to hunt for a misplaced .50-caliber machine gun.

"Comanche, we'll probably be leaving you in that area for a while," Byson said, radioing us later that night. "That's where the hunting seems to be best for you. Besides, we got the Tet truce coming up in a matter of days, and that's as good an area as any to get your men some well-deserved rest."

After thanking him and signing off, I passed the essence of his remarks along to Sergeant Sullivan, who was sitting beside me atop an empty mermite.

"Damn right, the troops need a rest!" he retorted. "Been up, walking and fighting for, what? Forty-eight hours plus? And how many assaults we made since leaving the bridge? How many different areas we worked?"

"Uh . . . I don't know myself, Top. A bunch."

"Hey, Six, I can't 'member neither and don't care to. And don't much care where we go or what area we work tomorrow, or the next day, or next week. And, sir, that's 'bout the way the troops feel."

He paused, grinned, and then continued. "Mean, shit, Six, when you reach the point that you can't remember where you've been or care 'bout where you're going, you're due for a break, right?"

"Right, Top," I said without elaborating. Because the Bull really didn't expect me to elaborate. I recognized the signs: my first sergeant was about to embark on another of his discourses regarding the haves and have-nots in the Nam.

But that's okay; he'll feel better when he's finished.

"Really, Six, what the hell do they expect out of snuffie? What more does he have to give? I mean, I've been in this man's Army for nigh on to a quarter of a century, and I've never seen anything like it! Shit, I know war's no cup of tea, but at least in the last two we had a line we either defended, or attacked, or withdrew from. Right?"

"Right, Top."

"And every now and then," he continued, as if not hearing me, "we'd be relieved, as a unit, from that line and stand down for a little refitting and relaxing. Here they say you're standing down if you're guarding the goddamn Bong Son bridge! Now, sir, you tell me the difference 'tween digging a hole to sleep in out here every night and filling those fucking sandbags on the bridge every day. None! Right?"

"Right, Top."

"Damn right, there's no difference! And they expect snuffie to live like this for twelve goddamn months! Twelve months of this stinking heat, dust, mud, rain, rotting fatigues, malaria tabs, bugs, leeches, cold charlie rats, sheer boredom, and, fuck, instant terror. I'm telling you, sir, many a normal man can't retain his sanity living like this for a goddamn year."

He paused briefly, then continued. "And that's not the real pisser of it, Six. I mean, if we were all living like this, it'd be different. But we're not! You got any idea how them support troops are living in An Khe and Qui Nhon? Or places like Cam Ranh, Danang, Long Binh?"

I had a very good idea, and he was right: it simply wasn't fair. But then, many things about the Nam were unfair.

"They're living like fucking kings!" he went on. "Got hot showers, starched uniforms, clean sheets, steak every fucking night, multiservice—if you know what I mean—maids falling all over themselves. Got their clubs with two-bit-a-shot booze and go-go girls, libraries, USO shows, PXs, class VI counters with two-buck-a-bottle Johnny Walker—Black Label! Got their enterprising—again, if you know what I mean—doughnut dollies. Shit, you name it, they got it!

"And, Six," he began to laugh, "those assholes are envious of them chairborne wimps stationed in Saigon, 'cause they have a *golf course!* You believe it, sir? A fucking golf course! Our generals couldn't manage this war without building themselves a fucking golf course."

He stopped laughing, paused, then said, "And our troops think it's Christmas when they get a single warm can of three-point-two beer. Shit, it ain't fair, sir."

"Of course it's not, Top," I replied, "but tell me something. Where would you rather be tonight, here or on that golf course in Saigon?"

"Right goddamn here! Right here sharing this stinking crap with snuffie! Shit, you know that, sir," he answered, defiantly. "'Cause snuffie here, well, he's . . . uh . . . mean, these are the greatest . . ." His voice broke, and his eyes suddenly moistened. He wiped at them with his hand. "'Scuse me, sir. Uh . . . I mean they're 'bout the most magnificent human beings walking this fucking earth."

He's right, of course, but perhaps he's also been out here too long. Or maybe just sent forward to fight one too many of his nation's wars.

Composing himself, smiling, he added, "Shit, you gotta love 'em, Six. Nobody else does."

And I did. We both did. Still do.

Early the next morning, Three Six, the most rested of the company's platoons, climbed our mountain and set up a standard two-point claymore ambush. Later in the day, One Six and Two Six conducted casual cloverleaf sweeps north and south of the company's base, looking for a new NDP in the process. Around one o'clock in the afternoon Two Six radioed that they had found such a site a klick or so to the north of us. We in the headquarters section and Four Six waited until One Six had returned from their sally to the south and then, joining forces with them, began moving toward our new NDP.

Shortly before closing Two Six's position, we heard the familiar report of a claymore's detonation, followed by the rhythmic pounding of an M-60 machine gun on the mountain towering to the left of us.

And we felt good.

"Three Six bagged 'em!"

"The sun shines today."

"Cloverleaves suck! The good hunting's always in the high country."

It was not that we were jubilant about the sudden violent demise of what I would moments later learn to be three NVA soldiers—three fellow human beings. It was simply that we had scored. That we had succeeded in doing what we had been trained and sent to Vietnam to do. The death of enemy soldiers at our hands quite simply produced a good feeling, a feeling of exhilaration much like that experienced when one's high school football team scores a touchdown. In this sense, we modern soldiers did not seem that far removed from our cavemen brethren or Genghis Khan's warriors.

After joining Two Six in our new NDP, I pulled MacCarty aside.

"Hey, Mac, how about putting your trick or treat, say, a squad or so, on the 506 'bout where Wester scratched those five NVA night 'fore last? I mean, they're obviously traveling the route, and we might get lucky again."

"506? Sir, that's nearly two klicks out. Quite a ways for a single squad to set up."

"Well, shit, Mac, beef it up a bit. 'Nother M-60, couple M-79s. Your call, but I want an ambush on the 506 tonight, okay?"

"Okay, Six. I'll take a squad plus. We'll leave the perimeter shortly after . . ."

"Mac, I don't want you going. Hey, you'll be leaving us in a day or two, and you've got good squad leaders—Baker's one of the best. You gotta give 'em room to grow, and they can't do that with you looking over their shoulder all the time."

He looked at me a moment, amused, and then smiled and said, "Right, sir. Kind of like you letting me grow while looking over my shoulder during our two-squad helicopterless false extraction, right?"

"Uh . . . that was different," I protested, blushing a little. "Mean, I was but a casual observer on that venture. Just . . . learning the ins and outs of a stay-behind. You know, being new on board and all, I just wanted to . . ."

"Or during our claymore forays up the mountain, huh?" He interrupted, grinning broadly.

"Well, shit, Mac, I can hardly sit on my ass with Four Six in the NDP all day, now, can I?"

"No, sir, you can't, and I copy you loud and clear," he said, still smiling. "And Baker it'll be, and he'll be augmented accordingly."

In the wee hours of the following morning, I was awakened by a very concerned Lieutenant MacCarty.

"Sergeant Baker's in a bind, sir. Says he's got what he thinks is a company of NVA on the 506 where it intersects with that secondary north-south trail we traveled the other night. Says they're just sitting there, like they're assembling or something."

"Is he in contact?" I said, hurriedly unwrapping myself from my poncho liner and getting to my feet.

"No, sir. Says they're not in his kill zone, and there's too many of 'em for him to take on anyway. But he's got 'em on the starlight scope."

Turning to Anderson, who was on radio watch, I loudly whispered, "Andy, go to Two Six's push."

"They're not in a posture to do much talking, sir," MacCarty commented.

"Understand that, Mac," I remarked, "but if he's got a company out there, and he can't take 'em on, we gotta get some red leg on 'em. Which means Baker and his people are gonna have to move."

He nodded and then took Anderson's extended handset, whispering into it, "Two Six Tango, this is Six. We're gonna be bringing red leg in on your target. If you can move, key your handset twice. Over."

We listened as the handset's rushing noise was interrupted by two distinct breaks.

"Okay, Tango, I copy. Now I understand that north-south trail is the same one we used when we left the red line the other night. If so, give us another two clicks and then haul ass and go for cover. Call me as soon as it's safe to do so. Over."

Again the handset's rushing sound was twice broken by Baker keying his push-to-talk.

"I'll get Brightly," the Bull, now also up, offered.

Lieutenant Brightly quickly plotted the grid and requested his fire mission. Moments later he said, in a louder voice than he should have, "Hot damn! They're gonna put a TOT on 'em! Been out here better than five months and ain't never seen a TOT fired." Time on target is a mission in which artillery fires from several firing locations are simultaneously massed on a single target.

"Uh . . . it'll take 'em a few minutes to crank it up, Boss," he added, turning to me.

"And it'll take Baker longer than that to clear the area. There ain't gonna be *no* TOT until he and his soldiers are safely tucked in somewhere," Sergeant Sullivan remarked, leaving little doubt in anyone's mind that he meant what he said.

"I copy that, Top," Slim Brightly said. "Not to worry. We don't shoot at the good guys."

"Probably ought to wait 'til Baker's a good six, seven hundred meters up range, huh?" MacCarty remarked more than asked.

"A klick would be better. Just to be on the safe side," the Bull said.

"Hey, they're even bringing an ARVN battery in on it," Brightly said, his handset to his ear.

"Better make that *two* klicks," the Bull said dryly.

"Hell, Top, if they fall back two klicks, they'll be sitting with us in the NDP!" Mac said.

"You're right, Lieutenant. And I don't know 'bout the rest of you, but I'm gonna *sit* this one out in my hole," Sullivan grunted.

A short while later, Sergeant Baker informed us that he and his patrol were out of harm's way, having retired to a ravine a klick or so south of the 506. Moments later, Slim Brightly, smiling broadly, gave a thumbs up: "Rounds on the way!"

Then we heard the shrieking, screaming sound of artillery projectiles passing over our heads from the southeast. Suddenly the northern horizon lit up in multiple vermilion-and-white flashes, and moments later we heard the crashing sound of the projectiles exploding on Route 506. The earsplitting display of firepower lasted several minutes.

"Divarty requests some feedback on the mission, sir," Slim said after it was over. "Wants to hear about piles of dead gooks out there."

"Well, ain't nobody going back there tonight," I replied. "Tell 'em we'll check it out at first light."

Baker and his patrol did just that but found nothing. No dead bodies, no weapons, no blood trails—nothing. And neither divarty nor battalion was happy about that.

That night, after the log bird had departed and while the Bull and I were in idle conversation, we received a call from Colonel Lich's executive officer.

"Comanche Six, this Arizona Five. Uh . . . we're a little concerned 'bout last night's fire mission. You know, large expenditure of class V with nothing to show for it. Request that you try to ascertain whether or not there was actually a large enemy force out there or whether your people might have just been seeing ghosts."

Why, you pompous, chair-warming sonofabitch!

"This is Comanche Six. Be advised that I am well acquainted with the soldier in charge of that patrol, and if he says there was enemy out there, there was enemy out there. And that's all the 'ascertaining' I intend to do," I said heatedly. "How copy?"

"Roger, I copy. Don't know if that'll satisfy higher, but I'll pass it along."

"You believe that, Top?" I said angrily. "Who the fuck is he to question one of my soldiers? And who the fuck made him keeper of Uncle Sam's artillery stockpiles?"

"Now, take it easy, sir," the Bull said, trying to calm me—the two of us reversing roles on this occasion. "The XO's all right. Sometimes can't find his ass with both hands, but he's all right. Probably just trying to answer the divarty commander's mail. Don't let 'em get to you."

"But shit, Top, what's the great concern? I'll bet they routinely fire these missions at a bunch of old tank hulls back at Sill trying to impress some fat congressman or civilian aide, and here we're at war and they start counting rounds on us!"

"Well, you're right there, Six. If the divarty commander is so god-damn interested in seeing where his precious rounds impact, why don't he come and sit his ass on the 506 one night 'stead of living in the lap of luxury back there at English!" he said, beginning to bristle.

"Right, Top!"

"I mean, just who the fuck is he to be questioning my commander!" he continued, his anger intensifying.

"Uh . . . right, Top, but actually we don't know if he even . . ."

"It's just like I said the other night. These fat fucks sit back there in their secure fire base, eating their goddamn steaks and drinking their goddamn booze while snuffie here . . ."

"Whoa, Top. Let's not get into another discourse on living conditions and the haves and have-nots, okay?"

He paused, smiled, and said, "Yeah, guess not. Guess we've pretty much covered that ground, huh?"

We sat in silence for a while, hearing only the low rushing sound emanating from the company's radios positioned a short distance away.

"But shit, Six, I know I'm preaching to the choir in your case," he remarked, picking up the conversation where we'd let it drop moments before. "Hell, you've paid your dues, what with this being your third tour and all. And I know you 'green beanies' suffered too, far as living conditions were concerned."

I merely nodded.

"Well, what about it, sir? Was it worse out there with Special Forces than it is here with us?"

"No, not worse. Sometimes, in some ways, it was better. I mean as far as living conditions go." Then, reflecting on it, I added, "And sometimes, in some ways, it was worse. But mostly, it was just different."

"Yeah, different. I know what you mean there," he responded. "At least here we got the whole fucking Cav behind us when we get into something. Whereas you all had what? Twelve men, brave and true, and a campload of gooks with no red leg or nothing else to back you up."

"Kind of like that."

"Where were you anyway, sir? Not here in II Corps? You know they got a team over in Happy Valley."

"No, not here. First time, back in '62, there weren't any 'twelve men brave and true.' Back then I was a young staff sergeant stationed in Nha Trang, living a hell of a lot better than we're living out here, Top.

"Second time I was on the Laotian border, at earth's end, not far from Khe Sanh." I smiled, reminiscing. "You know, Top, this place was so isolated, we used to go to Khe Sanh for R&R."

He grinned and asked, "What was the name of the place?"

"It was called ARO, although it beats the shit out of me why."

Later that night, as I lay in my piece of Vietnam's soil, my thoughts drifted back to those early years—so different, so young, so long ago.

Early Days

The first of three four-engine C-124 Globe Master transport planes began its lumbering descent into Tan Son Nhut, the international airport located on the outskirts of Saigon, in the country of Vietnam, a country few of us aboard had ever heard of six months before. The descending Globe Masters carried an Army Special Forces element referred to by its planners as "Force 76T." The seventy-six Green Berets aboard, however, referred to ourselves as the "seventy-six trombones," which was also a song from the then-currently popular movie, *The Music Man*. The Force would exercise command and control over all Special Forces operational detachments, or "A" teams, serving in Vietnam, teams that were presently controlled by the Central Intelligence Agency and, in most cases, working with the country's indigenous mountain, or Montagnard, tribes.

The C-124 taxied along Tan Son Nhut's tarmac to the military off-load area, then shut down its engines and opened its massive cargo doors. The humid, hot, and sticky influx of air hit us like a sledgehammer. Our Vietnam experience had begun. It would affect each of us differently. Some would rapidly grow to hate this country and everything about it—the climate, food, culture, deprivation, our mission, and most of all the country's people. Others would fall in love with everything our colleagues loathed and in so doing develop symptoms of a Far Eastern disease referred to by French Foreign Legionnaires as "yellow fever," a love of the Orient in general and Indochina in particular.

We were quartered in an old and beautifully preserved French villa on the outskirts of the city just a hop, skip, and a jump from Tan Son Nhut Air Base. Actually, the officers were quartered in the beautifully preserved villa; the peons, myself included, were quartered in peasant hutches *behind* the lovely villa.

Our job was to understudy the CIA, which would eventually relinquish to us its control of the Army's Special Forces in Vietnam. The code name for this transfer of responsibility was Operation Switchback, an operation that would take six months to complete.

Assigned to the command's operations section, I quickly discovered that our CIA counterparts were very good at what they did. In supporting our field teams, the Central Intelligence Agency's underlying philosophy was to ask the man on the ground what he needed to do the job and then see that he got it—without subjecting him to a lot of "first sign this in triplicate" hassle.

Most of these supplies were airlifted to outlying teams from our logistical support base in Nha Trang, and, within days of our arrival, that was where many of the "trombones" found themselves. The rest of us remained in Saigon.

Saigon was a beautiful city in the fall of '62, one of the most alluring in all of Asia—a pleasant mix of East and West, old and new, traditional and contemporary. I saw quite a bit of Saigon in those next couple of months. With the CIA still running the show, duties were not that taxing in our joint downtown TOC (tactical operations center), and since I didn't go on shift until four in the afternoon, I had most of the day to wander about exploring the city. And getting off shift at midnight, I had another two hours' play time before Saigon's 2:00 A.M. curfew closed the bars.

Meanwhile, the "little war" in the high country continued as our widely scattered twelve-man Special Forces A teams went about enlisting Vietnam's principal minority, the Montagnard, in the republic's struggle against the Viet Cong. Many a Montagnard and many a Green Beret were dying in the process. But they were also succeeding in the central highlands at a time when there were few successes to boast about throughout the rest of the country.

With the passage of time the CIA surrendered its control of these teams, and we found ourselves with fewer leisure hours to roam the haunts of Saigon.

NHA TRANG, VIETNAM: FEBRUARY TO NOVEMBER 1963

In February, with Switchback nearing its completion, we moved to Nha Trang, consolidating the seventy-six trombones at one location.

As was the case with Saigon, Nha Trang was a far different place in 1963 than would it be in the post-'65 period, after our ground forces entered the fracas. When we arrived it was little more than a picturesque fishing village astride a sparkling white beach on the South China Sea.

We lived in tents at Long Van Air Base, a couple of miles south of Nha Trang. However, our TOC, in fact, the entire headquarters with the exception of the logistical support center, was located downtown in a former legionnaire's barracks only a block or so from Marie Kim's bar, a colorful establishment that in years to come would serve as a gathering place for many a Green Beret migrating to and from his little piece of the war.

But we had little time to frolic in the waters of the South China Sea or lounge about Marie Kim's bar. Instead, we worked feverishly on OPLAN 1-63, a plan designed to put many of our Special Forces teams in a border surveillance role. Finally, having completed and staffed the plan, we briefed it to everyone and his brother until it received a stamp of approval.

There were some, however, who privately harbored doubts concerning the plan's feasibility in certain parts of Vietnam.

"You ain't never seen terrain like that," Sergeant Scuggs, one of the area specialist team leaders, commented, returning from an aerial reconnaissance of surveillance sites in I Corps. "I mean, it's impossible to move through that shit! Pity the poor bastards who get stuck in that godforsaken place."

"Where's that, Sarge?" Pfc. Chester, one of his assistants, asked.

"Right here," he said, pointing to a large map depicting prospective sites in I Corps. "On the map it's called ARO, although Lord only knows why, 'cause there's nothing there. I mean, there ain't *nothing* there! Just a hilltop in the middle of the jungle with nothing 'round it far as you can see 'cept more jungle. Ain't no sign of life anywhere, no people, no water buffalo, no hutches, roads, trails, crops, nothing 'cept that god-awful jungle. Like I say, pity the poor bastards who draw ARO as a duty site."

Chester and I just shrugged our shoulders. Duty at ARO was of no interest to either of us. Little did I know that within two years I would be one of those "poor bastards" who, along with eleven other valiant souls, would spend long hours atop that hill and in the "god-awful" jungle surrounding it, wondering what in the hell the Army could possibly have been thinking of in 1963 when it selected ARO as a border surveillance site.

But this was a challenge yet to be faced. In our downtown TOC on that bright and sunny day in 1963, looking at a "one over the world" planning map, ARO really didn't look bad at all. Besides, a desolate hilltop 250 miles away was someone else's problem.

Seasons change little in Vietnam. It's always hot, sticky, and dry or hot, sticky, and wet, so the transition from spring, and then to summer, went unnoticed. By this time our daily duties in the TOC were more than merely routine; they were just plain boring. Plot, type, monitor, brief, file, and then . . . plot, type, monitor, brief, and file some more. We existed in a perpetual cycle of trivial administrative minutiae.

Thankfully, our year in the Nam was rapidly drawing to a close. In the evenings, there was little talk of anything other than that magic fall date when we would go "wheels up" out of Tan Son Nhut, winging our way back to the "land of the big PX."

One day, while we were busy plotting, typing, monitoring, briefing, and filing, my boss, Sergeant Fallow, casually asked if I'd like to see some action.

Tongue in cheek, I retorted, "What you got in mind, Al? One of them new electric typewriters?"

"Hey, Jimbo, I'm serious. Team in Cheo Reo, up in Phu Bon Province, is opening a new camp at Plei Do Lim."

I nodded.

"Well, they've lost a couple folk to hepatitis and, what with being stretched between two locations, find themselves in need of a light-weapons man. Want to go up there and give 'em a hand for a couple of weeks?"

"Hell, yes!" I enthusiastically responded. I was on my way to Cheo Reo that afternoon.

In addition to its twelve-man Special Forces A detachment, the camp at Cheo Reo was populated by a Montagnard strike force of Jarai, Drung, and Bahnar tribesmen.

These tribesmen impressed me. As one of my adopted team members pointed out, other than providing them with a rudimentary knowledge of modern firearms and explosives, there was really little we could teach them. They were more adept at this type of warfare than we were. Wearing only a loincloth and armed with a medieval crossbow, these primitive warriors could live and fight indefinitely in the country's most impenetrable jungles. Moreover, they were unfailingly loyal to their Green Beret comrades, as they had been to our French counterparts during the first Indochina war. In both instances, the enemy, probably because he was Vietnamese, albeit *Communist* Vietnamese, had little success recruiting these tribesmen to his cause. Quite simply, the Montagnards, or 'Yards, disliked *all* Vietnamese. Many of them found it incredibly fortunate that with the coming of the second Indochina war it was not only permissible to kill these descendants of the Sino-Mongol race that had pushed their ancestors into the highlands centuries before, but that their Green Beret "round-eyed" compatriots would pay them a monthly salary to do so.

During my brief stay with these hardened warriors and the professionals who led them, I helped out where and when I could, shuttling myself between Cheo Reo and the new camp at Plei Do Lim.

The two weeks passed all too quickly, and before I knew it I was back in Nha Trang—plotting, typing, monitoring, briefing, and filing. The boring routine would be broken once more before the end of my tour.

"Pack it up! We're moving, lock, stock, and barrel," Sergeant Fallow yelled. "And I mean on the double!"

It was early afternoon on the first day of November, and we were assembled in our downtown TOC as he and "Quick Draw" McDawe, returning from an emergency session with the colonel's staff, charged through the door.

"Big fight going on in Saigon, maybe throughout the country," Major McDawe, our operations officer, said, stuffing papers from his desk into a laundry bag. "Nobody knows what's happening, but we're moving to Long Van. No security here in Nha Trang, and we don't want to get caught in the middle of this thing . . . uh . . . whatever it is."

Of course Quick Draw, and most of the rest of us, knew there was more to it than that. We had been told throughout the summer months of the possibility of a coup, and we knew that President Ngo Dinh Diem's palace guard, perhaps the only force that might remain loyal to him in the event of a coup, was the LLDB, Vietnam's Special Forces and our counterparts. And *that's* what we didn't want to get caught in the middle of.

Within a matter of minutes, we had everything loaded on trucks and were on our way to Long Van, where we set up operations in our alternate TOC, a sandbagged bunker. We stayed there for the next thirty-six hours or so as events in Saigon unfolded. Although we received some information from MACV (Military Assistance Command, Vietnam) and our Saigon liaison element, most of the news came to us via AP/UPI teletype. Midday on the second day, the teletype printed out a message stating that the president and his brother, Ngo Dinh Nhu, had committed "accidental suicide"—rather difficult to do with one's hands wired behind one's back.

The celebrations then began, and for the next several days an atmosphere of controlled anarchy prevailed throughout most of the country, especially in the larger cities. The celebrations would not last long, however. By every measurable standard—economically, politically, and most assuredly militarily—the country's fortunes would quickly take a turn for the worse. But by then I was on my long-awaited journey back home, to the land of round doorknobs and the big PX.

Fort Bragg, North Carolina: January 1964

Returning from that first stint in the Nam, I reported to the Fifth Special Forces at Fort Bragg, North Carolina, as ordered, only to discover I'd been reassigned in transit. My next stop was Infantry Officer's Candidate School at Fort Benning, Georgia, from which I was commissioned a second lieutenant of infantry the following June.

After OCS, I reported back to the Fifth Special Forces, whose group adjutant welcomed me with open arms.

"Got great news for you, Lieutenant. We're on our way to Vietnam! Whole group's going. We're replacing all the A teams from Okinawa and the Seventh. Gonna be strictly a Fifth Group show from now on. Assigning you to detachment A-104. Team's in predeployment training right now, presently conducting area studies." Then, after picking up a red-bordered folder stamped Secret and studying it a moment, he uttered his frightening pronouncement. "Your team's going into the northwestern part of the country. Place called ARO. Hummmm, never heard of it myself . . ."

Oh, no! I have!

ARO, Vietnam: January 1965

"Lieutenant, it beats the shit out of me why it's called ARO," Sergeant Grimshaw said grumpily but not unkindly. He was a senior sergeant of the Okinawa-based Special Forces detachment that had occupied this desolate hilltop for the past six months, a sergeant who was obviously anxious—as indeed was his entire team—to put both name and place behind him as quickly as possible.

"Don't even know what the word means, if it means anything. Hell, maybe it's Viet meaning 'forsaken,' or French for 'wilderness.' Or maybe it's Katu for 'white man's folly.' That would be more appropriate.

"No, sir, don't know why it's called ARO, and don't care. But I do know if those numbnuts in Nha Trang expect you all to spend a fucking *year* on this hill, your whole team will be 'looney tunes' time you rotate! Hell, we've only been here half that time, and ain't none of us quite right anymore. If we had to spend a year in this shithole, if you all weren't replacing us *now*, we'd go bugfuck, completely bugfuck!"

"That bad, huh?" I said, standing next to him atop a bunker in my brand-new "been-in-Vietnam-all-day" jungle fatigues, the two of us overlooking the hilltop Sergeant Scuggs had so graphically described to Chester and me two years previously.

"Yeah, that bad. Listen, sir, you got briefings on this place at Nha Trang and Danang . . . uh . . . camp's mission, surveillance strategy, and so forth, right?"

I nodded.

"Well, don't believe a fucking word of it! I'll give you the real skinny. First of all, our mission is interdiction, stop the flow of troops, arms, and supplies along the Ho Chi Minh Trail, right?"

He paused, so again I nodded.

"Well, know how many *troops* we've stopped in the past six months?

One! And I'm not so sure he wasn't just some poor Katu tribesman who got caught napping. Know how many arms and supplies we've quote, interdicted?"

I shook my head.

"None! Zero! Know why? 'Cause of that fucking jungle out there. See, the concept is—and I'm sure one of Nha Trang's little Napoleons told you this—we 'aggressively' patrol the area between us and the camps at Kham Duc and Ta Ko. Bullshit! If you took off overland today, you wouldn't reach either of 'em 'fore Christmas. You measure a day's walking in that jungle in meters, not klicks."

He paused, evidently collecting his thoughts, then continued, "And what about your strike force? See, the concept was to recruit the force from the indigenous Montagnard population, in our case, the Katu. Well, sir, I ain't never seen a Katu, much less recruited one. 'Cause the Katu, he's not like your Rhade or Jarai 'sign-me-up-for-a-can-of-rock-salt' Montagnard you got down south. He don't want nothing to do with nobody. Oh, he's out there, out there in that jungle. We run 'cross one of his hutches every now and then, but he's never at home. Don't have them tribal, you know, communitylike instincts other 'Yards have. Usually it's just him and his family, maybe two, three families, always on the move."

He paused, again as if he had lost his train of thought. Then he said, "Anyway, there's no way we're gonna enlist the Katu in our border surveillance program, right?"

"Suppose not," I replied.

"So Danang's mayor," he went on as if not hearing me, "him having his own problems with an overpopulated prison system, says, 'Hey, you looking for aggressive, tough young fighters for your strike force? I got 'em by the truckload.' And that, sir, is your strike force." He motioned toward an adjacent area of the camp where several of these soldiers were moving about in the late afternoon sun, two of them engaged in a heated argument over what appeared to be a can of Del Monte peaches.

"Pickpockets, petty thieves, beggars . . . shit, rapists and murderers for all I know. Perfect place for 'em. They can't desert; there's no place to go."

"Well, can they fight?" I asked. "I mean, are they good soldiers?"

"No on the latter, and beats the shit out of me on the former. Like I said, we ain't seen a lot of fighting. But on the other hand, guess maybe the answer's yes, 'cause they shoot one another every now and then. Uh . . . mostly as a result of gambling arguments. They play a lot of cards—not much else to do with their pay what with there being no village, or women, or booze, or anything else 'round here to spend it on. And you can't let 'em go back to Danang on leave to spend it. Shit, you'd never see 'em again."

And once again he paused, staring at the distant horizon as if hypnotized by the sun's setting over the Laotian mountains to the west of us.

Sonofabitch! I thought to myself. Maybe he wasn't kidding. Maybe this hilltop does play on a man's mind.

"So," he said abruptly, as if coming out of a trance. "Uh . . . let's see, I've briefed you on your mission and the troops you have available to accomplish your mission. Now, let's talk of logistics and how we resupply those troops as they go about failing to accomplish their impossible mission. See, the concept was to build an airstrip and then airland everything you needed to keep the camp going. You know, a little Dien Bien Phu. So Danang airdropped a bulldozer and road grader in and built us an airstrip." He gestured to our front at the dirt runway that ran the length of the camp from east to west.

"Know how many planes we've had land on it, Lieutenant?"

"No," I replied, shaking my head.

"One! Know how many planes have taken off from it?"

"One?"

"Nope, none!" he answered, directing my attention to a heavily sandbagged bunker, protruding from one end of which was the nose section of a two-engine CV-2B Caribou. Above the aircraft's windshield, affixed to the sandbagged roof covering the wingless, tailless fuselage, was a neatly painted sign:

HAMMOND HOUSE
Presented to the United States
of America by the people of the
Commonwealth of Australia

"See, Lieutenant, only trouble with our airstrip is it ain't very long, and, since they tried to cut it out of the top of the hill here, it's eight or ten feet lower on each end than it is in the middle. Air Force came out, surveyed it, and said, 'Hell no, we ain't gonna land no fixed-wing on it.' Which, when you think of it, I guess is understandable. *Our* pilots are a bit leery of landing fixed-wing aircraft on runways with a fucking hill in the middle of 'em!"

Then, smiling a bit peculiarly, he said, "Not so with the Aussies. Hell, no! If you don't know it yet, Lieutenant—and you don't—you'll learn it very damn soon 'cause you got two of 'em attached to your team here. Anything an American can't do, an Australian can. And anything we can do, they can do better. Uh . . . think, they've never forgiven us for saving their cookies in World War II."

He paused and then, a bit sheepishly, apologetically said, "Hell, shouldn't talk like that. Both our Aussies are with the Special Air Service, super soldiers and likable people, kind of folk you like to have around you in a place like this. Like I say, I've just been out here too fucking long."

I nodded understandingly.

"Anyway," he continued, "the Australians have an aviation contingent flying out of Danang. So they come out here after the Air Force survey and say, 'Sure, mate, we can put a Caribou in here in a flash. Nothing to it.' Well, couple days later, we're all sitting out here waiting for the first plane to land at ARO. And 'course our two Aussies ain't missing this opportunity to rub our noses in the dirt a little."

He started laughing. "Damn, I'll never forget it as long as I live. Plane comes in from the east, circles the camp a couple times, then approaches the strip from the west. And the 'Kipper'—he's one of your attached Aussies—says 'Now you Yanks gonna see a bit of flying skill."

"And we did.

"Plane hits perfectly, looks like it's slowing, but then goes over that hill in the middle of the runway, and, shit, all of a sudden it's airborne again! Comes back down on the far side, bounces a couple times, and then just keeps on going . . . off the end of the strip, through the wire, and into the fucking jungle, shedding pieces of itself 'long the way.

"Didn't phase the 'Kip' *at all!* Plane finally comes to a stop, and he says, 'What say, mates? You ever saw a Yank what could land a plane and clear fields of fire at the same time?'"

We both laughed, he in recalling the incident, and I in envisioning it.

"Pilot's name was Hammond," he said, wiping at his eyes. "He and the crew walked away from their Caribou laughing. Said they wanted to do their takeoff in a helicopter.

"So now it's our alternate command post, leastways the fuselage is. Used the wings and tail sections for revetment.

"Well, sir," he said soberly, "that about wraps up my orientation of your new home for the next year. I'm sure my boss is giving your boss a similar pitch, 'though I'll bet it's not quite so . . . uh . . . open minded. Now you'll probably want to be getting with our XO so as to figure up a fair price for the team rations we have on hand."

He strolled off toward the team house, undoubtedly having more important tasks to perform than explaining the pitfalls of ARO to a "butter-bar" lieutenant. I remained atop the bunker, spending a few additional minutes in the fading light, assessing our new home.

ARO sat atop an elongated, east-west ridge with its useless airstrip running the length of it. Actually, it was more three camps than one, with separate fortified positions at each end and midway along the airstrip on its northern side. A zigzag trench network (reminiscent of World War I trench systems), intermittently strongpointed with covered fighting positions and crew-served weapons bunkers, surrounded each of the three encampments. Forward, or on the enemy side, of these entrenchments, the camp's occupants had emplaced wire barriers composed of alternating runs of triple concertina, double-apron fence, and "tanglefoot," which, without going into a lengthy explanation, were merely three different techniques of employing barbed wire. On the enemy's side of the wire, at a distance of fifty meters or so, the jungle encircled the entire hilltop.

One of ARO's three strike-force companies, the best of the three according to Grimshaw, occupied the fortified position on the eastern end of the airstrip; the other two were encamped on the western end. Each of these companies was composed of eighty to a hundred "strikers" armed with light-infantry weapons of World War II vintage. Although the mainstay of this arsenal was the .30-caliber M-1 carbine, some strikers were armed with the M3A1 "grease" or M1A1 Thompson .45-caliber submachine gun, the .30-caliber M1918A2 Browning automatic rifle, or, in rare cases, the M-1 rifle. Their crew serves consisted of the .30-caliber M1919A6 machine gun, the 60-mm mortar, and the 57-mm recoilless rifle.

Our team and a Nung force of perhaps twenty-five men resided in the camp's center fortification, about midway between the two strike-force contingents. This position was dominated at its highest point by an above/belowground communications bunker, on top of which was a sandbagged observation post. From this vantage point, I could survey the entire hilltop, noting as I did so the other facilities composing our part of ARO. These included a combination cookshack and team house—a clapboard, tin-roofed structure in which the team ate and spent most of its leisure time; a small underground dispensary, which our senior medic, Sergeant Morgan, would soon relocate to the more spacious, dryer, and less rat-infested Hammond house; our sleeping, fighting bunkers, located at various points on the trench network; two 81-mm mortar pits and adjacent ammunition bunkers; and, on the northern side of the hill and lower on its crest, the Nung encampment from which the Nung force would rush to our aid should the Viet Cong attack ARO.

The Nung was a mercenary, a holdover from an earlier era in which the CIA, then controlling Special Forces operations in Vietnam, had hired these clansmen to protect U.S. team members from the Viet Cong or from their own strike force if it should turn upon them. He was a Vietnamese nationalist of Chinese origin who considered himself only Chinese, and understandably so inasmuch as he spoke Chinese, was of pure Chinese genesis, and, like the Montagnard, passionately hated the ethnic Vietnamese.

A loyal and ferocious fighter, the Nung would and often did unselfishly surrender his life on behalf of the Special Forces soldier he was paid to protect. But, as we would soon learn, because of his dislike of the Vietnamese, he was not always an asset in what we were trying to accomplish.

In any event, I decided there was scant likelihood this mercenary force would ever be called upon to protect us during an attack, since after listening to what Grimshaw had to say about ARO, I was convinced that the probability of such an attack was microscopic. Here on this barren hilltop we were sustaining a force of some three hundred men, but it was a force in limbo—a force that was inflicting absolutely no damage on the enemy yet was costly to maintain. Charlie was an astute tactician. I doubted he had any interest in running us out of ARO and seeing us employed in a more meaningful role elsewhere.

As the sun fell behind the Laotian mountains, I put aside my thoughts on the enemy's philosophy regarding our border surveillance program at ARO and returned to the team house, there to discuss the fair market value of a case of canned wieners with the outgoing team's executive officer.

Toward the River Boung: March 1965

Within days of our arrival at ARO, Captain Peterson, our detachment commander; Sergeant Matis, the team sergeant; and Sergeant Morgan, with a small contingent of Nungs and one strike-force company in tow, departed camp on the team's first long-range patrol. It was a ten-day venture that, not surprisingly, turned out to be little more than a walk in the weeds. Or, as observed by Captain Peterson, "A great physical conditioning exercise, but probably of little significance as far as the war's final outcome is concerned."

Sergeant Warner, the team's assistant operations sergeant, and I accompanied the next foray of this sort. It too was an exercise in futility, providing information of no great consequence other than the discoveries that Vietnam's jungle leeches could penetrate the smallest of openings in our clothing and that the Army-issue insect repellent was without question the most effective defense against them. We literally bathed ourselves in it.

We tried to keep at least one such patrol on the move constantly, screening our area of responsibility as best we could. With two or three team members accompanying each of these operations, any of the twelve of us would return to the bush on every third or fourth patrol.

On rare occasions, we greatly expanded our area of influence on these excursions by inserting our force via helicopters. In early March, Sgt. Ken Luden, our senior demolitions sergeant, Australian Warrant Officer Kipler (the "Kipper," or simply "Kip"), and I found ourselves involved in such a venture. And everything that could conceivably go wrong did.

"I've overflown your LZ and see no great problem," Yankee Papa's flight leader said, as we squatted in a circle on ARO's runway. Assigned to the Marine Corps 163d Aviation Battalion flying out of Danang, he was briefing us and his pilots on our pending assault. Six of his cumbersome H-34 helicopters, sequentially numbered YP-1, -2, -3, and so on, were lined up on the strip behind us.

" 'Course it's awful damn small," he continued, "but shit, finding a clearing bigger than a backyard garden in these mountains is like witnessing the second coming of Christ. See it as a two-ship LZ, so we should have you down in three quick touch-and-goes . . ." Then, turning from us to his pilots, he said, "Now we don't know what's out there, so we're gonna go in *hot!*"

Great! I thought to myself. That means an LZ prep, those Marine F-4Cs from Danang, gunships firing rockets, maybe even a little . . .

"That means your gunners are firing when you go in to set down. And I don't want to hear any gripes 'bout cleaning guns when we get back to the house . . ."

Door gunners! That's it? That's going in hot? No fast movers, no red leg, no gunships? Just helicopter door gunners spraying 7.62 around with their M-60s? Sonofabitch!

"Okay, that's it, then," he said, concluding our joint air-ground prebrief. "Load time is 0855, takeoff at 0900."

Having conducted our airmobile insert without incident, by nine-thirty we were moving generally in an easterly, northeasterly direction about twenty klicks from ARO. The operation was to be a ten- to fourteen-day foray during which we hoped to reach the Song (river) Boung, travel it west, then reenter ARO from the north. Accompanied by twelve Nungs and one company of strikers (which had fielded a force of approximately sixty men), there were about seventy-five of us fighting our way through the jungle on this the first day of an ill-fated mission.

In the late afternoon, shortly before dusk, we began searching for an acceptable RON (remain overnight—a position identical to an NDP, RON merely being the acronym in vogue in early '65). As we approached a small clearing that descended downward from the side of the mountain on which we were making our way, the patrol abruptly halted.

Moments later Luden approached the Kipper and me from the front of the column, saying, "Point man stepped in a pungi trap, sir. One of the spikes went all the way through his right foot; he isn't gonna walk much further."

Shit! I thought. If we hadn't come in by helicopter, if we weren't so far from home base, we could send him and fifteen or so strikers back to camp. We obviously can't carry him around with us for the next two weeks. That leaves only two options: dust off or scratch the op and return to ARO. Funny how we never really think of these things when we're planning these excursions. Always kind of assume we won't have wounded. Or if we do, they'll be walking wounded. Got to get a dust off, can't scrap the operation on day one.

"Gonna be hard to get 'em to fly a dust off," Ken commented, as if reading my thoughts. "If it were one of us, it'd be different. But you know how they feel about dusting off one of the little people."

He was right. Vietnamese wounded, paramilitary or otherwise, were supposed to use ARVN medical evacuation resources, not U.S. And there was a far greater likelihood of the tooth fairy flying into this jungle and whisking away our wounded soldier than of ARVN doing so.

Suddenly, while pondering our dilemma, we heard the familiar sound of an H-34 in the distance. It was evidently flying toward us from the southwest.

"H-34. Probably flying a milk run out of Kham Duc en route to Danang," Kipler said. "What do you think, Skip? Think they might make a pickup?"

"Can't hurt to try, Kip," I replied. "We got their push, Ken?"

"Yeah, should be the same one we used on the insert this morning."

Luden quickly located our PRC-10 radio, a little-used communications asset, since we depended primarily on a CIA-issued, single-side-band HT-1 radio for most of our communication needs. However, the HT-1 would not net with the Marine Corps helicopter.

"Uh . . . Yankee Papa, this is Roaring Tiger," I said, after Ken had calibrated and affixed the proper frequency to the Korean-vintage radio.

Silence.

"Yankee Papa, this is Roaring Tiger, over."

Then, after another brief pause, the H-34 pilot responded, "Roaring Tiger, this is Yankee Papa. Don't recognize call sign or push. Authenticate. Over."

Shit, we don't have their CEOI. How the hell can I authenticate?

"This is Roaring Tiger. Uh . . . don't have your go codes, but Yankee Papa inserted us this area, this morning." Then, concluding that a slight compromise in radio security was a minor price to pay for getting the wounded striker out of our hair, I added, "We're the Special Forces element out of ARO. Got one wounded, and our op can't go any farther unless we get him out of here. Over."

"Roger, Roaring Tiger, that's good enough for me. Let me take a look at your Lima Zulu and see what we can do. Can you pop smoke? Go."

Yankee Papa, now nearly overhead, began a lazy orbit as we prepared to mark our LZ, it being the small clearing extending downward from just below the top of the hill upon which we stood. Unfortunately, the hill's level crest was not part of the clearing.

"Slope's too great for him to set it down, sir. I'll bet on it," Sergeant Luden commented.

"May be right, Ken," I replied, "but it's his call. All we can do is mark it for him and hope."

He nodded in agreement, pulled the pin on a purple smoke grenade, and threw it down the hill, where it came to rest in a clump of dry elephant grass.

"Roger, Roaring Tiger," Yankee Papa transmitted, moments later. "Got your grape. Let me give it a quick look-see. Stand by."

After orbiting us once more at a lower altitude, he said, "Okay, Roaring Tiger. Think we can do it, but that hill falls off pretty damn fast, so I'll be setting down as close to the top of it as I can. I'm coming in now."

It almost worked.

Yankee Papa attempted to land his cumbersome bird parallel to the side of the hill as near to its wooded, fairly level crest as possible. Creating a mighty backwash, it descended slowly, not more than fifteen meters from where we stood watching.

The H-34 is a three-wheeled helicopter, its two weight-bearing wheels on the front of the aircraft's fuselage. As Yankee Papa's left-front wheel touched and began settling into the hill's soft upper slope, its right-front wheel, facing downhill, remained suspended above the ground. The helicopter started to tilt dangerously. Its pilot, belatedly recognizing that the hill's slope was too great, attempted to throttle back up and lift off again. But it was too late. Increasing the engine's RPM merely amplified the aircraft's downhill cant, hastening the inevitable.

The helicopter momentarily lifted itself off the ground and then, suspended in air and as if in slow motion, lazily rolled over on its side, its belly facing us and its main rotary blades—still spinning at top pitch—nearly perpendicular to the earth below. We watched in shock as it went plunging, crashing down the side of the hill. Within seconds the whirling blades struck the jungle's edge at the base of the clearing, throwing foliage, tree limbs, dirt, and dust into the air. Suddenly one of the main rotary blades freed itself from the aircraft's engine and, along with other debris, spiraled upward toward where we stood.

It crashed to the ground ten to fifteen feet in front of us. Then, for a brief moment, an eerie silence settled over the landing zone. The helicopter was obscured in a haze of dust and smoke at the base of the hill.

"Jesus H. Christ!" Luden said.

"Oh, shit!" I said.

"Think we're gonna need us another dust off, Skipper," Kipler commented, grinning at the two of us somewhat oddly.

"Uh . . . you got that right, Chief," I replied. Then, with the plight of the helicopter's crew in mind, I turned to Luden, only to find he had already grabbed a couple of the nearest Nungs and was on his way down the hill.

Turning back to Kipler, I said, "Kip, get hold of base and tell 'em what happened. Tell 'em to pass it on to Yankee Papa in Danang. Tell 'em we're gonna need a dust off. Tell 'em . . . oh, shit, just give 'em a sitrep. Okay?"

"Right, mate," he responded, as I began running down the hill after Luden.

I had moved but thirty meters or so before my right foot suddenly gave way from under me, and I felt a stabbing pain in my ankle. Retrieving my foot from the hole into which it had plunged, I saw a long slender bamboo spike protruding from my canvas jungle boot just below the ankle.

Holy mother of Mary! A goddamn pungi trap. What else can go wrong? I reached down and pulled the spike from the side of my foot.

Continuing down the hill toward the crash site, I ran into Ken, his Nungs, and Yankee Papa's crew moments later. The crew, carrying the helicopter's M-60 machine guns, appeared to be unhurt.

"Hey, sir, goddamn miracle. Not a scratch on any of 'em," Ken said. But *he* was limping badly.

"Uh . . . yeah, got a little problem here," he said, noting my concerned look and pointing to *his* right foot. It was much worse than my minor wound. The entire side of his boot and the flesh underneath lay open as if cut by a surgeon's scalpel.

"Fell into a damn pungi trap. You believe that? You believe anyone could be that fucking clumsy?" he said.

"Uh . . . yeah, I do, Ken," I replied. "And we got to get you out of here. Your whole foot's laid open!"

"Sir, it's really not that bad, and I'd prefer to stick with the patrol. Couple pills, a battle dressing—I can make it."

Of course we both knew he couldn't. However, before I could say anything else, the pilot of our bent and broken helicopter, a Marine Corps captain, came forward and with a stoic expression asked, "Who's in charge of this circus?"

"I am, I guess, sir," I replied.

"Well, Lieutenant—you are a lieutenant, I presume, noting that discolored bar on your collar—you owe the United States Marine Corps seventy-five thousand dollars for one H-34 helicopter. Now how do you like them apples?"

As I looked at him aghast, he smiled and said, "Hey, Army, just joking. My fault, and don't worry about it. Worthless piece of shit anyway, outlived its usefulness. Ah, now, have you called anybody 'bout getting us out of here?"

I told him we had, and we continued up the hill together. Nearing its top, just feet from where Kipler was standing, we were suddenly, apparently, taken under fire by an unseen enemy.

Bam! Bam! Bam! Bam!

We hit the ground. "

"Where's it coming from?" I yelled to Kipler.

"Coming from our LZ, Skip," he replied, standing above us and smiling as if this was turning out to be a pretty good day after all.

"Your marking grenade landed in some dead elephant grass down there. The bird's backwash blew us up a bit of a fire, which is now burning in a clump of bamboo. Mates, that's bloody bamboo you hear exploding."

He paused momentarily, allowing us time to regain our composure and to laugh at ourselves as we did so—although on the whole there was really very little to laugh about.

"Skip, called base and gave 'em a sitrep," he continued. "Sanford [the team's communications sergeant] just called back and said Danang's gonna have a Huey out here in thirty minutes or so. Same time, I told him to pass on that the crew's okay."

While waiting for the Huey, Kipler pulled me aside and suggested I accompany the others back to Danang to have my foot taken care of.

"May not be bothering you much right now, sir, but I promise you it'll be hurting like hell later on."

"No way, Kip! You'd be left as the only round eye on the op, and Nungs or no Nungs, we don't do things like that. 'Sides, it's a very minor cut. Once we get these people out of here, I'll take a couple no-sweat pills, slap a battle dressing on it, and be as good as new."

He smiled as if he knew better but said, "Okay, Skipper. You're the boss."

The sun had set and darkness was rapidly approaching when we heard the Huey overhead. Although I suppose one could argue as to which of us had proven ourselves *least* qualified to land a helicopter on our downward-sloping LZ, I decided to ask our visiting Marine captain, the pilot of the downed H-34, to bring the Huey in. He at least spoke the Huey pilot's language. Besides, if the government should find me liable for the loss of its H-34, one helicopter was all I could afford on lieutenant's pay.

After talking to the airborne Huey a couple of minutes, the captain turned to us and said, "Okay, he's gonna land in basically the same attitude I did . . . " Oh, that's just great! "Only difference, he's gonna touch down with only his uphill skid and then hover, so he wants us to load quick. Got an ACL eight; there's four of us. How many you gotta get out, Lieutenant?"

"Just one, Sergeant Luden. No, make that two. Forgot about our wounded striker."

"Super, that makes it six and no problem. Now listen up, since the Huey's gonna hover at a level keel . . . " He paused, smiled, then said, "Which, in passing, is the best way to land a rotary-wing aircraft. Landing or lifting off a helicopter at a cant can be disastrous! 'Course, we all know that now, don't we?"

His crew chuckled at this, and so did we.

"But seriously," he continued, "with the bird hovering like that while we board from the uphill side, those blades, which ain't that far off the ground to begin with, are gonna be low and dangerous. So keep your heads down and move under them in a low crouch."

Unfortunately, the Huey's onboard medic didn't hear the captain's warning.

The helicopter came in with its left skid uphill and began hovering. As soon as the skid touched ground, the medic, who I thought was the helicopter's crew chief, jumped from the Huey and ran toward us, in a crouch to assist with the wounded. He had barely gotten himself from underneath the periphery of the Huey's main blades—which, since the helicopter was maintaining a hover, were rotating at full pitch—before our boarding party, moving toward the helicopter, passed him.

Pivoting in midstride, he fell in behind Ken Luden and our wounded striker and started back toward the Huey. I fell in behind him, wanting to give the pilot a thumbs up in appreciation for flying this mission.

Approaching the medic in a low crouch from the rear, I heard a soft, swift zippp. Suddenly, my face and the front of my jacket were covered with blood! The medic had been hit squarely atop his head by one of the whirling main blades of the Huey. If he had been a fraction of an inch taller, or if he had stood a fraction of an inch higher in his crouch, the top of his skull would have been instantly crushed. As it was, the helicopter's blade merely skimmed the top of his head, separating his scalp from his skull and throwing it back on his neck like a toupee caught in a sudden gust of wind.

The medic looked up from the ground, perplexed, and said, "My hat! I lost my hat." The blood seeped down his forehead, forming little droplets on his eyebrows.

I yelled, "Medic!"

"Sir, I *am* a medic," he said, looking up at me, smiling. For a fleeting second all I could think was, will this day never end?

As the Huey's pilot looked at us in shock from behind his Plexiglas windshield, I kneeled; took the young man's scalp, which was still attached to his skull by a shred of flesh; and placed it atop his head as neatly as possible. Then I put one of his hands on top of his scalp, telling him to hold it there until he arrived safely in Danang.

Once we had the medic on board, I gave a thumbs up to the pilot and in a low, a *very* low, crouch, ran out from underneath the Huey's "kill zone" as the helicopter lifted off.

An hour or so later, my foot began to really hurt.

After the Huey's departure, Kipler had dressed the wound, noting in doing so that my foot had begun to swell. I was able to get my boot back on only with some difficulty.

Can't take it off again; I'd be going barefoot the rest of the op!

The Kipper, old bush hand that he was, knew I would be in pain by this time, so he suggested a shot of the big M. (On extended operations of this nature, one or two of the team members carried syringes of morphine.)

"No way, Kip," I said between gritted teeth as I lay wrapped in a poncho liner, unexplainably cold. "Don't believe in it. Don't want some mind-boggling drug messing up my thinking."

Yeah, as if a clear head had done anything for us thus far. Hell, things might take a turn for the better if I did start doing my thinking from cloud nine.

"Okay, Skip, you're the boss." Then, chuckling, he said, "Say, mate, what do you make of our op so far?"

"Great start, Kip," I said, with a straight face. "I don't see how our first day could have conceivably gone any better."

He laughed.

"Shit, Kip, after this is over, *Dai uy* Peterson probably won't even let me set foot on ARO. Probably just have me flown directly to Danang to issue toilet paper for the rest of my tour as the C detachment's new assistant to the assistant deputy logistics officer."

"Hey, Skipper, never setting foot again on ARO ain't punishment! 'Sides, you'd eat better in Danang."

He paused for a moment, then said, "But seriously, sir, I was just thinking. 'Fore we came over here all them experts in jungle warfare told us not to worry much 'bout pungi stakes. You know, at worst they're nothing more than a nuisance, a minor annoyance. But today, one fucking pungi stake compromised an entire operation, destroyed a seventy-five-thousand-dollar helicopter, and wounded four soldiers, three of 'em Yanks. Now I'd say that's a pretty good payback for a couple minutes' carving time on a sliver of bamboo!"

I nodded in agreement. The pain in my foot had progressed from a dull constant ache to throbbing torture. I couldn't understand it. The wound was so small. How the hell could it hurt so?

"Oh, yeah, forgot to mention it, Skip," Kipler said after a moment's silence. "Thought you might be sleeping and didn't want to wake you, 'cause you won't be getting much sleep tonight. You can bet on it. Anyway, Sanford called in and said your Marines are gonna have a crew out here at first light or as soon after as they can get a bird in. Gonna pull the radios from their H-34 here, then torch it. Want us to stay with the helicopter till they finish up and leave."

He paused and felt my forehead.

"Running a fever, mate, and it's gonna get worse, 'cause the gooks put all manner of shit on those two-minute pungis. Now let me tell you something, Lieutenant," he said forcefully. "Your foot's infected, and you can't walk, and you're gonna be out of here on that bird in the morning! And I think you bloody well know it."

Then in a softer voice, he said, "Come on, Skip. Let me give you a shot of morphine. Make the night go quicker, and you'll be in Danang with some little nurse in the morning."

"Like I said, Kip, no fucking way. I'm not leaving this op, and I'm sure as hell not taking any morphine. I can take the pain; it's part and parcel of the trade. Ain't taking no morphine, *period!*"

"Okay, Skipper, you're the boss," he said, getting up to leave.

Well, I guess I set him straight, I thought to myself as he wandered off toward his part of our perimeter. Hell, pain's part of the game, and I can play the game.

It was perhaps twenty minutes later when I crawled over to Kipler's hammock and, somewhat sheepishly, asked, "Uh . . . Kip, where's the fucking morphine? How many syringes do you have, anyway?"

And the next morning, as the Kipper had predicted, I departed the op aboard the Marine's radio-recovery helicopter. Kip had seen to it that I was ordered to do so, but that was really unnecessary. I would have gone anyway. I could no longer walk.

Farewell to ARO

Ken Luden and I were back at ARO, limping about, within a week or so. Although we wouldn't be participating in any long-range patrols for a while, that really didn't matter—for there were to be no more long-range patrols. Detachment A-104 had received new orders: destroy ARO.

It was not a trivial task, even though ARO was little more than a useless airstrip and a lot of holes in the ground. How does one go about destroying useless airstrips and holes in the ground? Or why would one want to? The Viet Cong had no air force, and none of us could see how our bunkers—our holes in the ground—could conceivably provide the enemy aid, comfort, or any material advantage if left intact. Clearly, he could not take these holes and use them against us elsewhere.

But orders were orders, so we spent the next month burning, dismantling, blowing up, and caving in bunkers.

The night before we bid our final farewell to ARO, we also bid a sad farewell to our two attached Aussies, neither of whom would be accompanying us to our new camp. The C detachment in Danang (our higher headquarters) was forming a Nung "Mike" force that could rush to the aid of any besieged Special Forces A camp in I Corps. It was a good idea and a necessary asset, as these camps were usually well outside the range of artillery support, ARVN could not or would not send forces to aid them in the event of an attack, and in the spring of '65 there were no American ground forces to come to their assistance. Unfortunately, the C detachment needed our attached Australians to organize and train this Mike force.

So on that last night atop a hill we'd never miss, we threw a party for a couple of Aussies whom we'd miss very much indeed. We drank, we talked, we sang. By any measurement, Kip and his companion beat the rest of us at all three—for no one can outtalk, outdrink, or outsing an Australian.

The following morning, we blew what remained of ARO sky high, mounted Marine helicopters, and journeyed our way southward to Kham Duc, another of I Corps' border camps.

HA THANH, VIETNAM: APRIL 1965 TO JANUARY 1966

On April 25, the day after ARO had become but another page in the history of I Corps' ill-fated border surveillance program, we boarded C-123 Providers and flew ninety miles southeast to Quang Ngai City, the capital of Quang Ngai Province. From there, we flew another fifteen miles or so in a westerly direction, once again via Marine Corps H-34s, to a hilltop overlooking a small remote village called Ha Thanh, the district headquarters of Son Ha District. We had arrived at our new campsite.

Son Ha was the westernmost of Quang Ngai's districts. It was a fertile rice-growing area dominated by its valley of the same name, which ran generally north-south through the district along the banks of the Son Ha River. To the north and west of the valley were the mountains in which the Viet Cong, and Viet Minh before them, reigned supreme. In the low-lying areas the district was inhabited by "friendly" Vietnamese, who lived primarily in the village of Ha Thanh, and Hre Montagnards, who lived mainly in the countryside. With a population of perhaps twelve hundred people, Ha Thanh was the social, economical, cultural, and most certainly political center of the district.

Our strikers fell in love with Ha Thanh the moment they disembarked the helicopters. Although the village was little more than a random assortment of thatch- and mud-walled hutches astride a dirt road, it had everything ARO lacked—food, sundries, beer, women. Understandably, we preferred Ha Thanh to ARO. Here there was a camp to be built instead of destroyed, a mission to be accomplished, a populace to be protected, assisted.

As an added incentive, within days of our arrival a helicopter landed at Ha Thanh, disembarking the newest members of our team. Clad, as were we, in "tiger" fatigues with green berets atop their heads, were three young and very attractive Vietnamese nurses. In the coming months, they would share our hardships, pain, and laughter as well as be a source of comfort and encouragement to the district's medically deprived.

Our camp was atop a small hill adjacent to the district headquarters on the western side of the village. The hilltop was barren except for a single mud-walled, corrugated-tin-roofed barnlike structure that sat in the middle of it.

There was much to be done. The airstrip, located outside our campsite at the base of the hill on its northern side, had to be extended, since it was then little more than a duplicate of ARO's runway, capable of receiving only rotary-wing aircraft. But the airstrip was of secondary importance. Our first priority was construction of the camp itself, a task that had to be performed from the outside first. Since we were vulnerable to an attack, we had to start on our defensive barriers around the hill before worrying about our living quarters.

Surrounding the base of the hill, we laid ten meters of tanglefoot (barbed wire strung randomly at ankle level). Up the hill, this was followed by a pyramid of triple concertina anchored on each side by double-apron barbed-wire fence. Then there were more tanglefoot and a second run of concertina and double apron, still more tanglefoot, and finally a third run of concertina and double apron. At critical junctures within this wire barrier surrounding our defensive perimeter, Sergeant Luden positioned command-detonated claymore mines and fugas. (Fugas was a napalm mixture contained in a fifty-five-gallon drum, the bottom of which was slightly submerged in the ground while its top faced upward and outward at an angle pointing toward the enemy. At the base of the drum, Ken rigged a command-detonated shaped charge that would blow both bottom and top off the drum when fired, igniting the napalm in the process and throwing it in a fiery arc for a distance of thirty to forty meters. In short, our fugas devices were stationary, homemade napalm bombs.)

Behind this wire barrier, around the hilltop's military crest, the strike force dug its fighting trenches. At several points on or behind these trenches, we constructed our two-man covered positions. In addition to our assigned M-16 rifle and .45-caliber pistol, each of these positions normally housed a .30-caliber A6 machine gun and an M-79 grenade launcher (as well as a hodgepodge of backup weapons that, depending on the preference of the individual concerned, might include a .45-caliber Thompson submachine gun, a .30-caliber M-1 rifle or M-2 carbine, a twelve-gauge shotgun, and an abundance of both frag and smoke grenades). Completing the camp's defensive infrastructure atop the hill, we dug an underground communications bunker and constructed two 81-mm mortar positions with their adjoining ammunition bunkers.

Our defenses were somewhat augmented by four mountaintop observation posts (OPs) a short distance to the west, northwest, north, and northeast of us. These OPs were manned by Son Ha's regional popular force, a paramilitary organization composed primarily of Hre Montagnards and commonly referred to as "Ruff Puffs." Unfortunately, our only means of communicating with these positions was through district headquarters, at best a time-consuming process.

Our mission in Son Ha was simple: pacify the district. And pacification was a simple process: protect and assist the populace on the one hand while destroying the enemy on the other.

A week or so after arriving at Ha Thanh, we conducted our first full-scale offensive operation, a two-company foray to the north of the camp. Sergeant Morgan led one of the companies and Captain Crawford the other. (Captain Crawford had replaced Captain Peterson upon our departure from ARO.) The two companies departed Ha Thanh around ten o'clock in the morning, and all went well until midafternoon, when Morgan's company found itself in trouble.

As Ken Luden, Sergeant Boyde, the team's weapons specialist, and I sat in our tented open-air team house, discussing where next to go on the camp's defenses, Phil Sanford ran out of our nearly completed commo bunker and, in a concerned voice, said, "Morgan's in a bind, sir! Says he's surrounded and can't extract himself! Got two dead on the ground, more wounded . . ."

"He's in a firefight?" I asked excitedly, then said to myself, well, that's brilliant, Lieutenant. What the hell do you think they're in with two dead on the ground?

"Yes, sir! Ambushed! Crawford's moving in to assist him, but he has a way to go." He paused, then said, "Hell, they're not too far from us. Here's his plot."

He showed us Morgan's plot on the map he always kept within arm's reach of his radios.

"Let's go talk to the *Dai uy*," I said.

Running toward the commo bunker, I thought, damn, the enemy! A firefight! We just got here, and we're in a firefight! Three months at ARO, and, except for an occasional sniper round, we never heard a shot fired in anger.

"Outbound Six, this is Base Five. Over," I said into the mike attached to our SSB base-station receiver.

"This is Outbound Six," Captain Crawford responded immediately, in a seemingly fatigued voice. "We're on the move. What you got . . ."

"This is Base Five. Outbound Alpha One says he's in trouble. Can we assist?"

Crawford replied, "Think we can get to him before you. Moving toward him fast as we can from the southeast. Don't know what he's into, but if you assist, try to come in from the west. Might be able to catch 'em between us. Use your own discretion and keep me informed. Out."

I liked Captain Crawford. Few commanders would tell a butter-bar second lieutenant to use his own discretion. Of course, being a butter-bar, I interpreted that to mean "do whatever you want."

"Okay, Sergeant Luden, Sergeant Boyde, saddle up 403d Company. We're moving!"

The two of them smiled broadly, obviously as enthused as I was over the possibility of actually, finally engaging our evasive enemy. None of the three of us, or Phil Sanford looking on, commented on the very apparent fact that the camp would be virtually defenseless if we sallied forth with the third of our three strike force companies. But that was really of secondary importance. We had some of our own in trouble to the north.

Within ten minutes we had assembled as much of 403d Company as could be found on short notice, approximately forty men, and began moving north across the valley's lush, green rice paddies and then into the low-lying hills beyond. After accessing the concealment afforded by the vegetation of these foothills, we began maneuvering eastward toward Sergeant Morgan's last reported location. Hopefully, we'd be entering the contested area from the west as Crawford approached it from the southeast. We had little trouble orienting ourselves in the right direction. We simply followed the sound of gunfire.

The sun had been shining and the sky nearly cloudless when we left Ha Thanh. Now, as was often the case in the Nam, it began to rain. Not a monsoon downpour, just an annoying, body-soaking drizzle. We continued moving, the gunfire becoming increasingly louder.

As we emerged from a tree line we saw in front of us, across a wide valley with a stream at its base, the hill that Morgan was supposedly on. But he wasn't. Charlie was!

Captain Crawford, as he predicted, had beaten us—only to find that Sergeant Morgan had already succeeded in extricating himself from his precarious locale. Having joined forces with Crawford at the base of the hill (the hill's right, or southern, flank from our perspective), the two of them were now exchanging fire with the enemy above.

For a fleeting few moments I had visions of conducting a classical textbook "fire-and-maneuver" assault against the enemy atop the hill to our front. Let's see, I thought quickly, I'll leave half the force here in the tree line. They'll lay down a good base of fire while the rest of us, using my OCS-taught fire-and-maneuver techniques, assault the hilltop. Yeah! The final coordination line will be the . . . uh . . . enemy hill's tree line. Right. When we reach that point, our base-of-fire element will shift their fires to the . . . uh . . . left. Sure, that's best. Keep their fires away from Crawford and Morgan on the right. I'll signal the shift with a smoke grenade. Then, we in the assaulting element will close and . . .

Pop! Pop! Pop! Rat-tat-tat-tat-tat!

We were under fire! The enemy, having become aware of our presence on his flank, was redirecting his fire and throwing everything he had at us!

My schoolbook fire-and-maneuver scheme was doomed the moment Charlie fired his first round. Because before Luden, Boyde, or I could utter a single word, our strikers ran—every single one of them. But not to the rear! As one they charged the enemy to their front, firing their weapons and, in a death-defying chorus, screaming a warrior's challenge at the top of their lungs. It was all we could do to keep up with them.

Damn! I guess these "Danang cowboys," these ex-prisoners, have just answered the question I asked Grimshaw that first night at ARO. They're fighters!

We ran down the hill, jumping the small stream at its base. Bullets ricocheted off rocks at our feet and took large chunks of bark out of trees at the water's edge. I looked wide eyed at Sergeant Boyde, running beside me.

"Sonofabitch!" he yelled. "This is just like the movies!"

Suddenly, the striker running in front of us caught a round in the side of his skull. In horror, I saw the other side of his head burst open, splattering the tree beside him with blood, bone, hair, and purplish fragments of his brain. It was a ghastly split-second image that would remain with me a long time.

We continued onward, upward.

But by the time we reached the hill's tree line, the fight was over. Charlie had picked up his marbles and retired from the scene to fight another day. Finding nothing in the tree line, we moved back down the hill and joined Captain Crawford and Sergeant Morgan in the paddy below. Then, as a light rain continued to fall, we wrapped our dead in ponchos, strung them beneath bamboo carrying poles, and began our trek back to Ha Thanh.

Walking beside me, Ken Luden commented, "Hey, sir, think we're in a new ball game here. Charlie's gonna fight for this place!"

"Yeah, think you're right, Ken. Sure as hell ain't ARO."

And it wasn't. Our operations differed greatly from those we had conducted at ARO. Certainly there was no need to make two-week forays in Son Ha, since virtually the entire district was within two days' walking distance of Ha Thanh. We at times ventured forth on three- or four-day patrols, but these operations were atypical. Instead, after discovering our comings and goings were always watched during the day, we normally departed Ha Thanh as stealthily and silently as possible at two or three o'clock in the morning, conducted our operation, and then returned to our campsite by nightfall.

Moreover, the nature of these operations differed greatly. At times they were strictly offensive, the best example of which was the search-and-destroy mission. On other occasions they were humanitarian, an operation such as a MEDCAP (medical civic action patrol). And at times they were a combination of the two, usually in the form of a cordon and search of a village. During a cordon and search we would surround a contested village at night, enter it at first light in the morning, and then kill or capture Charlie if we found him—and treat his family if we didn't.

Throughout our tenure at Ha Thanh, we attempted to keep at least one such sortie on the move constantly. We did not always succeed in doing so, nor did we always succeed in accomplishing what we set out to do on any given operation. As I suppose was the case with most A detachments in the Nam, we had our fair share of glistening successes and glaring defeats. On one venture we might kill some of Charlie, and on the next he might kill some of us. Or, as we'd later say in the Cav, "Sometimes you eat the bear, and sometimes the bear eats you!"

In the fall of 1965, we sat atop our campsite at Ha Thanh, waiting for the sky to fall. The repercussions of a battle in the Ia Drang Valley, nearly a hundred miles to the southwest, were being felt in Son Ha District.

America's involvement in Vietnam was escalating rapidly. Now U.S. warplanes were routinely bombing North Vietnam as part of the Air Force's ill-advised Rolling Thunder campaign; our forces totaled nearly 130,000 men; and U.S. ground forces, the infantry cutting edge of this commitment, were engaging the enemy in direct combat.

The first, and in one little-known respect the last, of these engagements occurred in October and November during the First Air Cavalry's Pleiku campaign, a campaign that later became known as the battle of Ia Drang.

Ia Drang had its impact on us only because the battle ended in such a debacle for the north. General Giap's greater strategic intent in his Dong Xuan (winter-spring) offensive, in addition to destroying a major U.S. force, was to score a spectacular victory by splitting the republic in two from the coastal city of Qui Nhon west to the Cambodian border. Failing in this, allied intelligence feared that rather than abort his plan, the general might look elsewhere to sever the country, perhaps where the country was narrower and where no U.S. forces were stationed. By late November or early December, intelligence sources reported the North Vietnamese might well have found such a place in Quang Ngai Province.

A military situation map of Vietnam in early 1965 would show that on a direct line running west from the coastal city of Quang Ngai across the country to the Laotian border, there were only two friendly outposts: an ARVN infantry battalion at Ba Gia, located between us and Quang Ngai, and our camp at Ha Thanh. But by the fall of that year, Ba Gia was no more. It had been overrun, literally eradicated in a predawn attack months before. And that was somewhat frightening, since it had been defended by an entire battalion reinforced with two 105-mm howitzers—both of which might now be pointed at us in Ha Thanh. Moreover, Ba Gia's attackers had defeated in detail a second ARVN battalion sent forth from Quang Ngai to reoccupy the garrison. And "defeat in detail" in this instance means Charlie tore the battalion to shreds! The rout was so complete that ARVN commanders tore their insignia of rank from their uniforms and, as common privates, tried to evade capture, leaving their American advisors to fend for themselves.

So Ba Gia was never reoccupied. Now there was only one outpost between Quang Ngai and the Laotian border—us.

As fall progressed, intelligence sources continued to identify new enemy units infiltrating into the district, first companies, then battalions, and finally regiments. In fact, at times it was difficult to believe that Son Ha District was actually large enough to hold all the enemy some of these sources said were there. We were convinced that all these enemy soldiers had but one mission order from General Giap: annihilate Ha Thanh; take no prisoners.

We patrolled by day, while the Air Force illuminated our camp at night and flew countless close tactical air sorties against real and suspected enemy emplacements, day and night. On occasion, VNAF (Vietnam's air force) assisted in these missions and, contrary to all we had been told, were very good at it. In fact, they were at times more daring and accurate than their U.S. counterparts.

Still the enemy made no deliberate, determined attack on our camp. With the passage of time, we began to breathe easier.

Until we awoke one morning to discover that OP 66, our most eastward observation post, had been overrun the night before. OP 66, a site garrisoned by perhaps half that many Ruff Puffs, had sat astride the Son Ha–Quang Ngai highway (an unimproved dirt road) about midway between Ha Thanh and the now-deserted garrison at Ba Gia. Its fall, coupled with the aforementioned intelligence indicators, convinced our C detachment it was now time to commit its newly formed Nung Mike force to the defense of Ha Thanh.

Then we really had a fight on our hands.

It was a dark, overcast, and drizzly afternoon, typical of the monsoon season, when the Mike force arrived at Ha Thanh aboard their Marine H-34 helicopters. Roaring up the valley in file, the helicopters were in fact flying NOE (nap of the earth), not because it was tactically sound or technically innovative to do so but because the low overhanging ceiling prevented them from flying at any greater altitude. Settling on our unimproved runway, they off-loaded the Mike force. The confrontation between the Chinese Nungs of the Mike force and the Vietnamese of our strike force began before the last H-34 had disappeared into the valley's mist.

The confrontation between the Nungs' taskmaster, an Australian warrant named Gundy, and me began almost immediately.

Setting my own faults aside for the moment, and they are many, let me say that Gundy was an arrogant, egotistical cretin, so much so that even his fellow Aussies, the most loyal of nationalists, avoided him whenever possible. On reflection, I don't suppose that bothered Gundy, since, as he often told anyone willing to listen, he didn't really consider himself an Australian; he thought of himself only as a Nung.

Within an hour of so of his arrival, while he and I were in our underground communications bunker arguing—*discussing*—how best to defend the camp, we suddenly heard a .30-caliber A6 machine gun begin firing.

Rat-tat-tat-tat-tat-tat!

"Fuck me, mate, this is it!" Gundy yelled, excitedly. "Guess *we* Nungs got here just in time, what say?"

"I think not," I replied, unsure of whether I was referring to the timeliness of the Nungs' arrival or his assessment of the tactical situation.

Seizing our weapons, we ran up the bunker's sandbagged stairs, emerging under the dull and dreary overcast sky to find the Nungs lined up on one side of the camp preparing to do battle, with our strikers aligning the other. The two forces were yelling and cursing in Vietnamese and Chinese, while Sergeants Luden and Warner stood between them, trying to defuse the situation.

Evidently, one of our strikers had fired a machine gun in the air amid a rampant verbal fray between the two groups, a fray that had broken out when the Nungs attempted to fill defensive positions previously occupied by our strikers. The striker, a man named Phan, the commander of 403d Company and one of the bravest of our brave, might have fired the machine gun in an attempt to restore order—and later that was his defensive plea. On the other hand, he might have fired it as a face-saving, fight-provoking gesture. (On reflection, I think the latter was the case.)

Warrant Gundy was enraged, to put it mildly, and started yelling about courts-martial, dawn executions, official reprimands, and so forth.

"Nobody shoots at my Nungs, Lieutenant. Nobody! Understand!"

"Now simmer down, Chief," I replied. "I mean nobody really shot at anybody, just fired the gun in the . . ."

"Bullshit! He threatened my Nungs!" he shouted testily, interrupting me. "And nobody threatens my Nungs. Nobody! I'll have that bloody Danang cowboy of yours hung!"

"Okay, Chief, we'll do it at sunrise. But right now, I think . . ."

"And I'll tell you something else, Lieutenant," he continued, again interrupting me. "I'm gonna report this incident to Colonel Aldorn forthwith, and I'm gonna use your name freely."

Oh, to hell with it, I thought, losing my temper. "Mr. Gundy, I don't give a good goddamn who you report what to, but it's gonna be dark soon, and I suggest we get our people in some sort of defensive posture. And if we can't do that, *I'll* call Colonel Aldorn and ask him to extract you and your fucking Nungs *forthwith!*"

"Oh, yeah! Well, Lieutenant, let me tell you something . . ."

The incident was not handled with a lot of professionalism by either of us, and I felt bad about it—but then, I was only a second lieutenant. And second lieutenants are not schooled in joint and combined warfare, nor is tact one of their more notable character traits.

After tempers had cooled, we divided the camp, assigning each of the two forces a portion thereof. Nungs and strikers remained in this posture for the next week or so, avoiding each other as much as possible. In the meantime, Warrant Gundy and I went about our business, we too avoiding each other as much as possible.

Then intelligence indicators began to reveal that the threat in Son Ha District was dissipating, the enemy supposedly retiring to do battle elsewhere. Warrant Gundy and his Nungs returned to Danang, convinced that their intervention at Ha Thanh had been the pivotal factor behind the enemy's decision to withdraw. Of course, we knew better. We knew Charlie was posed for an attack when the Mike force arrived. However, after observing our efforts at organizing a combined defense of the camp that afternoon, he had a good laugh and decided to move on. Why in the world should he waste his soldiers and ammunition on a camp that was about to self-destruct?

By mid-December only three of the original team remained at Ha Thanh—Jock Warner, Ken Luden, and me. Christmas came and went and with it Sergeant Luden. Jock and I spent New Year's Eve at the campsite, and then he departed. Three days later, on the next helicopter out, I left the Son Ha Valley, never to see it or its people again. But I think of them now and then—and dream of them often.

FORT BENNING, GEORGIA: FEBRUARY 1966

I spent the next eighteen months as an instructor in platoon and company tactics at the U.S. Army's Infantry School—watching our Army turn itself inside out. Overnight, the Army had turned its entire focus on Southeast Asia. Suddenly, no Army training post was complete without its media-oriented "Vietnam village." Doctrine was revised, stressing its adaptability to an insurgency. Training curriculum was changed, deemphasizing subject matter the Army had held so near and dear since 1945—how to fight on the plains of Europe.

We in the school's company operations department were charged with preparing young leaders, teaching them what cannot be taught, then sending them on their merry way and starting over again with the next class. It was not a thankless task, but a trying one of six- and seven-day weeks, of sixteen- and eighteen-hour days. Before very long, it got old.

One cold, sleety night on CP-77—a seventy-two-hour counterguerrilla field exercise we'd walk different officer candidates through once, and more often, twice a week—one of my fellow instructors, the two of us having recently been promoted to captain, said, "Called branch today. Asked them to send me back to the Nam."

"Why?" I asked.

"Why? 'Cause way I figure it, a man has to put in hours like this, he might as well put 'em in where it's warm and where he can kill someone a little bit."

Made sense to me. I had "yellow fever." And American infantrymen were in the fray now. Perhaps I could lead a company of them, perhaps a company in the First Air Cavalry. Hell, they were kicking Charlie's ass up one side and down the other.

The next day, *I* called infantry branch.

The Cav II

It was a bright, sunny Monday, like most January days on the Bong Son plain. For Charlie Company, it was another day of business as usual—the last day in the Year of the Goat to make a hit in the high country.

One Six and Three Six, headquarters section accompanying Three Six, sallied upward to establish their claymore ambushes on a mountain that reeked of the dead. Two Six, with a new lieutenant at its helm, worked the valley floor. Four Six, as was often the case, if for no other reason than to ensure that we had a secure LZ at our disposal, remained at last night's NDP, napping the day away.

Lieutenant Halloway, wisely, chose to access the mountain's main north-south trail at a point farther north than usual so as to put the remains of most of Charlie Company's previous victims to the south of us. He felt this was both tactically sound and gastronomically desirable, as it was nearly lunchtime. A short while later, we found an ideal ambush site, one in which the platoon could straddle a curve in the trail without being observed from the enemy side of either the north or south hit teams' positions—and one in which the stench was at least bearable. Still, when the wind occasionally shifted, we got a healthy whiff of our more recent kills.

Lunch in the Nam, in the Cav, was as often as not ignored. We were authorized two meals of C rations per man per day, but with C&D

in the morning and a hot A or B ration in the evening, most of us ate only portions of a meal during the day—whenever the mood struck us and we found ourselves in a posture to eat. "Sweet" Willie Dubray, however, was a three-meals-a-day man.

As we sat in wait midway between the two hit teams, Bob Halloway, Slim Brightly, and I idly talking of unimportant things, I casually watched Dubray—who was filling in for Anderson as my company RTO on this occasion—prepare his noonday fare. He first opened a couple of cans of crackers and then, using a Stateside "church key" can opener, poked several holes in the sides of the cans. In each of these make-shift stoves he placed a heat tablet and lit it, then he set a can of beans and wieners atop one and a can of pork-sausage patties atop the other. While his meal was heating, he opened small tins of jelly and peanut butter and spread it on his crackers. Between mouthfuls, he alternately hummed and sang something about a young man named Billy Joe who had evidently jumped off the Tallahatchie bridge.

Blair, lying on his side a short distance away, gazed at Dubray throughout these preparations, shaking his head in disbelief.

"Chow time," Dubray said in a low voice, removing the bubbling, greasy pork patties from atop the heat tab.

"Don't do that, Willie," Blair softly remarked. "Please just don't do it."

"Huh?" Dubray said.

"Willie, a sane and starving man doesn't eat charlie-rat pork-sausage patties in the dead of night, in the cold of winter, much less at midday in the Nam when the temperature's registering a hundred plus and the pungent fragrance of victories past are about us. Willie, that stuff's nothing but grease, pure grease. It'll kill you."

Dubray looked at Blair uncomprehendingly a moment and then, smiling and shoving the first of the pork patties in his mouth, said, "Shit, you ain't gotta worry yourself 'bout me, Blair. Ain't nothing's gonna make me sick."

"I know that, Willie," Blair responded quietly, almost as if to himself. "It's not your health that concerns me. It's mine. And if you put one more of those greasy patties in your mouth, I'm gonna heave."

Grinning, Willie said, "Well, you just stick to your fruit cocktail and peaches mixed with them teeny little old pound cakes and pass 'long your patties to me. I mean all that there fruit ain't no good for you, Blair, don't stick to your ribs. My pappy, he say meat, taters, and rice, that's what'll . . ."

"And did your pappy happen to have scurvy, Willie?" Blair asked, with a straight face.

Dubray looked at him thoughtfully for a moment and then, nonchalantly, said, "Naw. Had one when I was just a little fellow, but one of the wheels fell off, and Pappy, he never got 'round to fixing . . ."

Blair just shook his head in resignation and rolled over to his other side, mumbling, "Cretins. I'm surrounded by cretins."

I smiled and turned my attention back to Bob Halloway, who was somewhat frivolously discussing the strategical value of Secretary McNamara's electronic "wall," a barrier designed to curtail the infiltration of North Vietnamese soldiers and supplies into South Vietnam.

"See, the way I see it," he said, "we're really over here because it serves our national interests. No other reason, right?"

Slim and I nodded.

"Mean, the domino theory and making the world safe for democracy are all well and good," he continued, "but the bottom line is we're here so as to keep 'em off the shores of California, right? So why not just stretch the secretary's electronic barrier from Seattle to San Diego and save ourselves all this travel time. Hell, maybe Charlie Company could screen the L.A. area."

We smiled politely but said nothing.

"Seriously, sir," he continued after a short pause, "what's the answer? I mean we just keep on killing 'em, and they just keep on coming."

"Beats the shit out of me, Bob."

"Answer's *artillery!*" Brightly blurted out. "Just put all the artillery in the fucking free world, hub to hub, up there on the 'Z' where McNamara wants to put his fence, and then start plowing ground northward. Complete your mission, then roll forward fifteen or twenty klicks and do it again. Keep going till you get to the Chinese border."

"Red leg's not the answer to all our problems, Slim," I said. "We proved that the other night on the 506."

"Yeah, what do you think happened, sir?" Halloway asked.

"Beats the shit out of me, Bob."

"I'll tell you what happened," Brightly said. "Charlie moved, plain and simple. While we were cranking up the mission, and Baker's squad was going for cover, Charlie picked it up and moved elsewhere. Unobserved fire. Can't expect miracles from unobserved fire."

"Well, what do you think they were doing just sitting there in the first place?" Halloway asked.

"How the fuck should I know?" Brightly answered. "Maybe they were getting ready for Tet. You know, been raising Cain here on the plain for the past year, and now they're returning to the hills for a little rest and relaxation during the truce."

"Hey, how long does the truce last, anyway?" Halloway asked.

"Depends on whose you're talking about," I replied. "Theirs is supposedly seven days; ours lasts only thirty-six hours beginning at 1800 hours tonight."

"Think they'll stick to it, sir?"

"Beats the shit out of me, Bob."

It was an uneventful afternoon, and with its passing Charlie Company had failed to accomplish its primary mission, that of closing with and destroying the enemy. Our foe was simply not traveling the mountain that day, nor was he on the plain.

"Perhaps Charlie finally got to wherever he's been heading the last couple months," Lieutenant Brightly jokingly remarked.

Around three o'clock we decided to pack it up and begin journeying back toward the valley floor. I radioed Bill Norwalk, telling him to do the same. It was the time of day we liked most, when day's work was over and we were moving effortlessly downhill toward our NDP, a hot meal, and a night's rest instead of struggling upward into the unknown. But it was always more satisfying to be descending our mountain after a successful hit.

As we worked our way downward along yet another east-west trail, I took note of Three Six's riflemen. As usual, they were moving as riflemen should move when in Indian country—with weapons at the ready, distances maintained, and a warrior's silence. Still, there was a certain aura of laxness on this occasion. Perhaps it was the result of having made the up-down sally so many times before—routine is the greatest ally of laxness—or perhaps it was simply in anticipation of the pending truce.

Two Six had selected an NDP in relatively flat terrain a klick or so from the base of the mountain but a short distance from Daisy. As the company began its nightly ritual of digging holes, clearing fields of fire, and emplacing claymores and trip flares, its platoon leaders, attached FO, first sergeant, and I assembled for our evening parley. Unlike my tête-à-têtes with the Bull, these sessions were usually brief affairs, restricted to the company's business at hand—the platoon leaders had little time for casual conversation until after their defensive preparations were complete. We first shared any lessons learned on that day's operation and then turned our attention to the next day's activities. At the conclusion of our get-together, the platoon leaders would show me where they proposed to put their LPs and trick-or-treat sites that night, and I would routinely approve their recommendations without comment. Slim Brightly would then plot these locations on his map.

On this occasion, talk immediately turned to the next day's activities.

"Where we gonna do this train-fire stuff, sir?" Lieutenant Norwalk asked.

"What train fire?" I asked in return.

"I propose we set the range up on the west side of the perimeter," Lieutenant Halloway said. "Use the mountain as a backdrop. 'Course there aren't that many villagers around here anyway, so maybe . . ."

"What train fire?" I repeated.

"Not enough range," Bill Norwalk said in response to Halloway's suggestion, as if not hearing me. "If you're gonna even approximate the firing tables, you're gonna need at least . . ."

"What train fire, goddamn it!" I snapped, feigning anger.

Silence. All heads turned toward me, then to my first sergeant.

"Uh . . . hadn't had a chance to get with you since you came off the hill, sir," the Bull said. "Sorry. Anyway, this afternoon your XO called and informed us in passing that he couldn't find any silhouette targets, so he's gonna send us out some charlie-rat cases that his folk have done some painting on. Seems the old man wants us to use this downtime to 'enhance our marksmanship abilities.'"

"Okay, understand. Thanks," I said and then, turning to the others, asked, "Well, what about it? You all think we need a little marksmanship training?"

"Fuck no! . . . sir."

"No way! Colonel ought to ask Chuck about our marksmanship abilities."

"Didn't know we had a choice, sir."

"Don't know if we do," I said. "But let me try to get to the bottom of this."

I got up and walked the few meters to where Blair and Anderson were digging the hole they would share that night.

"Blair, my good and faithful servant, would you be so kind as to go to our log push. I would speak to my XO."

He made the frequency adjustment.

"Comanche Five, this is Comanche Six, over."

"This is Five Alpha. Uh . . . the Five ain't in the area right now. Can I assist? Over."

"This is Six, Roger. What do you know about train-fire activities tomorrow?"

"Five Alpha, not much. The Lieutenant had us making up these targets this afternoon. Rumor is that the colonel wants you all to do a little target practice during the stand down."

"This is Six. Okay. Thanks. Out."

"Back to command, please," I said to Blair. He again quickly changed the radio's frequency.

"Arizona Three, this is Comanche Six. Over."

"And this is Arizona Three, over." I could hear the faint, familiar *whump, whump* of a Huey as Major Byson keyed his push to talk. He was airborne somewhere over Bong Son's plain.

"This is Comanche Six. Is there some last-minute change to our marching orders for the truce? Uh . . . has the Six put out anything on marksmanship training, or some such?"

"Not that I know of. Six says it's pretty much your call. You know his philosophy on that. Man on the ground and so forth. 'Course, you've got to keep yourself in a strong defensive posture. I recommend aggressive defensive patrolling during the day and the same nature of ambushing at night. Copy?"

Just another rumor that somehow nearly became fact. Story's old as the Army. Wonder how many operations have gone afoul—or succeeded—because of it.

I walked back to our assembled council.

"No train fire," I reported. "We aggressively defensively patrol during the day and defensively ambush at night. In short, we do what must be done to protect our own, okay?"

"Sir, might you tell us the difference 'tween *defensive* and *offensive* patrolling and trick-or-treating?" Bill Norwalk asked, smiling.

"I'll tell you the difference, sir," Sergeant Sullivan replied. "The difference is we do the same thing we do every other fucking day of the year, 'cept we don't hurt anybody, don't shoot anybody, in the process. Jesus Christ, what a war."

"Couldn't have said it better myself, Top," I commented.

We wrapped up our session by planning those defensive precautions we'd undertake over the course of the next two days in order to "protect our own." In the main, One Six and Two Six would screen our perimeter the next day, and if the truce held Three Six, augmented by Four Six, would do the same the following day.

The method by which the two platoons would accomplish the next day's mission was pretty much standard. After the LPs and trick or treats returned to the NDP and the morning log bird departed, One Six would move out of the perimeter, due north for one klick. Two Six would do the same, moving due south. Then both platoons would circle us at a distance of one kilometer in a half-moon fashion, moving clockwise. Both would remain an equal distance from us, with our NDP separating them. At day's end, One Six would rejoin us from the south, and Two Six from the north. In essence, this maneuver provided us our own moving "doughnut ring."

Of course, these preparations were all for naught. The next day we'd find ourselves doing anything, and a bit of everything, except patrolling defensively.

Slim Brightly remained behind as my platoon leaders returned to their sectors of the perimeter. First Sergeant Sullivan, with tour-extension papers in hand on one of Three Six's soldiers, accompanied Lieutenant Halloway.

"So what say, Slim? Understand you're gonna be leaving us shortly."

"Yeah, guess so," he said, smiling. "My six months are up in another couple of weeks. Gotta move on to bigger and better things."

"And what might that be?" I asked.

"Well, getting promoted 'bout the same time I ferry out—least that's when I hit my twenty-four months. Colonel says he's gonna give me a battery. 'Course that's what I want, a command."

"Sure you do, but it can weigh on you. Especially assuming the reins same time you go double on your silver. Nervous?"

He looked at me as if unable to comprehend my question, then said, "Hell, no! Ain't nothing to commanding a battery, particularly over here where your soldiers and soldiering are 'bout the only thing you have to worry about. I mean, you don't have the wives and family problems, or the socials, fund drives, parades and reviews, Saturday-morning inspections, police and support details, and so on and so forth. All you gotta worry about is making sure your soldiers can put iron on a target quicker and more accurately than any other battery in the fucking division. And my people will damn well be doing that soon enough after I take over!"

False modesty was not one of Lieutenant Brightly's character flaws. He was confident almost to the point of cockiness. There was little doubt in my mind that he would be an outstanding commander.

"Hell, maybe I don't understand the question, sir," he continued. "Mean, were you nervous when you took the company on the bridge?"

"Damn right I was. Still am. Every goddamn day."

My response seemed to surprise him. Then, shrugging his shoulders, he said, "Well, you shouldn't be. Company's turned itself around since you took over. Shit, we ain't done nothing but kick Charlie's ass up one side and down the other since leaving the bridge."

"Yeah, but Slim, I've had very damn little to do with that, and you know it. We've just been lucky as hell these past couple of months. Could've just as easily gone the other way."

"Whoa there, Six," he said, grinning. "*Lucky!* Wasn't it you who told me he didn't believe in luck that first night when I said we were having damn little of it?"

I smiled and said, "Well, let me rephrase that. The gods of war have smiled on us these last couple of months. Okay?"

"Yeah, I copy that, and you're right, they have. And I do believe in luck, but the company had problems other than just the lack of it before your arrival." He paused and then, in a more serious vein, said, "See, your predecessor was one of the finest officers, one of the finest men, I've ever known, in the service or out. Loved his soldiers, looked over each and every one of them like they were his children. As a good commander should."

He breathed deeply. "And the colonel was right in relieving him. And every one of your leaders knows that 'cept your first sergeant, and down deep he knows it, too. 'Course, he won't admit it to anyone except maybe himself, and you can't fault him for that."

I said nothing, so he went on.

"He loved his soldiers *too* much. And after he lost a couple of 'em, he simply went too far in trying to keep the rest of the company out of harm's way. Sort of got his priorities mixed up—you know, accomplish the mission, but *first* take care of the troops.

"Hell, I don't know, maybe he just wasn't ready for command. Maybe we're making our lieutenants into captains too soon."

Changing the course of our conversation, I asked, "Hey, Slim, you gonna fire a registration tonight?"

"Naw, don't need it. I can work off Daisy's RP if need be.'

The evening log bird landed minutes later and Lieutenant Brightly strolled off to see if it might have brought mail for him.

"Maybe he just wasn't ready for command." Well, hell, who is? But he's right, as was I. Although we rarely admit it, because it can't be taught in leadership courses, the difference between a successful and an unsuccessful commander in combat is, as often as not, a matter of pure luck, fate, the fortunes of war. And we had been lucky. What if we had been caught in an ambush on one of our early forays up the mountain? "Why were you on a trail, Captain?" "Did you have flankers out, left and right?" What if the five NVA had been quicker with their AKs than Wester had been with his twelve-gauge the other night on the 506? "And what were you doing moving bold ass down a highway at night, Captain?" "Did you have flankers out . . ." Yeah, I'm nervous. Stay nervous.

At dusk, after the company had messed and began settling in for the night, my first sergeant came over and sat down beside me atop an overturned five-gallon water can. In each of his hands he held two cans of beer.

"Battalion sent out two cans per head count tonight, Six. Guess because of Tet."

"Kind of wish they hadn't, Top. Gotta keep our people on their toes."

"Well, yeah, but we're still abiding by our two-beer-limit rule, sir," he retorted.

"Hey, Top," I replied a bit testily. "You know, and I know, that there are nondrinkers in the company, and not one of those beers will go undrunk tonight. Which means some of our folk are gonna break the two-beer rule, right?"

"Well, yeah, guess that's so. But shit, Six, what with the thirty-six-hour stand down and all . . ."

"Sure, it'll be all right. Guess I'm just nervous, that's all." Stay nervous.

We sat in silence for a while, sipping our beer and watching the last light of day fade over Vietnam's Annamese cordillera.

"Guess Mac is winging his way home now," I offhandedly remarked.

"Not yet, Six. He'll probably be leaving An Khe tomorrow or the next day, then Cam Ranh, then home. Good officer. We'll miss him."

"Yeah, wish he'd stay in, but think there's little chance of it happening."

"Naw, he's not career, sir. None of your officers are, with the possible exception of Lieutenant Norwalk, and he's undecided. But MacCarty will get out, you can bet on it. Don't know anything about his replacement. Halloway will get out. Fact, don't know if he could go career even if he wanted to. Him being Reserve and all."

"Well, hell, Top," I interrupted, "all our officers are Reserve."

"Yeah, but he's *reserve* Reserve. Mean, he wasn't commissioned active in an indefinite status. He's an inactive who volunteered for an active tour so as to do a stint in the Nam. Old-fashioned patriot."

Shame on you, Captain. You should've known that.

"One exception, 'though he ain't really our officer," he continued. "That's Brightly. He's career through and through. He'll stay in and might even make general." Pausing, he smiled, "If he doesn't, it won't be because he didn't think he was capable of handling the duties of a general officer."

I laughed softly. "Yes, he is a confident young man, isn't he?"

"To a fault, Six."

After a short lull, he said, "What about you, sir? Ever had any doubts 'bout staying in?"

"Nary a one. Can't ever remember a time I didn't want to be a soldier. Mac says it's 'cause of World War II. Hell, might be right. That's the time of life I first remember, and everybody was in uniform except Mom. What about you, Top? You grow up wanting to soldier?"

"Hell, no! Never even thought about it till the war came along. Joined up at seventeen—it was expected of me—but knew I'd be back on the farm soon as the thing was over."

"So?"

"Well, I never saw much of the war, you know, just the tail end of it. Spent some time guarding a muddy ordnance dump in France and saw war's end in Austria. So, anyway, I was high on the list for occupation duty. Pulled it, then, just 'fore my hitch was up, and as I was getting ready to come home, it suddenly struck me. Hell, I don't want to be no farmer. Soldiering is more fun than farming. Occupation duty's better than digging taters."

"Found a home, huh?"

"Yeah, guess so. Next day told the first sergeant to whip another four on me. He did. Figured I'd pull that tour and then maybe get out— my folks really wanted me back on the farm. But four years later, I was running for cover at a place called Chipyong-ni, cursing the Chinese birthrate while I was doing so."

I laughed. "What outfit, Top?"

"Why, the 'First Team,' of course. Fifth Cav, as a matter of fact. Joined it as a replacement in '51."

"They were at . . . uh . . . Chipyong-ni?" I asked. I recalled some of the old-timers talking about the battle but remembered few of the details.

"Yeah. Some of the Second Infantry's folk were surrounded, and the Fifth Cav went in to relieve 'em. Task Force Crombez, remember it well. Cold enough to freeze brass balls off a monkey; damn, it was cold. That's the one good thing 'bout this war, Six. Don't have to worry about freezing your nuts off."

I nodded.

"Anyway, went into Korea as a corporal and came out of it with two rockers—one of which I was allowed to keep. By then, there's no question of getting out. Goddamn Army was in my blood, know what I mean?"

And I nodded again.

"There'll be some of these kids, these men, come out of this thing the same way. None of 'em might believe it right now. Probably tell you you're out of your goddamn mind if you even suggest such a thing. But there's some of 'em who'll stay in and others who'll go back on the farm, or on the street, or wherever, and suddenly find they're bored as hell. Find themselves missing a little bit of everything they're cursing right now. And sooner or later, they'll find their way back in."

"Suppose you're right."

"And them that don't, with very rare exception, will harbor few regrets for having been here—although again, they'd tell you you're out of your goddamn mind if you suggested such a thing tonight."

He paused as if in thought, then said, "Don't know why that is. Way of war, I guess. Or maybe it's because very damn few of our soldiers, of us, will ever again do anything as . . . uh . . . as *big* in life as we're doing right now. Am I making any sense, sir?"

"Yeah, you are, Top. And you said it better than I ever could."

He smiled and let his thoughts drift for a moment. I did the same.

"Think the truce will hold, Six?" he asked, opening the second of our two beers and passing one of them to me.

"Like I told Halloway, Top, it beats the shit out me. But, yes, I think it'll stick. North seems to want it; least that's what the papers say. Christmas truce held up pretty well. You know, couple flare-ups here and there, but guess that's to be expected."

"Well, hope you're right. Snuffie could use a little downtime. 'Course, like I said at our parley, difference 'tween offensive and defensive humping is goddamn little."

Darkness had fallen, which meant we could no longer smoke openly, and neither of us could enjoy what remained of our second beer without an occasional drag on a cigarette. Putting his head under a poncho, Sergeant Sullivan lit two cigarettes, and then, cupping them closely, we continued our conversation.

"Dirty filthy habit," he said. "Ought to give 'em up. And by God I will! I'll give 'em up 'fore I do ROTC duty. Don't want them cadets influenced the wrong way."

"Shit, we ought to both give 'em up, Top. ROTC duty aside, it'd make the hump here on the plain easier. 'Course, if we quit tomorrow, might catch an AK-47 round through a healthy lung next week, huh?"

He smiled. "Yeah, you're right. Wait till this thing's over. Then we'll both give 'em up the day we hit the good old U.S. of A. Okay, Six?"

"Okay, Top."

"Shake?"

We did.

And again there was a lull in our conversation as each of us, I suppose, tried to think of other things to talk about. Because this evening discourse was important, refreshing. Neither of us could talk to others in the company quite as candidly as we talked to each other. We were both somewhat distanced from the others, he as the company's senior NCO and me as its commander.

"You hear about Cooper?" he asked, suddenly.

"Our sergeant major? No."

"Got himself a direct commission—to *captain!* Getting himself a company in the mech battalion. You believe that, Six?"

"Well, shit, I'm happy as hell to hear it. You know, Top, he said he was gonna do it, back there at An Khe. Don't think any of us took him seriously at the time. Uh . . . he's younger than you, isn't he?"

"Sure. Couldn't have got a commission if he weren't. But see, I'm having more fun than he is. Least I was 'fore he got a company. But he'll make a good commander. Jess is a soldier's soldier."

And so are you, First Sergeant, I thought to myself. You could take a company right now without missing a beat.

"And he's worked with mech before," he continued, "back in the late fifties, in Germany. He'll do well."

We sat in silence for several minutes before I asked, "Anything happening on the admin side I ought to know about?"

"Naw, just routine. Gonna have to get Young in 1st Platoon in to English for some emergency dental work, got a tooth that went bad on him. Smathers, also in 1st Platoon, is complaining of dizzy spells. Doc Heard says we don't have no choice but to send him in for a look-see. I'll have both of 'em on the morning log bird. Burke, Three Six, signed his extension papers this evening and is catching hell from the rest of the platoon, none of whom think he's quite sane. But he wants to be a door gunner, so we'll probably be losing him 'fore too long.

"Uh . . . let's see, anything else? Oh, yeah, Sweet Willie's Pfc stripe came down. Shit, Six, we ought to have a little ceremony . . ."

Suddenly we heard a faint fusillade of small-arms fire somewhere in the distance.

"Probably a bunch of the little people celebrating Tet," the Bull remarked, then a bit moodily, "wish I was somewhere celebrating something, anything."

"Well, when this thing's over we'll do that very thing, Top."

Brightening, he said, "Goddamn right we will, Six! When we get back to the States, the two of us, just the two of us, will get us a bottle of Rebel Yell and sit down in the sand someplace and get drunk as skunks, okay?"

"It's a promise, Top."

But we wouldn't. We'd never see each other again—which I suppose is also the way of war.

First Day of the Tet Offensive: 30 January

"Arizona Three, this is Comanche Six. Over."

"This is Arizona Base. Go."

Go? Where did this guy learn his radio procedure? Been talking to too many helicopter pilots.

"This is Comanche, Roger. We had an enemy probe of our November Delta Papa. Burst of automatic-weapons fire about zero five ago. I've got one lightly wounded. Do not, I say again, do not require medevac before first light. Request dust off at that time. How copy? Over."

"Roger, Comanche. Solid copy. Uh . . . dust off at first light . . . break. Be advised we're under attack at this location. Out!"

Well, that's a switch! Hell of a way to start a truce—shooting at us in our NDP and then attacking what had always been a sacred refuge for us boonie rats—battalion headquarters.

The Bull, having just returned from One Six's piece of the perimeter, informed me our injured soldier had indeed suffered only a minor, somewhat embarrassing, flesh wound to his buttock, one that required little more than a Band-Aid.

"It's not a good wound, Six," he said. "Certainly not good enough to return him Stateside. Fact, I'll bet it gets him no farther than the battalion aid station. Probably be back out here on the evening log bird."

He paused for a moment and then said, "On the other hand, hope it ain't a bad omen. You know, we haven't had a single soul so much as scratched since leaving the bridge. Hell, we ain't even ever been fired on in our NDP!"

"Yeah, we've been lucky. Just glad the young stud's okay. And I don't believe in omens, Top."

He nodded, smiling.

"But you know, Top, it was sort of strange the way they hit us here tonight. As if they were just passing by and decided to throw something our way—almost like an afterthought. What do you make of it?"

"Beats the hell out of me, Six." Then, grinning and looking at his watch, he said, "But it was a hell of a short truce, wasn't it. Must have lasted all of seven or eight hours. And shit, don't think I've ever heard more red leg than they're throwing downrange tonight . . . uh, this morning. Sure as hell ain't H&I."

"Yeah, I noticed that, too," I replied. "By the way, when I reported our wounded soldier to battalion, know what the Three's radio man said? Said *they* were under attack!"

"Hitting battalion?" he asked, obviously surprised. "Well, *that's* something new. Can't recall that ever happening before." Then, again grinning, he said, "Wonder what they want us to do about it. Send 'em reinforcements?"

I smiled. "It'd be a hell of a walk, wouldn't it?"

"Three's on the horn, sir," Blair said in a low voice, yawning.

"Comanche Six, this is Arizona Three. Pass line number on your WIA. Over."

"This is Comanche Six. Roger. Wait. Out."

Turning to Sergeant Sullivan, I asked, "Got a line number on our wounded man, Top?"

"Just a sec," he replied, pulling his copy of the company's roster from a cargo pocket. Bending over it with a red-filtered flashlight, he squinted for a couple of moments and then said, "Shit!"

He passed the roster and flashlight to Blair. "Uh . . . give me a line number, will you, Blair?"

Noticing the subtle smile on my face, my first sergeant said, "Don't say it, sir. It ain't the eyes. Hell, I'm seeing at twenty twenty. It's just them red filters . . . uh . . . they mess up a man's night vision."

Which of course was untrue, and we both knew it. Red-filtered flashlights protect one's night vision.

Then, grinning a bit self-consciously, he said, "Ah, sweet youth, Six. Age does take its toll, as you'll learn soon enough."

"I copy that, Top," I replied, as Blair said, "Bowers, line thirteen. Shit, unlucky number."

Retrieving his handset, I said, "Arizona Three, this is Comanche Six. Over."

"This is Arizona Three."

"This is Comanche Six. Reference your last, line one three. Copy?"

"Roger. Good copy. Line thirteen. Now, what happened? Over."

"This is Comanche Six. Received a single burst of automatic-weapons fire—think it was an AK, 'bout one five ago from the western side of the perimeter. Man in question was simply in harm's way. Minor wound. No need for dust off before first light."

"This is Arizona Three. Okay. Had a similar incident in Running Navaho's sector about an hour ago. As I told him, I don't want you to wait for wounded to report these contacts. Anytime you hear a round fired in anger during the next thirty-six . . . uh . . . twenty-eight hours, I need to know about it. Gotta keep book on the enemy so that higher can tabulate their list of 'shame-on-you' truce violations three days hence. Copy?"

I said I did and returned Blair's handset to him.

Turning to Sergeant Sullivan, I said, "Seems Delta Company also had some sort of contact tonight. Byson wants to make sure we report as much as a single sniper round during the truce."

"Well, shit, we knew that, sir. Same as Christmas, right?"

I nodded. "Blair, my good man, how about giving One Six a call-up and tell 'em I'm on my way over."

I found our wounded soldier lying a bit uncomfortably on his stomach, on an air mattress, next to Norwalk's command post. Kneeling, I put my hand on his shoulder and asked, "How's it going, Bowers?"

"I'm okay, sir. Just burns like hell."

"Sure, it burns," Doc Heard snorted. "Let me give you a shot of morphine, and it won't burn, least you won't notice it as much."

"No."

Faintly experiencing a feeling of déjà vu, I said, "Come on, Bowers, let the doc give you a shot." Make the night go quicker, mate.

"No, sir. It ain't that bad, and I don't like shots—or morphine. I can take the pain."

Ah yes, Top. Sweet youth, indeed!

Getting to my feet, I pulled Heard aside and whispered, "Prognosis?"

"Aw, he'll be all right. Still, it is painful, and more serious than some—including our first sergeant—might think. Bullets destroy meat tissue no matter where or how lightly they hit you. Probably keep him at battalion for a couple days or so." Then, looking at Bowers grit his teeth, he whispered, "I could give him the shot anyway, sir. I'm authorized."

"No, it's his call, or should be. Besides . . . uh . . . he might very well change his mind before the night's over."

"You see where it came from, Bill?" I asked, sitting down next to Norwalk atop his hole's parapet.

"No, sir. Somewhere to the west of us. No one saw the flash or anything. Just heard the pops as the rounds came through our perimeter."

I nodded my head. "Bastard."

"What do you think, sir? One of the 10 percent that never gets the word?"

"That's my guess. Either that or one of the 90 percent that does and just doesn't give a shit. Both sides have 'em."

"Guess that means we still do defensive patrolling tomorrow . . . uh . . . today, huh?"

"Yep, we'll patrol defensively, and we'll abide by the truce even if Charlie doesn't—'less of course we run across the one that shot your soldier."

"And they all look alike, don't they."

"That's what they say, Bill. Anyway, thought I would tag along with you, okay?"

"Sure, sir. Happy to have you."

But of course he wasn't. Platoon leaders don't like having their commanders looking over their shoulder all day.

Rising to leave, I said, "Ought to get some sleep, Lieutenant. Still have another three hours before dawn."

The enemy had probed our perimeter in the wee hours of the morning on the first day of the Chinese lunar new year. Referred to by the Vietnamese as Tet, it was the most celebrated of the year's holidays—Christmas, New Year's, Thanksgiving, and the Fourth of July all rolled into one. In 1968, the Year of the Monkey, it was also the first day of Gen. Vo Nguyen Giap's Tet offensive.

During the next ten days, the pace of Charlie Company's operations would be frantic—always moving, always fighting, sometimes conducting two and three combat air assaults a day. In the morning we might find ourselves searching for remnants of the evading enemy in the dense, triple-canopied jungles of Binh Dinh's mountains, then fighting him in the province's coastal areas that afternoon, only to move again that night to some desolate hilltop and begin digging the residue of the general's retreating army out of its rocks.

There was no C&D that morning. Shortly after first light, as most of us were downing a charlie rat, Blair passed me his handset, saying, "Three's on the horn, sir."

"Comanche, this is Arizona Three. The truce is terminated in your Alpha Oscar. I say again, the truce is terminated! Take appropriate defensive precautions . . . break. Comanche, stand by for mission orders. Acknowledge. Over."

"This is Comanche Six. Roger, acknowledge truce terminated. Standing by for orders."

Within twenty minutes or so he radioed us again. "This is Arizona Three inbound in one five with a zero, plus three, plus zero. LZ secure. I'll be talking to you on the ground!"

Plus three. No slicks, no gunships, all hooks. Well, at least we won't be fighting our way onto a landing zone.

The three large troop-carrying helicopters ferried us fifteen klicks or so southeast, landing adjacent to a small cluster of villages astride

Highway One. Major Byson met us on the LZ. As he did so, I noticed an ARVN contingent maneuvering through one of the villages on the eastern (coastal) side of the highway.

"Hey, Jim, gotta get out of here, so let me give this to you quick and dirty. NVA attacked throughout the province last night, actually all across the central part of the country. Looks like a coordinated offensive. 'Though info's still real sketchy, seems to be confined mainly to the populated areas, places that haven't heard a round fired in anger in a long time."

"Yeah, understand they even hit *battalion* last night."

Oh, shit! Wrong thing to say.

He looked at me sternly, but not unkindly, and said, "Listen up, Captain. I've heard my share of rounds fired in anger."

"Uh . . . yes, sir. That's not what I meant, really."

Then, smiling, he said, "But yeah, Chuck did throw us a couple rounds last night. Nothing serious. In fact, he seems to be pretty much leaving our folk alone. Concentrating on villages and cities, shit, in some cases district and maybe even provincial capitals."

I nodded, making notes as he spoke.

"But our concern right now is Binh Dinh," he continued. "NVA went through these supposedly secure villages last night. ARVN's now in the process of digging out those still in the area. Want you and your folk to do the same. Highway's your boundary, little people on the left . . . coastal side, you on the right. I brought along a Kit Carson who may be of some help to you." He grinned, "Doesn't speak much English, but he's really fluent in Vietnamese.

"Jim, everything's up in the air right now. Don't know if you'll be staying 'round here tonight, or moving on, or what. But I'll promise you one thing; you'll go wherever we find Charlie. So hang loose, or as we say in the military vernacular, stay flexible!"

We wished each other well, and he departed aboard the battalion's C&C ship.

Minutes later we began our sweep of the villages with One Six tying into Highway One on the left, Two Six on the right, and Three Six, followed by Four Six and headquarters, in the center. We found no enemy. We found only scared and crying children and their shocked elders wailing over their dead as only the Vietnamese can wail over their dead. Most of the demised were village officials, and most had been executed with a single shot to the base of their skull. We would later learn that such atrocities were the norm throughout Vietnam on the nights of 30 and 31 January and 1 February 1968; and for a longer period in the city of Hue.

Within two hours of his departure, Byson called with a change in our orders. "This is Arizona Three. Want you to move to the red line and prepare for attachment to Prairie Schooner in two zero. You'll be conducting combined arms sweep of an area . . . oh, say, seven klicks to your north. Prairie Schooner's in command; however, if you have any problem with that just give me a call. How copy? Over."

"This is Comanche Six. Solid copy. Where on the red line do we marry up with Schooner?"

"This is Arizona Three. Just assemble your element on the big red. Schooner has your push. He can't miss you."

Turning quickly to Blair, I asked, "Who the fuck's Prairie Schooner?"

He was already thumbing through his CEOI codes and within moments said, "Prairie Schooner's . . . hot damn! It's the mech folk; looks like we ride for a while."

Thirty minutes later, we were barreling north on Highway One atop Prairie Schooner's M-113 APCs (armored personnel carriers). Captain Rogers, commander of the mech company to which we were attached, and I had agreed that my men would ride on top of the carriers, while his soldiers occupied their normal positions inside the vehicles. A mechanized rifle company is organized very similarly to an airmobile rifle company (the main difference between the two being that they sometimes walked but usually rode, while we sometimes flew but usually walked), so crossattachment of our two commands proved relatively simple. One Six merely joined forces with Schooner's One Six, Two Six with their Two Six, and so on.

Our objective was a large low-lying hill mass on the right, eastern, side of the highway about six klicks from our pickup point. According to some of the villagers in the area, remnants of an NVA force were now hiding in the hill's vegetation.

The carriers slowed and then, each suddenly braking on its right track, turned sharply ninety degrees to the right—and stopped. We were now facing the hill, with a distance of ten to fifteen meters separating each of the fourteen carriers on line at its base. Riding with Rogers atop his track, I asked what our plan of attack was.

"Plan?" he replied. "We're gonna recon by fire with the fifties . . ."

(referring to his .50-caliber machine guns, one of which was mounted on each of the APCs) ". . . and then roll forward."

"Fine," I replied. "You want my people to dismount and follow, or what?"

"Naw, that'd just slow us up. 'Sides, we don't really know if Charlie's up there or not. Why don't you keep your folk mounted, and then if we run into something, you can dismount at that time."

"Sounds good to me," I responded, being anything but an expert on mechanized warfare.

He talked briefly into the mike attached to his helmet, and then fourteen .50-caliber machine guns instantaneously began firing into the hill mass before us, their third-round tracers plunging brilliantly into the lush, emerald green elephant grass covering the hillside and then ricocheting crazily upward.

Bam! Bam! Bam! Bam!

It was an incredible earsplitting display of firepower. We of Charlie Company, having never seen so many .50-calibers firing simultaneously, watched in fascination as the tracers swept the hillside, back and forth, from its base to its crest.

Finally Rogers gave the signal to cease fire. The tracks began moving forward, slowly at first as they negotiated the highway's embankment, which jutted downward at a steep angle, and then gaining speed as they started up the hill, crushing the dense foliage before them.

We had moved perhaps fifty meters, less than a third of the way up the hill, when we ran into—no, over—Charlie. The enemy had dug himself into the hill's side, underneath its tall, thick, grassy covering, but in so doing had postured himself to hide, not fight. The track to our immediate right ran over the first of these positions, and as it did so an NVA soldier popped from his place of hiding and quickly pointed a rocket propelled grenade at the rear of the vehicle.

"RPG!" yelled one of our riflemen as he fired his M-16, killing his opponent before he could loose the grenade.

Moments later we heard an exchange of gunfire fifty or sixty meters to our left, where another of the tracks had uncovered a similar position.

That's it! I said to myself. Enemy's here, he's got RPGs, and there ain't no reason for Charlie Company to be riding atop these tin coffins.

I tapped Captain Rogers on the shoulder, pulled his helmeted headset aside, and said, "I'm dismounting my people, now!"

He gave me a thumbs up and signaled his tracks to stop momentarily, while we quickly dismounted. Then, after forming up behind the APCs, we continued up the hill afoot.

It turned out to be a very successful engagement. On our initial sweep, we netted ten or twelve of the enemy; on our return trip down the hill we killed another two or three. Finally, a horizontal sweep across the hill's face, with us once again mounted, turned up nothing.

Upon completion of this maneuver, Rogers assembled his tracks in a relatively flat area at the base of the hill, circling them into a "covered-wagon" defensive perimeter. We broke for lunch while awaiting new orders; and they were not long in coming.

"Comanche Six, this is Arizona Three inbound with four, plus two, plus two in one five. Gonna put you into your old stomping grounds. Getting reports of movement there. Looks like Charlie's using that general area as one of his routes of regress . . . break. Good show with Schooner, Over Trail Six passes 'well done.' As do we. You are now detached from Schooner. I'll see you on the ground in about one five. How copy? Over."

"This is Comanche Six. Solid. Standing by."

After quickly passing the gist of Byson's conversation to the platoon leaders and designating Bob Halloway's Three Six as our assault element, I turned over the business of moving the company to Bull Sullivan.

Twenty minutes later, we were sitting in the Huey's door frame, basking in the coolness of its ninety-knot backwash.

One of the fringe benefits of being in the assault element, I thought to myself. For a few brief moments aboard your doorless slick you can escape Vietnam's torrid heat while the rest of the company, following in the hooks, continues to sweat. Of course, if the LZ turns out to be "red," you may find yourself getting your clock cleaned while the rest of the company orbits above, sweating in safety. Is there a moral here? No, I don't think so. It merely means that in the Nam, the smallest of luxuries are often but a matter of chance and usually costless. But on occasion, suddenly and unknowingly, they are purchased at the price of life itself. Or, as the Bull would say, "Sometimes you eat the bear, and sometimes the bear eats you!"

I put my philosophical wanderings aside as we touched down on a green LZ a short distance from Daisy.

Attempting to cover as much of the area as possible in interdicting the enemy's withdrawal from Binh Dinh's populated areas, we kept two of our rifle platoons on the valley floor, sweeping the plain's approach routes into the mountains. One Six moved due north while Three Six, accompanied by the headquarters section, moved south. The 3d Platoon, Two Six, charged straight up the mountain to the west of us, accessing it by means of the same trail we had first discovered upon departing the Bong Son bridge two months before—the trail from which we had evacuated our nearly dead captive strapped to a jungle penetrator.

Neither of the valley platoons found Charlie, though both ran across evidence, hoofprints and so forth, that he had been traveling the area recently and extensively. In the process of making these discoveries, Lieutenant Norwalk found a suitable NDP site, and by 1500 hours One Six and Three Six had converged at this location.

Lieutenant O'Brien, MacCarty's replacement, remained on the mountain with Two Six. But not as long as he should have.

Within minutes of joining forces with Norwalk, we heard an abrupt explosive blast of automatic-weapons fire intermingled with the detonation of 40-mm grenades. O'Brien was evidently in contact! Concerned at not having heard a claymore explosion precede the sudden outbreak of small-arms fire, I took Anderson's handset from him and attempted to contact O'Brien.

"Two Six, this is Six. Give me a sitrep. Over."

Silence. No response from O'Brien, and the firing had stopped as suddenly as it began.

"Two Six, Two Six, this is Six. Over."

"This is Two Six. Uh . . . Roger, ran into something big. Think a large enemy force. We've succeeded in breaking contact and are now regressing down the hill. Looking forward to marrying up with you in about two zero."

You only think you're looking forward to marrying up with me, Lieutenant. Regressing, indeed!

"This is Six. Do you need dust off? Red leg? Over?".

"This is Two Six. Negative. Over."

"Okay, Two Six, I'll see you on the floor in two zero. Out."

I wanted to give our new platoon leader every benefit of the doubt, but the doubts were surely there. They'd been nagging at me since his arrival and Mac's departure two days previously. Of course, snap judgments based on first impressions are dangerous and often faulty, but I made them routinely. And although I hardly expected a platoon leader to report in with a bayonet between his teeth screaming, "Can do, Sir!" O'Brien thus far impressed me as someone who would really rather *be* anywhere else, involved *in* anything else, and doing it *with* anyone else. I missed Mac.

I didn't know what had happened on the mountain minutes before (and never would); however there were several unsettling adjuncts to the incident: Why had O'Brien broken contact? Where were the casualties? His or Charlie's? Why no request for fire support? Or assistance from us down here below?

In a matter of far less than twenty minutes, Two Six entered our perimeter. Taking Lieutenant O'Brien aside, I asked, not unkindly, "You got any wounded? We need a dust off down here?"

"No, real lucky there, sir. All of us are okay, but it was close, *real* close!"

"Okay," I replied. "Well, tell me about it, Dick. I mean in your own words, what happened?"

"Well, see, sir . . . uh . . . don't know *exactly* what happened. Mean, I was pretty far back in the formation . . . not really far, but, you know, 'bout midway, where I could best influence the outcome of any encounter . . . uh . . . like they taught us at Benning. But, anyway, shortly after we hit that main trail paralleling the mountain, all hell broke loose up front, and since we were in a draw, obviously at a tactical disadvantage, I thought it prudent to withdraw before we got someone hurt."

"Okay," I said—my initial response to his account of the encounter on the mountain, *our* mountain!

And then, perhaps because it had been a long day—and the day wasn't over yet—I lost my temper.

"Now listen and listen closely, Lieutenant," I said as calmly as I could. "I don't know what you may think they taught you at Benning, but let me assure you, you can best influence the outcome of any encounter by being as close as possible to that encounter when it happens! And if you're in Europe conducting a reconnaissance in force, perhaps midway in your formation is an appropriate place to be. But we ain't in Europe. And if you're conducting a retrograde movement, the rear of your platoon is where you should be. But we don't do retrogrades in Charlie Company! In this environment, in this war, things happen from the *front!* And that's where you should always be, *always!*

"And, goddamn it, if you can't see your point man, *always* see your point man in front of you, you're shirking your duties, and I won't tolerate it!"

I paused a moment to let our new lieutenant digest what I had said, words I perhaps should never have uttered. Then I continued.

"Finally, getting someone hurt is what we do around here, and we've been doing it rather well lately.

"Now, I want you to understand something, Lieutenant. You have, without question, one of the finest fighting platoons—undoubtedly the best platoon sergeant and point man—in all of Vietnam. I will not allow you to change that in any way. Understand?"

He nodded obediently.

"Dick, that mountain behind you there," I said in a somewhat kinder voice, "belongs to Charlie Company. It's our playpen, and nobody runs us out of our playpen. So I want you to take your platoon and get back up that mountain, find that large enemy force, and kick the shit out of 'em. Understand?"

He did.

As he was turning a very disgruntled platoon around and starting back up the mountain, I walked over to Lieutenant Norwalk. "Hey, Bill, saddle up One Six. We're going up the hill. Bring your claymores."

O'Brien and Two Six accessed the mountain by way of the main east-west trail, their route of regress just minutes before. In the meantime, we began working our way upward along a secondary trail (one we had used several times in the past) fifty or sixty meters to the north of Two Six. It was about three-thirty in the afternoon, still plenty of daylight left. Still time to make a hit!

Shortly after reaching the main north-south trail running parallel to the mountain's face, we were suddenly overwhelmed by the stench of rotting flesh. These were the decaying corpses of enemy soldiers who had fallen victim to our claymore ambushes over the course of nearly two months. The odor was nauseating, and several of us found it difficult to refrain from gagging.

"Whew! Talk about *ripe!*" Andy commented.

"Yeah, and to think we did this to ourselves," Blair responded.

Norwalk, meanwhile, began searching for an ambush site, preferably at some point on the trail without enemy dead astride it. Within ten minutes or so he found a place tactically sound and where, if the breeze remained calm, the stench was bearable.

While Norwalk set up his two-point north-south ambush, I contacted O'Brien, passed our location to him, and asked for a sitrep.

"This is Two Six. Enemy seems to have withdrawn from the area. No sign of Charlie now. Over."

"This is Six. Roger, go into a trick or treat somewhere in that general area. Maybe one of us will get lucky. Good hunting. Out."

So our two platoons went into ambush and waited for the enemy that had wreaked havoc on the people of Binh Dinh the night before.

"What do you think happened last night, sir?" Bill Norwalk whispered as we sat straddling the trail about midway between the two ambush sites. "I mean, with Charlie hitting all over the province like that."

"Beats the shit out of me, Bill. I'm more concerned 'bout our new platoon leader right now. What do you think he ran into?"

"Beats the shit out of me, Six," he responded, smiling. "Could've been a sniper, chance engagement, or maybe just overwhelmed by his own imagination, you know, being new on board and all . . . or maybe he just couldn't stand the stink."

"Well, I can relate to that! Damn, we gotta find us a new mountain to play on, Bill. It's all I can do to keep from puking anymore. Mean, this is a facet of combat they never taught us about at Benning."

"Yes, sir! Ought to have subjects in the curriculum like 'Coping with the Messy Battlefield' or 'Secondary Uses of the Gas Mask.'"

I nodded, grinning, then said, "But shit, Bill, I don't know how we could've done it any different. I mean, we couldn't have carried 'em out of here, and there's no way we could've buried 'em."

"Yeah, I know. But it sure brings it close to home, doesn't it? I mean, the sight of them, still in their uniforms, rotting away like that. And you notice the uniforms are okay, but their flesh has turned that ghastly greenish gray, and you think to yourself, I'll bet when he put that uniform on he didn't know it'd outlast him—and then you find yourself starting to look at your own uniform."

"Yeah," I said, "there but for the grace of God, and so forth. Bill, you still philosophizing?"

"No, sir. No one ever accused me of that except Mac, and *he's* the one who majored in it!"

He paused a moment and then said, "But speaking of Mac, I wouldn't worry too much about his replacement. He'll come along. Just takes time. These first few days are hard on a new platoon leader. Big adjustment, from a Stateside BOQ. Mean, here's O'Brien, Army puts him through the basic course and then lets him spend five, six months in a training command—which does absolutely nothing to prepare him for what he's about to be thrown into. Then one bright and sunny day he steps off a slick and it's welcome to the real world, or maybe that's the *surreal* world, Lieutenant! It's tough.

"At first you're kind of numb, but then after three, four days, maybe a week, you're suddenly struck with the awesome realization that you're gonna live this existence, *if* you live, for the next twelve months! And that can be a very traumatic awakening. Fortunately, it doesn't last long. Pretty soon you reenter the numb phase, just living from day to day, looking neither forward nor backward."

"Until you pack it up and go home, huh?" I commented.

"No, sir. Not according to Mac and others. They say you've got one more phase to go through, maybe the toughest one. That's the short-timer's phase, when you start to look forward again, and in doing so get nervous, cautious, hell, even paranoid in some cases.

"But your new lieutenant doesn't have to worry 'bout the trials of the short-timer for a while yet. And again, I think he'll do just fine."

Norwalk was right, of course, and Dick O'Brien would turn out to be a fine combat leader. As were all the lieutenants in Charlie Company.

"But you did the right thing by sending him back up the hill," Norwalk commented. "He'll sleep better tonight because of it. Just like getting back on a horse."

"Why, thank you for your confidence in my decision, Lieutenant," I jested.

"Also did right by putting us up here in a posture to give him an assist if need be," he added.

"Well, thank you again . . ."

Whoom! The claymore exploded! Our hit man to the north had a target.

Rat-tat-tat-tat-tat! The M-60 machine gun sprang to life; and so did we.

Being within thirty meters of the ambush site, we reached it in a matter of moments. The machine gunner was still working the area in and around the fallen bodies when we arrived.

"Got four of 'em, LT!" the hit man said excitedly, still clutching the claymore's electrical detonator tightly in his hand.

Norwalk and I stare momentarily at the shattered, lifeless bodies lying in disarray at our feet. And their uniforms have outlasted them. Indeed, such is the way of war, Bill.

"Good show, One Six. Super!" I said. "Now retrieve their weapons, do a quick body search, and let's go back to the ranch."

I called O'Brien and told him to "regress" to the NDP.

By dusk we had our night defensive positions dug and awaited the evening log bird, thankful that one of our longest days in the Nam was about to end.

But it wasn't.

"Three's on the horn, sir," Blair said.

Uh oh! He can't move us again, not now! Shit, it'll be dark in another forty-five minutes.

"Comanche, this is Arizona Three. I'm inbound with twelve, plus zero, plus two in zero seven. Got enemy on a hill up the coast and gonna put you on top of them. It's a 'needlepoint,' so be prepared for insert on a two-ship LZ. Once you go green, I'll have charlie rats, water, and any class V you need en route. Get your class V wants to your trains soonest if you've not already done so. How copy?"

"This is Comanche Six. Good copy . . . uh . . . poor timing, but good copy. We'll be ready for pickup. Over."

"Roger, Comanche. They told us there'd be days like this, but they never said they'd come like bananas, huh? And I'm light on the skids, inbound in seven. Out."

First Sgt. Bull Sullivan was pissed . . . really pissed!

"Goddamn it, sir. What do they want from us? How many times we moved today? Shit, up last night with the probe, hit the villages first thing this morning, linked up with tracks, back up here to the mountain! How many fucking chinks we killed today?"

Yes, he's really pissed, I thought to myself. When he slips into his Korean-vintage referral to the enemy as chinks, you know he's pissed!

"Fourteen, sixteen? I tell you, Six, the troops are tired! The troops are beat! Didn't have C&D this morning, ain't gonna have a hot tonight—and they'll forget to send the fucking mail out with the charlie rats, just wait and see! I mean, what the fuck they want out of us?"

"Take it easy, Top," I said rather sternly, but I hoped also compassionately. "I know how you feel, but nothing we can say or do is gonna change it. And, Top, you and me been 'round long enough to know that, right? And we've also been 'round long enough to know something big is happening right now. So how about whipping us up a quick air-movement order, cause we've already wasted two of our seven minutes in getting out of here."

He stared at me fixedly, almost rebelliously, for a brief moment. Then, suddenly smiling, he said, "Shit, you're right, Six. Hell, let's go see some of the country!"

Turning from me, he yelled, "Okay, drop your cocks and grab your socks. We're moving! Want to see my platoon sergeants up here, *now!*"

Concurrently, I called the platoon leaders forward and passed on Byson's warning order, emphasizing that we were all going in aboard slicks on a two-ship LZ. Five minutes later, with the last rays of sunlight disappearing over the western horizon, we were on our way to another of Binh Dinh's mountains.

Our flight of twelve Hueys orbited the mountain's pinnacle in a wide circle and then, flying in trail, prepared to land on our needle-point LZ. Because there were other friendly forces in the area, many of them on the mountain or at its base, Major Byson had decided against an artillery prep. However, this did not prohibit our accompanying Cobra gunships, suddenly roaring by us as we sped toward the LZ, from plastering the hilltop with aerial rockets and 40-mm grenades.

Whoom! Whoom! Whoom!

With the wind of the Huey's backwash in our faces, we watched the oncoming LZ explode in brilliant orange-and-red flashes, each immediately followed by an erupting pillow of black-and-white smoke intermingled with dust, dirt, and bits of foliage and rock, all of which was thrown asunder into Vietnam's darkening sky.

The lead Huey slowed, assuming a nose-up attitude, as we quickly maneuvered ourselves onto its skids. We leaped just before they touched the LZ's rocky surface.

Two at a time the other Hueys followed us in, discharging their soldiers in a matter of seconds; then, nose down and gaining airspeed, they were away. The LZ, as usual—and thank God for it—was green. But Charlie was here, hidden among the hill's crevices and rocks with his defenses oriented downhill. Within a matter of minutes we would find him.

As the *whump, whump* of the Hueys faded in the distance, we moved off the mountain's peak down a long, loosely vegetated ridge with One Six on the left, Three Six on the right, and Two Six straddling the ridge a bit in front of the other two platoons. The headquarters section followed Two Six. Moments later there was the abrupt crack of an

AK-47 round on Two Six's right flank, followed by an immediate fusillade of M-16 and M-60 machine-gun fire.

"We got one, sir!" O'Brien yelled excitedly, looking over his left shoulder toward us. "No, I think two! And a weapon—got us an AK!"

"Great!" I yelled back. "Let's see what . . ."

Suddenly, two blurry figures flashed across our front, between us in the headquarters section and O'Brien's platoon. They had obviously been well concealed but, like frightened quail in a cornfield, had been unnerved by the sudden exchange of gunfire. Their decision to flee was not a wise one. It was an especially unfortunate choice for the one who carried an explosive satchel charge strapped to his chest.

Still, they nearly made good their escape. Neither we nor the soldiers of Two Six could bring weapons to bear on the fleeing figures for fear of hitting each other. Then our attached Kit Carson screamed, *"Chu Hoi!"* One of the two evading enemy fell to the ground, placing his hands behind his neck.

The other enemy soldier, running down the ridge to our left toward One Six, quickly scrambled into a thicket of bamboo. It offered little protection. While the Kit Carson picked our new captive up from the ground, Two Six and the headquarters section began tearing the bamboo thicket apart with automatic-weapons fire.

Suddenly, our elusive quarry exploded! Pieces of bamboo intermingled with bits of cloth and flesh fell about us.

"Jesus H. Christ!" someone said after a moment's silence. "Must've had a charge on him."

"He did. I saw it! Had a yeller or khakilike satchel charge on his chest!" Sweet Willie said, his M-16 still pointed toward the bamboo thicket. "It was one of our rounds that hit it and sent old Charlie there to Ho Chi Minh heaven."

"I doubt it, Willie," the Bull said. "Ain't no M-16 round gonna detonate a satchel charge. More likely he self-destructed." He paused and then said to no one in particular, "You know, I'm getting short, and this is only the second time in this fucking war I've had a chance to shoot at somebody—and I rather like it, especially today. I feel like shooting somebody today! Shit, thought I saw our S-3 running into that clump of bamboo."

"Well, Top, glad we could make your day."

That was to be all of Charlie we'd find on the hilltop. Once it was secured, the company wasted no time in establishing its defensive perimeter. It was getting dark.

The Bull and I listened in as our Kit Carson conducted an informal interrogation of our NVA captive, who might have been sixteen years old but looked younger. Perhaps four feet nine or ten inches tall and weighing under a hundred pounds, he did not appear to be a formidable foe; he looked more like a frightened child.

The Kit Carson offered the NVA a drink of water from his canteen. He refused it. The Kit Carson then drank from his canteen and again offered it to the NVA "boy" soldier, who gingerly accepted it and drank as if he'd had been without water for days.

Blair offered the captive a cigarette, which he accepted, after staring at it hesitantly a moment, flashing Blair a brief smile. And I found myself unexpectedly thinking, I hope this young man, this boy in uniform, makes it through this mess. I hope he lives to return to his family.

"Someone give him a can of charlie rats," I said.

Blair pulled a can of ham and lima beans from the leg pocket of his jungle fatigues, opening it with the can opener he kept attached to his dog-tag chain.

"Who's got a clean spoon?" he asked, passing the can of beans to our startled prisoner.

Dubray pulled a plastic, cellophane-wrapped C-ration spoon from one of his pockets and handed it to the boy. Our captive looked at it a moment, apparently fascinated by the cellophane wrapping, and then stuck it into his can of limas.

"Not like that, asshole!" Dubray said, grabbing the spoon and removing its wrapping.

"Gawd, look at him go at them limas!" Anderson said. "Anyone can eat cold ham and limas gotta be starved."

"To him, it's probably a gourmet delight," Blair responded and then, turning back to our prisoner, said, "Just another of America's delicacies, my newfound friend, prepared for those of truly distinguished tastes in some of our country's finest dog-food-producing facilities."

By now, in between bites, boy soldier was smiling, talking freely, and sometimes even laughing at something his ex-NVA compatriot, our Kit Carson, said.

A short time later the evening log bird landed on our needlepoint LZ, dropping off ammo, water, more C rations—and the company's mail. The battalion S-2, accompanying the log bird, picked up boy soldier and flew him away.

A half hour or so after they had departed, Major Byson called, passed along another well done, and, tongue in cheek, said he had decided to leave us where we were for the night. I thanked him profusely.

The first day of the 1968 Tet offensive had ended for Charlie Company.

SECOND DAY OF THE TET OFFENSIVE: 31 JANUARY

At first light, Charlie Company descended the mountain, searching for remnants of its evasive foe on the way down. We found nothing other than a few enemy corpses that would later be tabulated into a "we-they" body count ratio at echelons far above ours.

Upon reaching the valley floor, we set up a hasty perimeter and awaited the morning log bird, hoping it would have aboard it a substantial C&D—a mermite of coffee would be especially welcome. In the meantime, the less optimistic broke out their heat tabs and charlie rats. They were premature in doing so. Minutes later the log bird landed, bringing with it an assortment of fresh fruit, scrambled eggs, bread, SOS, milk, and, of course, hot coffee.

We were enjoying this breakfast feast when Blair passed me his handset, reciting his familiar, "Three's on the horn, sir."

"Comanche, this is Arizona Three inbound your location to parley. See you on the ground in 'bout one zero."

The Bull and I met the battalion C&C when it landed in a paddy a short distance from our perimeter ten minutes later.

"How's it going, Jim, First Sergeant?" Major Byson said, more as a greeting than a question. "Got us a hell of a war going now, don't we?"

"Yes, sir," Sullivan and I said in unison.

"Well, listen, I want to pass on what we know of the situation, so you all can get the word down to your troops before they read 'bout it in *Stars and Stripes*. And I gotta be frank with you. We still don't know a hell of an awful lot. Still real sketchy.

"Anyway, seems to be a general offensive going on throughout the country. As you know, Charlie hit Binh Dinh night before last.

Think the situation here's pretty well stabilized; however, last night enemy struck big time both north and south of us, again mostly in the populated areas. They hit Hue! They hit Saigon! They attacked Tan Son Nhut. Last we heard Charlie was in the U.S. embassy! Believe that? Our goddamn embassy in downtown Saigon!"

He paused momentarily to allow us an opportunity to appreciate the gravity of his words. He needn't have. We both knew that if the enemy had captured our embassy (they had not, by the way), the situation was serious indeed.

"From what we gather—and again, info's still real sketchy—there's a hell of a fight going on in and around Saigon. President Thieu will probably declare martial law 'fore the day is out, if he hasn't already.

"One of the problems, of course, is that we had no combat troops in the city. Hell, they're using cooks, clerks, and jerks trying to defend the air base . . ."

"Super!" the Bull interrupted, grinning broadly. "That should keep them off the golf course for a day or two!"

"Uh . . . private joke, sir. Please continue," I said soberly, as Major Byson looked at the Bull, baffled by his remark.

"Right. Well, that's really about all we know right now. Intelligence thinks Charlie may have screwed up here in Binh Dinh. Got his dates mixed up and hit us a day early, either that or hit last night's targets a day late. But from what we hear coming out of Saigon, it didn't make a lot of difference. Our folk were still caught with their pants down.

"Anyway, the point you all should stress to your men is that the enemy, so far, hasn't done a goddamn thing except piss the population off and lose an awful lot of his soldiers. I mean, yesterday's numbers are phenomenal! Here we been waiting years for Charlie to surface and fight, and now he's doing just that—and getting his clock cleaned! Good chance he'll never recover from it. Stacking up to be a great tactical error on his part."

Again he paused as Sullivan and I continued to jot notes.

"Appreciate the info, sir," I said, "and we'll pass it along. Been getting some questions, but to tell you the truth, it's pretty much been business as usual for us out here. 'Course, like Sergeant Sullivan said, it was a hell of a noisy truce that first night. What about us now, sir? What you got in store for Charlie Company?"

"Nothing for the next couple of hours or so. Got other inserts going in, so air assets are a bit scarce right now. Besides, you all could probably use a little rest, right? If nothing else comes up, I'll probably be moving you back to your old stomping grounds later this afternoon—say, 1500 hours. And that'll be a four, plus two, plus two, by the way. Any questions?"

"None here," I responded.

"No questions," Sullivan said, "but, sir, how about seeing what you can do 'bout getting us in for a shower? Troops ain't had access to a fucking shower head . . . uh . . . bath unit since we left the bridge."

"Good point, Top," I commented. "They need it, and I should've thought of it myself."

"You *all* need it," Byson said in jest. "That's why I'm standing upwind from you. Seriously, everybody's in the same boat right now, but soon as things return to the norm, I'll get you in for a hot one, promise."

We gave him a snappy Fifth Cav "Ready" salute, and he departed. After the helicopter had lifted off, the Bull turned to me and said, "Gee, sir, I hope they didn't hurt the golf course."

We spent most of the second day of the Year of the Monkey in a "combat recoup." The log bird had dropped off clean sets of jungle fatigues and socks and our (usually) weekly issue of sundries. These so-called comfort packs contained cigarettes, toiletries, pens and stationery, porgy bait (candy and gum)—in short, the little necessities and luxuries our soldiers would have spent their money on in a PX if they had had access to one. So we cleaned our weapons, did what we could to clean ourselves, napped, and talked of those things that soldiers talk about when they are far from home. And we wrote letters.

"Hey, Short Round," one of our less than highly literate soldiers, sitting under a palm, his back against its trunk, yelled. "How you spell 'caress'?"

"Crest?" Short Round replied. "What are you doing, asking your old lady for a tube of toothpaste?"

"No, man, goddamn it! *Caress, caress!* You know, I'm trying to tell her, in a nice way, what I'm gonna do to her as soon as I get back to the world."

"Oh! Well, in that case, you spell caress f-u-c-k."

"Fuck you, Short Round!"

"And your mother, Knife."

Short Round, Knife, Lean Man, Boom Boom. Where do they get

these names for each other? Hell, they all have given names like Tom, Dick, Bill, and Joe. Why don't they use them?

Sweet Willie Dubray, meanwhile, was telling us of his recent R&R exploits in Bangkok. "Yeah, you can pick one out right at the airport when you land. Or, if you're wanting to, you can wait till you get to the hotel, then do it. And for fifty U.S. dollars she's yours to boom-boom the whole fucking week—do anything you want, I mean around the world and back again, turn you every which way but loose. But that ain't all. She'll help you shopping too, show you where's the best buys. You know, gold, jewelry, clothes—shit, you can save fifty bucks right there. And if you're wanting to, she'll even take you 'round and show you the sights, you know, temples and stuff like that. 'Course, I never bothered with none of that shit."

"You are a *cretin*, Dubray, you know that?" Blair remarked. "You had an opportunity to learn something about one of the world's oldest and richest cultures, and you forfeited it merely to satisfy your repulsive, insatiable, putrid appetite."

Dubray looked at Blair inquisitively a moment and then said, "You talking 'bout food? Let me tell you 'bout that! See, three or four of us, we went to this here special restaurant we heared about for lunch. Lunch! You fucking believe it! They sit you down at this big round table what has on it a long tablecloth, and after they bring you your chow, they stick a girl under the table. And the first one what smiles—well, he gotta pay for lunch!"

"A dullard. You're an absolute, completely immoral dullard, Willie," Blair said, smiling in resignation.

The afternoon of the last day in January 1968 wore on, and around two-thirty Byson informed us our pickup had been slipped to 1600 hours.

Fine, an extra hour of downtime won't hurt any of us. Besides, they can put us down anywhere near Daisy and we'll find a good NDP in a matter of minutes.

At 1545 hours the company was in stick order, awaiting its liftoff birds. But they didn't arrive at 1600, or 1610, or 1620. Becoming concerned at not hearing anything from Major Byson, I gave the S-3 a call, only to be told, "Stand by. Out." Minutes later, Byson was on the air.

"Comanche Six, this is Arizona Three. Change of mission. Say again, change of mission. Inbound with twelve, that's one two, plus zero, plus two in one five. Arclight has opened up enemy bunker complex on hilltop to your southwest. It's another needlepoint one-bird LZ. How copy? Over."

"Roger, good copy. Standing by for pickup."

"One-ship LZ!" the Bull said. "Now, where the fuck are they putting us down, atop the Washington monument?"

"Naw," Dubray chimed. "Ain't you heared, Top? Old Ho Chi Minh, 'cause he's getting his ass kicked so bad like on this here 'tack of his, up and died last night with a hard-on, and we gonna set down atop his . . ."

"Okay, that's enough," I said. "Let's saddle up and get ready to move."

How does Dubray come up with these stories? If he lives through this, he ought to publish a book. Wouldn't be "socially redeeming," but it sure would be spicy reading!

Waiting for our lift-off, I found myself reflecting back on Dubray's somewhat precarious initial tenure with the company. I recalled that first time I had heard his name mentioned, back on the bridge the morning after I'd arrived in the company.

"Sir, got papers here on one of my men," Lieutenant MacCarty said. "Chapter case . . . uh . . . unsuitability. Name's Dubray, Private E-2 'Sweet' Willie Dubray. Outgoing Six was gonna sign them, but now that you're in command, guess it's up to you."

"What's his problem?" I asked. "Pee in bed or something?"

"No, sir, nothing like that. He's just a screwup, and I don't think intentionally so. I mean he's just not too smart, you know, comes from somewhere in the backwash of Arkansas's swamps and can't seem to do anything right."

"Sorry, Lieutenant," I said, "I'm not tracking. What specifically is the young soldier's problem?"

"Okay. Well, he was assigned initially to Three Six, but that didn't work out, so the old man put him in Four Six. But he couldn't even figure out how to cut charges, and no one in the company wants someone on our tubes who cuts the wrong charge. So I took him, but shit, he was tripping over his own trip flares and spooking the hell out of my people. So . . ."

"Right. I get the picture, Lieutenant MacCarty. What about Dubray? Does he want to be chaptered?"

"Well, honestly, sir—no. But I really feel . . . *we* really feel that it's best for the company, and in the end, for the soldier concerned, to proceed with an administrative discharge."

"Okay. I'll read this over tonight and talk to the young man first thing in the morning."

And I did.

"Private Dubray, do you know what this is?" I asked the following morning, gesturing at the administrative packet atop the army field desk.

"Yes, sir," Sweet Willie Dubray responded, rather bleakly. "It's a chapter discharge. Means you all gonna throw me out of the Army."

"Not throwing you out, Dubray, *processing* you out on the grounds of unsuitability. Which is not something to be ashamed of. It merely means you don't adapt suitably to those tasks commonly required of an infantry soldier. It's a discharge that's normally granted without prejudice, in other words, under honorable conditions."

"Yes, sir, I understand that," he replied, meekly, his head lowered.

"Fine. Now if I sign this, it's only a recommendation that you be processed for such a discharge. However, I want to be level with you. Although anyone in the chain of command above me can reject my recommendation, they usually go along with the individual's—that's you, Dubray—commander's recommendation.

"So, what'll it be? If I sign it, we can have it out to battalion on the evening log bird, and you could be on your way back to the States in a week or so. Want me to sign it?"

For a brief moment he looked at me uncomprehendingly, and then, suddenly aware that our meeting was more than a mere formality, and that his fate was not necessarily foreordained, he said, "Don't you sign it, sir! Sir, I ain't wanting to get out of the Army! Hell, my pappy, he'll beat me like a hound that won't point if I get kicked out of the Army."

"But, Dubray, it appears from what's written here and from what your leaders tell me, that you simply can't adjust. Hell, you've been from rifleman to weapons platoon ammo bearer and back to rifleman again and haven't performed adequately in any of these positions."

"Yes, sir, I know. That's surely the truth. But I try. I really do, sir. And I'll try harder. It's just—well, I don't catch on quick like, you know, like the other fellows. I ain't meaning to mess up all the time. It's just that, shit, seems sometimes like I'm the only fellow what can take a silk purse and turn it to a sow's ear."

I had to smile at this colorful self-appraisal. Then, regaining my composure, I looked at him sternly and said what I'd pretty much decided the night before. "Okay, Private Dubray, I'm not gonna sign this. I'm gonna hold onto it for a month—thirty days—and see how you perform in a new, *final* job. If you do well, I'll tear this thing up a month from now. If you continue to screw up, I'll just redate it, and you'll be on your merry way home. Fair?"

"Yes, sir!" he replied enthusiastically. "I'll soldier my fucking ass . . . uh . . . my shorts off! Just wait and see!"

He paused and then innocently said, "Uh . . . 'course, we don't wear no shorts here in the boonies, 'cause they rot so quick like. Cause jungle rot on your private parts, too. Mean, you just getting here and all, sir, you probably ain't knowing that, huh?"

"Well, no, I didn't, Dubray," I replied, aware that I was losing control of our counseling session but unsure how it had happened.

Buoyantly, smiling broadly, he said, "Well, I'll tell you, sir, I didn't neither, and 'bout a week what with being in the boonies, my nuts got 'bout big as ripe crab apples—'bout as red too. And burn and itch, whew! I tell you, sir, I was a feeling like one 'em hounds that wouldn't point right, and Pappy, he not wanting him 'round the house no more, took a corncob and rubbed his ass raw, then he took a good dab of turpentine and . . ."

"Uh . . . yes, Dubray, I get the picture. And I understand you're gonna do the best you can to soldier your way back for us. Now let me talk to First Sergeant Sullivan about your new duties. In the meantime, you report back to Lieutenant MacCarty and tell him . . . well, just tell him to come and see me. And that'll be all now, Dubray."

He departed, and I went searching for my first sergeant. Upon finding him, I said, "It's about Gomer Pyle, First Sergeant."

"Who, sir?"

"Dubray, 2d Platoon's chapter case."

"Yes, sir. Mistake, and I told the young lieutenant as much. Willie's only problem is he's just a little bit slower on the uptake than the rest of us. But he wants to do right, and, by God, I'd rather have a dumb soldier who wants to soldier than a college draftee who doesn't!"

"Glad to hear you say that, First Sergeant," I replied. "He's yours."

"Ah, say what, sir?"

"I'm holding the chapter in abeyance for thirty days pending an evaluation of his performance in a new job. Sergeant Sullivan, please find Sweet Willie Dubray a new job."

Sullivan looked at me suspiciously a moment, and then a glimmer of a smile formed. "Okay, sir. Think I might have just the job for him."

Later that afternoon, sitting in my sandbagged CP on the bridge's southern approach, occupied with a change-of-command inventory, I overheard the Bull conversing with our problem child just outside the bunker.

"Now listen, Willie, and listen closely. From now on you're attached to company headquarters, and you have only one task to perform. That's to make goddamn sure me and the old man always—and Willie, I mean always—have hot coffee. I don't care if it's night or day, sun or rain, moving or stationary, you make sure me and the old man have our coffee. Understand?"

"Yes, First Sergeant," Dubray complaisantly replied.

"Now, Willie," Sullivan continued, "that means you don't have to worry 'bout cutting charges, or aligning aiming stakes, or plotting fires, or anything else. All you gotta do is make sure me and the captain have our coffee."

A somewhat unorthodox approach, but I guess it's a start.

It was a good start! The Bull had found the key to Sweet Willie. He wasn't a bad or a dumb soldier, merely a young man who lacked the educational advantages enjoyed by most of us. A young man who had been given too many things to do too quickly and had lost confidence in himself. But he soon excelled in preparing hot instant C-ration coffee under the most trying of conditions. Rain or shine, dark or light, on valley floor or in mountain's tropical rain forest, Willie was always there with a canteen cup of coffee in his hand.

Of course, we weren't serving in the British army and thus weren't authorized a "batman" at taxpayers' expense. So once Willie proved to us—and more importantly, to himself—that he could do one thing really well, the first sergeant had Blair and Anderson begin teaching him radio telephone procedures. Within a short time, Sweet Willie became a capable RTO. If his voice transmissions weren't always procedurally perfect, they were always colorful!

But, as we soon learned, Sweet Willie's real forte lay in the field of logistics. A couple weeks into his probationary month he approached me with a suggestion for resolving our uniform quandary. And, indeed, it was a problem. In the boonies, one did not have his own uniforms; our laundered jungle fatigues came to us weekly on the evening log bird. All sizes were intermingled, and it was every man for himself. You might end up with size small faded trousers, and a brand-new extra-large jacket.

"See, sir," Sweet Willie drawled, as we sat sharing a cup of his coffee, watching the sky darken, "this uniform thing's pissing everybody off, and hell, I don't see no reason for it. I mean, ain't no reason for us to dive into a bundle of jungles like we be a bunch of porkers at swill time."

"I know, Willie," I responded. "And the problem is high on my list of priorities. However, there are . . . uh . . . other priorities. But if you have a suggestion, I'm all ears."

He brightened. "Well, sir, I've been a doing a little figuring here, and what with I knowing 'bout the size of every swinging dick . . . uh . . . Richard in the company . . ." He grinned at what he had just said. "As you know, one time or 'nother, I been assigned to most of it. Uh . . . anyway, way I figure it, you take the extras, you know, the extra smalls and extra large, and put 'em aside. I mean, fuck, ain't that many of 'em anyway, and them what needs 'em, we can order special like of something. Then it's kind of simple like. You just have the smalls, mediums, and larges."

"Okay, Willie," I said, not knowing what else to say. Because I had no earthly idea what he was talking about.

"Yes, sir, then you have trains break out the company uniform dump into four bundles. That there's the three line platoons and one bundle what's for us in headquarters and Four Six. In each of them bundles, they put the uniforms what fit the guys in that platoon. Like in Two Six, I figure we need six smalls, twelve mediums, and nine large . . ."

"Yeah, but Willie," I interrupted him, "those sizes are changing constantly. I mean, we have soldiers rotating in and out of the company on nearly a daily basis."

"Yes, sir, but that don't matter none. Mean, we 'port our foxhole strength for issue of charlie rats. Ain't no reason can't do the same for uniforms. Hell, it be even simpler, seeing we'd only be a doing it once a week 'stead of everyday like we do the foxhole."

"Okay," I somewhat warily replied, still not comprehending the mechanics of his proposal.

Dubray, interpreting my "okay" as approval, handed me a dirty piece of notebook paper, at the top of which was scribbled "WEAKLY UNIFORM RPT." Then, with increased enthusiasm, he said, "See, sir.

Can't nothing be more simple. Just send this here uniform report in to trains each week, telling 'em the sizes what fit the guys in each platoon by line. Hell, I could handle it myself, sir. Just check with the platoon sergeants every week 'fore the uniform dump."

Unable to think of a single reason why his proposal wouldn't work, I said, "Willie, you're a goddamn genius! Do it! You're in charge. Use my name freely."

He did, and the following evening I got a call from my executive officer at company trains.

"Comanche Six, this is Comanche Five. We got some sort of request back here to break out uniforms by subunit and sizes. Think it came from Two Six's chapter case. Anyway, it's just impossible to do that—just takes too much time. Six, it's 'bout all we can do to get you the right number and a good assortment of sizes. Uh . . . what's your guidance on this thing?"

"This is Comanche Six. Be advised that the individual to whom you so callously refer as 'Two Six's chapter case' is my field logistics NCO, and when he speaks it is as if I had spoken. How copy that, Five?"

"This is Comanche Five . . . uh . . . Roger, good copy. Wilco."

"This is Comanche Six. Great! And, by the way, I want you to get my field logistics NCO promoted to Pfc forthwith. Any questions? Over."

He had none, and overnight Sweet Willie went from company idiot to company idol, loved by all who from that point on wore uniforms that actually fit.

Willie later assumed other logistic responsibilities, accomplishing them without ever missing a beat. He was serving his country and his fellow soldiers well, but more importantly, the war was serving him well. And no one could ever take that away from Willie.

The sun was fading over Vietnam's western horizon when we touched down, one ship at a time, on our second needlepoint LZ. Within moments of jumping from the lead Huey, I radioed Byson that our LZ was green.

"Well, we sure as hell ain't gonna NDP here tonight!" First Sergeant Sullivan said as the last of our twelve slicks lifted off. And he was right. The mountain peaked so abruptly that there was virtually no room for the company to stand atop it, much less defend it.

"Maybe it'll level off some when we reach Charlie's bunker complex," I replied. "And we better be getting a move on down the hill; it'll be dark in thirty minutes."

Assembling quickly, we began our movement down the mountain's steep slope toward the Arclight site, Three Six leading. Upon entering the cratered, rearranged jungle of the strike area, we discovered that our bunker complex had been an underground hospital. Various medical supplies were scattered about, some of Chinese and Czechoslovakian origin, some of French and U.S. origin. None of it was produced in North Vietnam.

We counted the dead, many of them still wearing battle dressings on wounds previously suffered, conducted our bomb damage assessment, and moved through the area as quickly as possible—which wasn't very quickly. Movement at night through a forested jungle was always difficult; but now, after the Arclight, movement was at a snail's pace and exhausting: over the fallen and shattered palms, through the interwoven wait-a-minute secondary foliage, under the giant teak, down into the bomb crater, through its knee-deep water, up the other side—where there were more fallen trees. But we had no choice other than to continue our trek downward. The mountain's face was simply too steep to establish an NDP unless we intended to sleep standing up.

In the early morning of February 1, after four or five hours of this torture, we found ourselves nearing the valley floor. Our jungle began opening up somewhat, and the mountain's face started to level off.

Suddenly, the soldiers in front of me were silhouetted against the darkened early morning sky by the flashes of the point man's M-16 and, a split second later, the lead machine-gun team's M-60.

Bob Halloway and I charged forward.

"Got both of 'em, Lieutenant!" Three Six's point man said, a little nervously. "Uh . . . one of them's a girl. But, shit, I didn't know that, and she had a weapon. Hell, don't even know what it is. Never saw one like it before."

I looked at the submachine gun. "French piece. MAT-49—don't see many of 'em around anymore."

The girl, shot several times in the face and upper torso, was perhaps seventeen and wore the familiar black garb of the Vietnamese peasant. A khaki pith helmet lay next to her head. The other lifeless body was clad in the customary khaki uniform of the NVA regular.

"Must've been VC," Halloway said. "I mean, the way she's dressed and the frog weapon and all."

"Yeah," I responded, "probably a local guide. Could've been taking her northern friend here up to the nonexistent hospital. Hell, maybe they were supposed to conduct a bomb damage assessment for Charlie. Well, anyway, you did a good job, Point. Now let's get it moving again. Think we're nearing the floor."

Soon afterward, we descended into one of the valley's rice paddies and a short time later found a suitable NDP in which to spend the few remaining hours of darkness.

THIRD DAY OF THE TET OFFENSIVE: 1 FEBRUARY

A few hours later, with February's first day of blistering heat well under way, we found ourselves again feasting on a full breakfast. As I ate, I looked up to see a concerned Lieutenant Halloway standing in front of me.

"Problems, Bob?"

"Uh . . . not really, sir. Just wondered if you might talk to 'Hard Times' . . . Crumbley, that is. He was the point man last night. Seems to be pretty upset about the girl. You know, the men were ribbing him 'bout it. I put a stop to that, but hell, I don't know, maybe it's 'cause none of us ever killed a female before."

"You talk to him?" I asked.

"Of course!" he replied somewhat indignantly. I suppose I should have realized that he had.

"Well, sure, Bob, I'll talk to him, but I really don't know what to tell him. I mean, I don't see where gender comes into play when you have two armed soldiers run into one another."

"That's what I told him, sir. But it didn't seem to make any great impression."

Crumbley was an eighteen-year-old draftee, and he cared very little about talking to me or anyone else. I sensed that he wanted to be left alone, to reconcile in his own mind what he had done.

"Crumbley, Lieutenant Halloway tells me you're a little upset 'bout last night's action," I said. He sat on the paddy dike beside me, the two of us nursing cups of battalion's fresh-brewed coffee.

"Naw, sir, that ain't it. I mean, the guys are pumping me a bit about it, but, shit, she had a gun! Could've greased me quick as I did her, right?"

"Absolutely!"

Following a long pause, he said, "Shit, sir, it's just that I ain't never shot no female before. Hell, I ain't never shot *nobody* before!"

He was visibly shaken, and why not? He had just killed two human beings in a war he hadn't asked to come to and probably knew little about. Nothing I could say would change that.

"Well, listen, Hard Times. That's what they call you, right? Hard Times?"

"Yes, sir, don't really know why." He smiled fleetingly and then said, "Well, yeah I do. Seems I'm the guy what always gets the pork-sausage patties in the charlie rats and the kents in the comfort packs. Always ended up with the buffalo trousers and the smallest jacket in the uniform dump 'fore Willie got it straightened out. Only man in the company to miss his R&R flight going *out* of the country."

Hell, I'm sorry I asked! I really don't have time for an open-door complaint session. But maybe he just feels better talking around last night's incident.

"Last time in Bong Son, you know, on LZ English stand down . . . that's 'fore you got here, sir. I was the next guy in line, looking out in case the LT comes back, 'cause we had a whore . . . uh . . . well, anyway, that's when the LT comes back. Don't guess I ought to be telling you some of this, huh, sir?"

I merely smiled.

"But, shit, sir, none of that means anything. Don't mean nothing and don't bother me none. But the girl . . . well, I figure I might be seeing her a lying there like that for a long time."

"Well, Hard Times . . . Crumbley, I don't know what I can tell you or do to make you feel better about what happened last night. I mean, our country's at war, and you and I are part of it. And a big part of it is killing the enemy."

That's all true, but it sounds so goddamn trite and obviously does little to console this eighteen-year-old sitting beside me. Ought to be more forceful. Ought to just lay it on the line!

"Listen, Crumbley, the girl was an enemy soldier with a red star on her helmet and a submachine gun in her hand. If she had been a

better soldier and had seen you first she'd now be evading us in the
weeds of that mountain, and you'd very probably be lying wrapped
in a poncho just feet from where we now sit, waiting for the C&D
bird to backhaul you out of here 'long with the mermites and water
cans. And tonight, I'd have to draft a letter that would do very damn
little to console your family.

"Now, goddamn it, you did a good job this morning. You met the
enemy face to face and defeated him. And that's the only thing you
should ever remember for the rest of your life! Shit, if you hadn't been
quicker than them, there might be a bunch of the rest of us dead! You
understand what I'm saying, Crumbley?"

"Uh . . . yes, sir, I do. The LT told me all that."

Oh!

"Sir, can I go back to my platoon now?"

"Yes, of course. And you should be proud of what you did on that
trail. It was the right thing to do."

A short time later, as we were waiting for Byson's inbound
flight of slicks to fly us to other parts of Binh Dinh, Lieutenant Halloway cornered me and asked, "Hey, sir, you get a chance to talk to
Crumbley?"

"Yes, I did, Bob—but it didn't seem to make any great impression."

Byson set us down on Daisy, and within an hour or so we were
once again confronted with the stench of our mountain. We need not
have endured it, since this last day of General Giap's three-day offensive
was to be a day without sunshine for Charlie Company. We retreated
from the high country that evening scoreless.

By evening of that third day, the '68 Tet offensive was pretty much
over in Binh Dinh Province. But there would be little respite for us.
Although Giap's great gambit had ended in utter failure throughout
most of the country, his troops were still firmly entrenched in the ancient
imperial capital at Hue—in I Corps.

And Charlie Company was on its way to I Corps.

BACK TO I CORPS: FEBRUARY 1968

We spent most of the next week or so in the vicinity of Daisy doing
what we did best, catching a still unsuspecting foe in our claymore

ambushes. And our enemy body count climbed while we remained unscratched. But that would soon change.

One early February morning, Major Byson visited our NDP to tell us of what was then felt to be the probable outcome of Giap's great gamble. I suppose other operation officers and their commanders were doing the same thing throughout Vietnam; it was a time "to keep the troops informed." He was all smiles as he spoke to the Bull and me, our platoon leaders, and several of their platoon sergeants.

"Hell, probably the greatest tactical defeat ever suffered by an army in the field in the annals of modern warfare. Numbers are still being tabulated, but it appears he lost nearly five thousand of his folk in the first two days of the offensive, while our dead in the same period were under three hundred. Course, that's a hell of a lot more than we normally lose in two days' fighting, and it's not setting very well in the Stateside press right now. But, shit, look at the kill ratio—nearly seventeen to one!"

Byson was right on both counts. We had kicked Charlie's ass royally and were continuing to do so, but the whole affair would be viewed as anything but a triumph by America's news media.

"And that's only a small part of it. See, it appears, you know, from what we've learned from captured documents, prisoners, and so forth that General Giap had called for a general uprising among the country's population. Well, that's falling on deaf ears. Fact, it looks like just the opposite's happening. Those that had been straddling the fence are now rallying to the side of the government."

History would prove Byson correct on this point also. After the Tet offensive, the country's populace did indeed rally to the republic's cause—in droves!

"Moreover—and this is really significant, guys—it appears North Vietnam, you know, to bring about this general uprising, ordered their Viet Cong henchmen to surface countrywide. So this elusive foe we've been searching for, hell, for nearly two, three years now suddenly comes out into the open to do battle—and he's being torn to shreds! He'll never recover from it, never. His infrastructure is being destroyed from the bottom up."

Again Byson would be proved correct. After the general's great gamble, the Viet Cong would no longer be a prominent participant in the war. As it turned out, perhaps by design, he would also find himself left out of the peace that followed.

Major Byson's optimistic, upbeat appraisal of the war was understandably contagious. We had fought the day-in, day-out battle so long without seeing any tangible results. It was extraordinarily uplifting to hear that a corner had now been turned, that something decisive had finally occurred.

"You mean it's over?" Lieutenant O'Brien asked, straight faced. "Hell, I just got here." Then, turning to me, he asked, "Was I here long enough to qualify for my combat infantryman's badge, sir?"

"You'll get your CIB, Dick," I replied as we laughed, collectively and somewhat nervously, at his comment.

"No, it's far from over, guys," Byson said. "Country's in a hell of a mess right now, and there's a lot of mopping up to do. Fighting a big battle up in I Corps, and Hue's still firmly occupied by the NVA.

"But what I'm saying is we're winning big time! Charlie's getting his ass kicked from the seventeenth parallel to the Cau Mau Peninsula. And I think I can safely say, without fear of future contradiction, that this will prove to be the turning point of the war."

Unfortunately, he was right again.

Ending his discourse on this high note, Major Byson pulled the Bull and me aside while the others returned to their platoons.

"Listen, fellows, what I mentioned about I Corps and Hue isn't any joke. Our Marine friends are having a hell of a time up there, and there's a rumor floating about that we may be pulled out of Binh Dinh and join the rest of the division in I Corps. I mention this 'cause if it should happen, it'll probably happen quick—you know, like everything else around here."

Sergeant Sullivan and I nodded in agreement. Things did indeed happen quickly in the Cav. The tempo of our operations since the start of General Giap's little ado amply demonstrated that!

"So keep it in the back of your minds and stay flexible. Just consider it one more contingency that you should be prepared for. If you receive a call from me saying I'm inbound for a long haul, you'll know what I'm talking about. Means we're heading north. Questions?"

"Yes, sir. If this does come about, will we be going back to Radcliff first?" the Bull asked, referring to the division's base camp at An Khe.

"Doubt it, First Sergeant. If we get the word to pick up and move, I'll probably extract you, along with the other companies, from wherever you're then operating and put you down wherever the Air Force tells me to for a fixed-winged deployment. Probably Qui Nhon or Phu Cat."

Very soon thereafter, while sitting in claymore ambush atop our mountain with Three Six, Blair passed me his handset, whispering, "Three's on the horn, sir."

"Comanche Six, this is Arizona Three. Inbound your location at one six hundred hours with zero, plus three, plus zero for a long haul. I say again, long haul. How copy? Over."

"Solid copy. We'll be standing by for pickup vicinity last night's NDP."

I turned to Lieutenant Halloway and said, "Okay, Bob, let's pack it up and get off this mountain posthaste." Then I made a quick net call, informing the other platoons to assemble at the NDP in preparation for "long haul."

Retrieving his handset, Anderson asked, "What's long haul mean, sir?"

"Think it means we ain't gonna be killing no more NVA on this mountain, Andy. Think it means we're going north to I Corps."

"Great!" he responded, as the breeze shifted a bit. "Just hope to hell Charlie buries his dead in I Corps."

He didn't, of course; but on one occasion the Cav would.

Back at the NDP, we found the rest of the company in high spirits, looking forward to the long haul north. This, I suppose, is a natural phenomenon among infantrymen since they look upon routine, be it in garrison or combat, as their most hated enemy. It was not that they expected life to be easier or death less threatening in I Corps; indeed, quite the contrary proved to be the case in both instances. They merely looked forward to a change, something different.

"Yeah, I tell you, you're a bunch of lucky shits to be going to I Corps," Slim Brightly was saying to no one in particular and everyone in general. "You all are gonna have a great time up there. No more of these endless, fruitless searches for our elusive foe, no, sir! 'Cause up there Charlie really *is* behind every rock—shit, there's a fucking million of 'em in I Corps. And no more of these beat-up Korean war–vintage war trophies. Up there you'll be getting bright, shiny new AKs, the ones with *plastic* stocks. Awards and decorations, you ask? Shit, they'll be bringing 'em out by the bucketful with your C&D every morning. And promotions! There'll be all kinds of vacancies to be promoted into once you start seeing action 'round Hue."

For a moment, I thought of tactfully asking our young artillery lieutenant if I might have a word with him in private. Then I saw, and it should have come as no great surprise, that those listening to him were enjoying his monologue mightily. And so was I.

"Now, men," he continued, an aura of seriousness about him, "I had hoped I could be with you as all these glories unfold. However, as you know . . ." A broad smile began to radiate across his face. "I just have *three* fucking days 'fore I take command of my battery!"

Then, pointing to Lieutenant Moseley, our new FO, who had arrived with the C&D bird that morning, he said, "So I want you men to make sure my cannon-cocker replacement here has ample opportunity to get one of 'em plastic-stocked AKs and his own bucket of medals."

"Hey, LT," Sweet Willie asked, "what you gonna be doing while you're 'placement here gets all them medals? Mean, don't hardly seem right, what with you a being with us so long and all, that you ain't gonna share a bit in all 'em good things what's gonna happen to us in I Corps."

"Ah, yes, Willie," Brightly answered. "But such is the way of life, and such is the way of war. However, rest assured that while I'm sitting there in that secure fire base, in the evening, after a hot shower, Johnny Walker in hand, waiting for that doughnut dolly to make fact of my every fantasy, my thoughts will be with you of Charlie Company as you go forward to smite our ungodly foe, whenever and wherever he may be found."

"LT," one of those listening said, "you can have the hot and the doughnut, but how 'bout sending the JW out to us?"

"Goddamn right!" Lieutenant Brightly replied, now serious indeed. "If the Six here would permit it, I'd have a fucking case of the stuff on every log bird flying!"

What he didn't say—but I guess he did, in his way—was that he was going to miss the men with whom he had served and suffered for the past six months.

Arriving on time, the hooks picked us up and then ferried us northeast to a newly constructed airstrip not far from the coastal city of Phu Cat. Upon landing we were met by one of Major Byson's menials, who told us to set up adjacent to the runway and prepare for an early morning departure via C-130s. Our destination was to be the city of Quang Tri, a province capital thirty miles north of Hue.

We rigged our poncho shelters on a muddy embankment beside the runway and settled in for the night.

Shortly after dark, as I sat atop an empty mermite enjoying the first of my two cans of beer, First Sergeant Sullivan joined me for our evening parley.

"Pull up a mermite and pop a beer, Top."

As he was doing so, I asked, "And what is the state of the command tonight, First Sergeant?"

"State of the command is good, Six. Troops are still in the fucking mud, still sleeping under ponchos, and still need a shower, but morale is high 'cause battalion sent 'em their mail and two cans of beer per, and 'cause they're going to I Corps tomorrow. And though none of 'em know what the fuck that means, they know it ain't Binh Dinh, and they're fed up with Binh Dinh."

"Great. Your assessment of the command's state parallels mine to a tee."

"They're also in high spirits 'cause I . . . uh . . . perhaps prematurely lifted the two-beer limit tonight. I hope you concur in my decision to do so."

"Well, I can hardly countermand it *now*, can I?" I retorted, annoyed at him for not having come to me first.

After a brief, somewhat awkward pause, I said, "Aw, shit, it was a good call, Top. They deserve a blast, and no one's gonna bother us here tonight."

"Should've talked to you first, sir. Sorry."

"Forget it. But where are they getting the beer? Make a run on the Air Force club 'cross the way there?"

"Naw, villagers have a stand set up outside the gate. Sergeant Marvel 'rented' himself a jeep somewhere and is running a shuttle service. Some of our snuffies did ask if they could visit the Air Force's establishment, you know, 'just to have a quiet beer and watch the go-go girls a bit, Top.' Well, I gave a firm and final no on that one. Wouldn't be in that club ten minutes 'fore our boys in blue thought they were in the *second* Tet offensive, if indeed they saw anything of the first."

"Well, I support you on *that* call."

"Yeah, they'll be fine right here tonight," he continued. "Bunch of 'em will end up with a little buzz, some of 'em will get laid, but all of 'em will be fit to travel at first light. And that's 'cause they're young. Youth recoups a lot quicker than us old . . ."

"Laid!" I said, interrupting him. "Who? Where? How?"

"Huh? Oh. Well, you saw them villagers assembling 'round the outer fence 'cross the field there just before dark, didn't you?"

I nodded.

"Well, Six, them girls ain't selling ice cream. They're probably working their way through the wire right now. Shit, I saw it at English; them whores can penetrate wire barriers that'd stop a VC sapper cold!"

Yeah, but shouldn't we try to stop our soldiers.

"And, Six, the best thing to do about it is just look the other way. I mean, if snuffie can smell it, he'll find a way to get at it, and ain't nothing we can do to stop him 'cept maybe look like fools trying to."

He was right, of course.

"Okay, Top. Tonight it's see no evil, hear no evil. But you better tell Doc Heard to prepare himself for several cases of 'lower urinary tract infection of an unknown origin.'"

He smiled and said, "Not to worry, Boss."

We sat in silence for a while, listening to the faint rumblings of what was probably a locally hired rock-and-roll band coming from the base's club in the distance. The base, in the light of day, appeared to be little more than a couple of tented maintenance facilities, several sandbagged POL (petroleum, oil, lubricants) points, some communications vans, and a bunch of tents with wooded and screened sidings.

"See, that's what I mean, goddamn it!" the Bull exploded, ending our repose. "Here we sit on a fucking mermite, in the fucking mud, while those goddamn Air Force wimps over there are drinking their booze, eating their barbecued steaks, and diddling their maids. And they won't even let us use their goddamn shower facilities!"

Where had I heard this before?

"Hey, Top, we'll be at Camp Evans by noon. Should be able to get everybody showered tomorrow."

"Yeah, but still . . ." he grunted in response.

After another brief pause, he asked what I thought we'd be doing in I Corps.

"Beats the shit out of me, Top. Guess same thing we've been doing in Binh Dinh—looking for Charlie and killing him when we find him. 'Course, really don't know how accurate Brightly's assessment is regarding our greater opportunity of doing that in I Corps."

"Think we'll be going into Hue, Six?"

"Hell, I don't know. Come on, Top, you know as much about what the powers have planned for us as I do."

"Yeah, guess so. Just wish the fucking Marines would finish up in Hue so we could put this whole Tet thing behind us. Tired of reading about it. Mean, the fucking papers, *Stars and Stripes* and those coming through the mail, ain't printing a fucking thing 'bout Byson's great victory—it's all gloom and doom."

"Yeah, Top, but . . ."

"And now," he continued angrily, ignoring me, "when we should be going for Uncle Ho's jugular, I read that our senators, Morse and Fulbright at their helm, are 'probing' the goddamn *Maddox* incident! Well, shit! What the hell's that got to do with where we are today? I mean, goddamn, sir, these are the people who sent us over here, and now that we're finally kicking the shit out of Charlie—and dying in the process—they're probing the fucking *Maddox!*"

I nodded but said nothing. He really didn't expect me to. Besides, he was right.

"Why don't they probe the fucking *Maine?*" he said, now really steamed. "I mean, there's probably a hell of a lot fewer Spanish War veterans to piss off, and them that are still around sure as hell ain't gonna be fighting in Cuba while their senators are conducting their probe. Fuck it!"

"Take it easy, Top. You worry too much about the small shit. We can kick Charlie's ass with or without the support of Senators Morse and Fulbright, or any of the rest of those Washington wimps."

But I was dead wrong about that.

"And I hope you're right, sir. I just got a gut feeling, you know, reading the papers and so forth, that this whole thing's turning sour. And if it does, it's gonna be a dirty rotten shame, and somebody ought to pay for it. By God, *we've* paid!"

After a short lull, he said, "Well, anyway, right or wrong, good or bad, for better or worse, looks like Tet's pretty much history now—I mean except for Hue. Guess we'll just have to wait and see how it's written up. Right, Six?"

"Guess so, Top."

Later, lying wrapped in my poncho liner, mindlessly listening to the faint sounds of the rock band, I found myself mulling over Sergeant Sullivan's comments.

What did he mean by "turning sour"? Why worry about a bunch of mindless politicians? Shit, we've turned the corner; Charlie has finally come out to play and is sorely sorry for having done so! We're tearing him apart!

After pondering these tactical realities, I dismissed my first sergeant's concerns as but another example of his tendency to overreact to minutiae and misinterpret the facts.

I was remiss in doing so. The Bull was far more politically astute than his commander. A short time later, while lying in a hospital bed in Silver Springs, Maryland, I would find myself utterly bewildered by what my country had done to its soldiers, its allies, and itself in the aftermath of the 1968 Tet offensive. Indeed, I remain just as bewildered now, over twenty years later.

CAMP EVANS, I CORPS

"Damn, it's cold!" Dubray said as we disembarked our C-130s on the southern end of Quang Tri's airstrip.

"Monsoon, Willie," Sergeant Sullivan said. "I Corps's in the middle of the winter monsoon now."

It *was* cold, at least compared to the blistering heat we were accustomed to on Bong Son's plain. Although it wasn't really raining, the darkened gray overcast sky emitted a steady drizzle, the kind that in time penetrates every fiber of your clothing, chilling you to the bone. And the weather's gloom was only heightened upon our learning that, due to a mix-up in flight scheduling, the trucks that were to take us to Evans had not yet arrived.

"Yo, sir," Lieutenant O'Brien yelled, running toward me as I stood talking to Lieutenant Norwalk and the first sergeant, the three of us discussing what to do next. "The air-transport officer says we ought to dig in right here on the southern end of the runway. Says the North Vietnamese have the northern end ranged all the way from the fucking DMZ!"

"Okay, fellows, you heard the man," I said. "Let's get 'em into a hasty perimeter. Looks sandy, easy digging, so may as well play the game and scratch out prone shelters just in case we do receive incoming."

I wondered if the enemy really did have the strip ranged all the way from the DMZ, or if some disgruntled and bored Air Force captain might have just seized the moment to vent his frustrations on our newly assigned second lieutenant.

How far are we from the Z? I asked myself. Eighteen, twenty miles? Shit, guess it's possible, but don't think we have red leg that'll reach that far. Not unless it's mounted atop a battleship.

So we sat in the wet sand beside Quang Tri's airstrip, ponchos about our shoulders, warming our coffee on heat tabs and complaining about the weather and battalion's failure to have transportation awaiting us upon deplaning. And we wondered what the future might hold for us.

It held very little that was good.

By midafternoon we were defending a portion of Camp Evans' northern perimeter, which, as it turned out, was one of the safer places to be at Evans. When darkness settled over the camp, most of the company had already showered, and some of us had even managed to get a haircut.

In the days that followed, as the constant soaking drizzle continued, interrupted only by brief rain showers, we spent most of our time filling sandbags and reinforcing our bunkers. We approached this task with a bit more enthusiasm than we had on the bridge, since Evans, unlike Bong Son's bridge, was vulnerable to rocket attack. Of course, these duties did not preclude the men of Charlie Company from doing some of those things they had been unable to do in the boonies: things such as visit the PX, mail packages home, take a steam bath, drink something a little more potent than 3.2 beer, and perhaps take in an open-air movie while sitting on an empty ammo crate, in the mud, in the rain.

Had the sun been shining, Camp Evans would still have been a pretty depressing piece of real estate. An Khe, though we rarely saw it, had a sense of order and tidiness about it. Its hardened streets and wooden troop billets provided a semblance of semipermanence. Most of the camp's division staff had been housed in prim, neatly aligned mobile homes, while the division commander and his major subordinates occupied splendid brick cottages atop a small hill adjacent to an elaborate underground TOC. It was a "1965" camp constructed for the long haul in a war that had not yet gone haywire. At An Khe, one rarely heard a round fired in anger.

Camps Evans, in contrast, had a distinct sense of disorder and untidiness about it. It was for the most part a hodgepodge of tents, bunkers, trenches, wire barriers, and sandbags, set atop a low-lying hill on the western side of Highway One south of Quang Tri and north of Hue. Supplies were stacked or thrown helter skelter, either by design or as a result of the most recent rocket attack. Everyone slept underground or in a posture that permitted them to go underground at a moment's notice, because at Evans hearing rounds fired in anger was the norm.

"Incoming!" someone screamed shortly after nightfall on our second day in I Corps.

Whish! Whish!

We dove into our trenches and then, looking up, gazed at the rockets' orange trails as they sped across the darkened overcast sky before falling within the camp's perimeter. Transfixed, we watched the second or third round land squarely on a supply-laden truck; silhouetted against the rocket's fiery explosion we saw boxes, debris, and what appeared to be a man blown high in the air.

"Mama, sweet Mama," Dubray moaned, "Binh Dinh weren't never like this!"

"Battalion wants an azimuth, sir!" Blair yelled from across the trench. "Wants to know if we can give 'em an azimuth for counterfire!"

"Roger!" I shouted back and quickly pulled out my compass, only to see that our new forward observer, Lieutenant Moseley, was already tracking the incoming rockets.

"Coming from the northwest. Looks to be . . . oh, say, 5200 mills."

As he sent this azimuth through his fire-control channels, I did the same via the battalion's command net.

You're right indeed, Willie. Binh Dinh was never like this.

A few days later we were relieved of our defensive responsibilities at Evans in order to start working the boonies of I Corps. Our initial operational area was a stretch of coastal plain referred to as the "street."

THE STREET TO HUE

Bernard Fall's *Street Without Joy* was not a street at all but a coastal area in the northern part of the republic bordered generally by the city of Quang Tri on the north, the ancient imperial capital of Hue on the south, Highway One on the west, and the South China Sea on the east. As Fall notes in his book, this area was usually a hotbed of insurgent activity, controlled initially by the Viet Minh and later by the Viet Cong and NVA. In Tet's aftermath, the enemy used the street—so named by the French Expeditionary Force during the first Indochina war—to reinforce and resupply its 5th and 6th Regiments, which had captured Hue on 31 January. Later it served as a route of withdrawal for these units. Allied responsibility for interdicting this route of resupply and regress rested with elements of the First Air Cav.

We were one of those elements.

In these waning days of February, we worked the street generally from the city of Hai Lang in Quang Tri Province to the village of My Chanh in Thua Thien Province, conducting usually fruitless search-and-destroy missions during the day and trick-or-treating Highway One at night.

On one of the first search-and-destroy forays, I accompanied One Six as they worked the area east of Highway One between Hai Lang to the north and the river Hoi Dao—which was little more than a stream—to the south. It was another walk in the weeds.

Around two o'clock in the afternoon, we halted our futile trek, taking a break next to a cluster of hutches, under a dark overcast sky that continued its constant drizzle.

"Coffee, Willie," I said in jest to Dubray, who was again filling in for Anderson.

"Coming up, sir."

"Hey, Willie, I was just joking."

"It ain't no problem, sir. 'Sides, I'm wanting a little myself. This here weather's chilling me something awful. Need something hot."

I smiled. Goddamn, you're a better man than me, William Ambrose Dubray. When this is all over, and you get back to Arkansas, I hope every good thing in your world happens. "Okay, as you wish. Carry on, Willie."

Blair looked on as Dubray took one of his makeshift C-ration-can stoves from a cargo pocket, lit a heat tab and dropped it in, and then put a partially filled canteen cup of water over it.

"Willie, I never thought I'd say it, but you're right," Blair said. "I Corps' climate does call for something hot. And I never thought I'd say it, but a couple of pork-sausage patties would taste kind of good right now. Jesus, this weather!"

Dubray smiled mightily. "Well, I ain't got no porkers, but I got a can of ham slices. Want to share 'em?"

"Yeah, Willie, I'd be honored," Blair said, grinning.

"You think the sun's ever gonna shine again, sir?" Lieutenant Norwalk said.

"Beats the shit out of me, Bill. Hope so. We could use a little drying out."

He looked at me in silence for a moment, as if thinking "a little drying out" was a major understatement. Then he said, "I don't know, sir. Never seen anything like it in my life. You know, back in the States, in the spring and summer it'd rain like hell, but then the sun would come out. Or it'd rain for a while, and then you'd have these drizzling skies for a day or so. But here, it comes down in buckets intermittently and then just dribbles forever!"

"Yeah, I know, Bill. And we're nigh constantly soaked. By the way, you checking your people's feet?"

"Yes, sir. Squad leaders are doing it, and I'm checking theirs. No problems so far. Every other stitch on us is wet, but we're making sure all our men have dry socks once a day . . . on those days the log bird flies."

Yeah, and that's a problem. Cav's lost too many of their birds from rockets at Evans. Whereas they logged us nearly every night and morning on the plain, they're skipping many a night up here.

"Shit, I don't know, sir," Norwalk continued. "Wish the Army would come up with something 'sides the poncho to keep a man dry." He paused, smiling. "Funny, isn't it. They give you a shelter half to make a tent, and it's not worth a simple shit—and a poncho to keep you dry, and it won't, but it makes a super tent."

"Yeah, I often wondered who sold the pup tent to the Army. It's undoubtedly the most worthless piece of gear in the inventory, yet it seems to have been around forever," I replied.

"Coffee's hot, sir," Sweet Willie announced a few minutes later.

So, on a dismal afternoon in I Corps, the four of us sat in Quang Tri's wet sand sipping coffee from Willie's canteen cup as he and Blair shared a can of ham slices and a pecan roll.

"Heard about Sergeant Major Cooper, sir?" Dubray asked.

"Captain, ex-Sergeant Major Cooper? No, not recently. Why do you ask, Willie?"

"He's dead."

Shit, not Cooper!

"Where? What happened? Where did you hear this, Willie?"

"One of the fellows what was coming back from An Khe the other day, he say Ser . . . uh . . . Captain Cooper was shot while he was commanding a mech company down south. Say Charlie put a round right through his heart."

"Damn, hate to hear that," Norwalk said. "I liked the Coop. Gonna miss his cocktail parties."

"Yeah. Hell of a note," I said. What else was there to say?

"I saw one of our own get it the other day, sir," Norwalk said. "First time, and it wasn't a pretty sight."

"Where was that, Bill?" I asked, baffled by his remark. I knew we hadn't lost anyone.

"Last day at Evans. You know, when we were pulling the road-clearing detail."

"Oh, yeah. Providing security for the engineers opening the highway in the morning, you mean."

He nodded. "Right. Anyway, had some of my people on their dump and the rest of the platoon trailing their sweepers on each side of the road, forty, fifty meters back. And suddenly we heard a boom! And the guy sweeping the right side of the road was no more. Don't know what he stepped on or why his detector didn't pick it up, but it sure made a mess of him.

"And shit, sir, he was just a kid."

"They all are, Bill."

But it ages them fast. How old are you, Lieutenant? Twenty-three? Twenty-three and referring to a younger dead soldier as a kid! War's made you older than your years, Bill.

"Well, what say, Bill, we 'bout ready to continue our stroll north?"

He nodded, got to his feet, and signaled his soldiers to do likewise. And once again we began our sluggish, phlegmatic movement northward toward Hai Lang.

Twenty minutes later, Blair handed me his handset. "Our Three's on the line, sir."

"Comanche, are you in a posture for a pickup? Over."

"This is Comanche Six. Negative. Have two of my subs working sector. The other's at last night's NDP adjacent to the big red . . ."

"This is Arizona Three. How long to consolidate? Over."

"This is Comanche Six. About six zero . . ."

"Okay, Comanche, I'll be inbound with four, plus two, plus two in six zero. Make that sixteen hundred hours for the pickup. Gonna put you in at point of origin PORE, I spell Papa, Oscar, Romeo, Echo, left three eight, up one three. How copy? Over."

"This is Comanche Six. Roger. Papa Oscar PORE, left three eight, up one three . . ."

"This is Arizona Three. Good copy. Got reports of some activity west of the ville there. Want you to check it out and then sweep generally northeast. You can log somewhere in that vicinity tonight."

Taking Dubray's handset from him and signaling Norwalk's RTO, who was standing but a few feet from me, to disregard, I made a net call to assemble the troops.

That afternoon's assault on the village of Thon Truong Tho and its aftermath were uneventful. Byson set us down in the low-lying foothills along the river O Khe on the western side of the village. As the hooks ascended, we received a couple of sniper rounds fired by a very poor marksman; that was all we heard from Charlie that day.

The villagers of Thon Truong Tho looked more like lost souls than the enemy. In fact, they looked very much like the villagers of Happy Valley, with that surreal aura of fear about them as if the ax were about to fall. Perhaps it already had, during General Giap's recent offensive.

After moving through the village, we continued northeast for a kilometer or so and then set up our NDP next to a cemetery, a short distance from the republic's little-used railway. Cemeteries were often the best defensive setting in paddy country, since they were usually higher and drier than the surrounding terrain. Of course, one had to use care in digging his foxhole.

"And how is morale tonight?" I asked, opening our regular planning parley.

"Lower than whale shit, sir," the Bull said gloomily.

"And that's at the bottom of the ocean," Halloway remarked, completing Sullivan's assessment.

"Not to worry, men. The one thing you can count on is that nothing stays the same. If the sun's shining, sooner or later it's gonna rain. And if it's raining, sooner or later . . ."

My remark brought forth little more than dutiful, strained smiles. The weather and lack of contact were not setting well with Charlie Company's rank and file. There was little I could do about either.

"Well, anyway, turning to tomorrow's op, we'll be doing 'bout the same thing we did today—most of the day, that is, disregarding our little Thon Truong Tho excursion. But let's flip-flop—One Six works the western side of the highway, Two Six the eastern. Okay?"

Norwalk and O'Brien nodded.

Turning to Lieutenant Halloway, I said, "And, Bob, your folk can nap the day away here—after trick-or-treating the highway tonight, of course."

"Of course," he replied, smiling.

"And where are our trick or treats tonight?" Lieutenant Moseley asked, unfolding his map.

Later, while waiting for a log bird that would never come, Sergeant Sullivan and I talked briefly.

"How was your day, Top?"

"Wet. Yours?"

"Ditto."

"Tagged along with Two Six today," he said. "And, sir, you might want to spend some time with that young platoon leader of yours, O'Brien."

"Why is that, Top?"

"Hell, I don't know what it is about him. It's not that he don't want to do well or ain't trying. It's just that . . . that he's so goddamn young or something. Naple's running the platoon while his boss is asking everything but telling nobody to do anything."

"Well, hell, Top, we were all young once. And asking's the best way to learn. He'll come along; just give him time," I said, echoing Norwalk's advice.

"Yeah, guess so. But damn, he's so . . . so *young!* So goddamn gullible." Smiling, he added, "Know what he kind of reminds me of, Six? Kind of reminds me of an earlier Willie Dubray in officer's clothing."

I laughed softly.

"Know what he told me today?"

I shook my head.

"Told me he didn't like this place. Well, of course, I was surprised—hell, *shocked* to hear that. Can you believe it, sir? He doesn't *like* this place! So I asked him why on earth not, and he says 'cause it's not what he expected. And I asked him what is was that he expected."

He paused and started to laugh. "Know what he says? Says, 'Well, I . . . uh . . . kind of thought it'd be more like camping.' *Camping!* You know, where's the campfire, and when are we gonna sing 'On top of Old Smoky'?"

"Okay, Top, I get the message," I said, unable to control my laughter. "I'll tag along with Two Six tomorrow."

"Hey, Six," the Bull said after a brief lull, "you like this place? I mean, are you enjoying your command here, even in I Corps' dark and dreary mist?"

"Hell, yes! Like you say, I'd much rather be here than on that golf course, Top."

"Well, that's good," he said in a serious tone. "Ought to enjoy it; it'll probably be the last one you'll ever have."

I was startled by his remark. "What do you mean, Top? You know something I don't? Did my court-martial papers come down with last night's mail?"

Smiling, he said, "Naw, nothing like that. You'll go on to be Six at other echelons, but you'll never again be commanding soldiers. You'll be commanding other commanders, and *their* soldiers *through* them. Company command is the first and, in many ways, the last real command an officer gets, especially in the infantry. Ought to enjoy it."

And, I would discover in years to come, that, as usual, the Bull was right.

The following morning I, along with Blair, Anderson, and Lieutenant Moseley and his recon sergeant, accompanied Two Six on its sally east of Highway One. The platoon was to make a large circular sweep of an area south of the one that One Six had worked the day before. Around midday, we came across a couple of deserted hutches virtually hidden by a small grove of bamboo and tropical foliage. In the process of clearing the area, one of Two Six's soldiers discovered a five-hundred-pound bomb under a rice bin, haphazardly covered by some matting and rice straw.

Second Lt. Richard O'Brien felt we should destroy the bomb in place. "Let's blow it, sir," he said.

"And just how," I asked, "do you propose to do that, Dick?" We carried no explosives, detonators, or time fuse for that sort of thing.

"Well, we can put a claymore up against it, or maybe tie a couple grenades to it, see. Then we tie a long piece of string or maybe some commo wire to the pins, move over there behind that paddy dike, give the wire a tug, and watch the fireworks! What do you think?"

What I thought was can you really be this naive? Do you have any idea of the lethal radius of a five-hundred-pound bomb? My first sergeant is right. You're not learning the trade quickly enough. Then I noted Blair and Anderson, staring at the ground, to conceal the smirks on their faces, and I said, "I don't think so, Dick. For reasons that we'll talk about another time."

"Well, hell, maybe if we fell back a ways and hit it with a LAW," he said, now seeing the fallacies of his proposal, but, observing the faces of those around him, not wanting to admit his mistake.

"No!"

"Could work," Moseley said, tongue in cheek, as O'Brien strolled back toward the rice bin. "Might I suggest we move downrange a klick or so and leave your young lieutenant here holding the string."

I didn't smile.

"Want me to call battalion, sir?" Blair asked. "See if they can get a demolitions team in to us?"

"No, not yet."

Lieutenant O'Brien did have a point. Charlie was obviously the new owner of this piece of Uncle Sam's ordnance, and if we ignored it, it would eventually be used against us. However, if I called a demolitions team forward, it would take hours.

Talking it over with Lieutenant Moseley, we decided to keep moving and then to hit the hutches with an artillery strike after we were out of harm's way. This might detonate the bomb or at lease sensitize it so it would explode prematurely when Charlie tried to move it—in which case we'd kill four or five of his men while ensuring the thing was not used against us.

Twenty minutes or so later, Moseley requested his mission. We stopped in place briefly and watch the rounds impact, hoping for a secondary explosion. There was none.

As we continued our movement eastward, I overheard Anderson offhandedly ask, "Wonder if the LT's a West Pointer?"

"Naw, Ivy League. You can bet on it," Blair responded. "Only an Ivy Leaguer thinks on that plane."

The log bird flew that night, bringing with it steak and, for the first time in what seemed a long time, a ration of beer and coke.

"How'd Two Six's op go today, Six?" the Bull asked, passing me a beer.

"Just another fruitless walk in the rain, Top."

He grinned, obviously having heard of O'Brien's proposal for ridding ourselves of an unwanted five-hundred-pounder. "And how did our new lieutenant do?"

"Moseley? Super. He's filling Slim's boots without missing a step. Couldn't be happ . . ."

"No, damn it! You know who I mean, sir. Our camper. Lieutenant O'Brien."

"Oh. Well, he's coming along. Just takes time." Smiling, I added, "But, Top, in the meantime, I'm sure as hell glad he's got Sergeant Naple as his number two."

He laughed. "I copy that, Six."

"Anything on the admin side tonight?" I asked, thinking of little else to say.

"Normal stuff. Pay complaint in Three Six. Letter of indebtedness in One Six . . . uh . . . Edgerton. Talked with him about it. Says his wife's running up the bills in his name. Letter says if they don't receive payment in ten days, they're gonna serve a warrant on him. 'Course, that worries the shit out of Edgerton. Says, 'Well, serve me, Top! I'd be more than happy to go home and get this thing cleared up.'

"Anyway, I'll have the XO get the standard 'although the U.S. Army is not a collection agency, we will so on and so forth' letter out for your signature.

"And Dejohn's sister was killed in an auto accident. Got him out on the evening log bird."

We talked a bit longer as the late afternoon faded to dusk. Then, getting to my feet, I said, "Think I'll mosey over to Two Six's part of the world, Top."

He nodded understandingly.

Second Platoon had rigged themselves a three-poncho CP. One covered their position on a relatively flat plain about three feet above the ground. The other two, snapped to the first, extended downward and outward, their bottoms staked into Vietnam's terra firma. Inside, O'Brien, Naple, and their RTO sat huddled around a single candle, which offered little heat but did give the appearance of warmth and dryness.

"Come on in, sir," O'Brien said. "Got a fire in the fireplace."

"Thanks," I said, bending over and crawling inside. It appeared that he and Naple were sharing their CP, and the two of them knew I took a dim view of platoon leaders and platoon sergeants sharing the same defensive position. But I said nothing. O'Brien had been chastened enough for one day. Then, perhaps this wasn't the case. Perhaps Naple was simply taking the time to talk to, to teach, his young lieutenant. No matter.

"Want a beer, sir?" Naple asked. "We got a couple the nondrinkers turned in."

"No thanks. Had one."

Turning to the platoon's RTO, Naple asked, "Nadolski, you change your battery yet?"

"Naw, Sarge. Willie ain't got 'em broke down."

"Think he has now. You run along and see, okay?"

Specialist Nadolski looked at Sergeant Naple inquisitively for a moment and then, after looking at me and back to Naple, said, "Uh . . . yeah, probably does." As he departed, Naple crawled out behind him, saying, "Think I'll go check the line, sir."

"Well, how do you like the Nam, Dick?" I asked.

"It's okay, sir. Of course, I still have a lot to learn."

That's true.

"Mean . . . uh . . . that was a pretty dumb idea I had today, wasn't it?" he said.

"Not the brightest, Dick, but don't worry about it. Shit, it's a small thing and it's in the past, okay?"

"Yeah . . . uh . . . yes, sir, but the men are all laughing about it behind my back. Don't know what I was thinking of at the time."

"Hey, Lieutenant, put it behind you. Tomorrow someone else will do something less than brilliant, and the company will be laughing at him. Might very well be me."

"Kind of doubt that, sir."

"Well, you shouldn't. Hell, we were all second lieutenants at one time, and we all made mistakes. And those that went on to make good first lieutenants—and captains and colonels and generals—were the ones who learned to put their mistakes behind them and get on with the business of soldiering."

He flashed me an unconvincing smile, sighed, and said, "Well, yeah. Guess so."

"Dick, you know what I was called when I was butter bar?"

He shook his head.

" 'Shape Charge.' Or Lieutenant 'Shape Charge,' depending on who was addressing me or talking about me. Want to know why?"

He nodded.

"Well, after I got out of OCS, I reported in to the Fifth Special Forces, which at the time was undergoing predeployment training, getting ready to come over here. And one block of this training concerned demolitions. Well, one day, after a brief description of the forty-pound shape charge—during which I was either napping, or not listening, or simply unable to grasp what was said—when the instructor asked if there were any questions, I, for reasons only God knows, raised my hand and asked how you *held* the charge when firing it."

O'Brien looked at me in utter disbelief and then, brightening, said, "You've got to be kidding! Really?"

"Absolutely. And you can well imagine what I suffered for *a while* after asking that dumbest of dumb questions. Hell, your idea today pales in comparison! But as you can see, Dick, I survived that and other similar dumb things said and mistakes made. And you can, too. And you will.

"Tell you what an old major told me one time. Said, 'Jim, you don't have to be the brightest or best-educated officer to outshine those around you. All you got to do, before you go to sleep each night, is take a few minutes to think about what you did that day, starting from when you got up, and then plan what you're gonna do the next, starting when you get up. Takes no more time than a good prayer and might well pay bigger dividends.'"

Smiling broadly, O'Brien said, "How do you *hold* a forty-pound shape when you *fire* it? Damn, sir!"

"Hey, Lieutenant O'Brien, gotta promise not to tell anybody about that, okay?"

"Of course not, sir!"

But of course he would. And that was okay. Hell, it's not that unbelievable. Could've even happened. Probably did to someone, sometime.

Getting up to leave, I asked, "By the way, Dick, where'd you go to school?"

"Brown, sir. Why do you ask?"

"No reason. Just wondered. Uh . . . better blow the candle; it's getting dark."

"Roger that, sir, and . . . uh . . . thanks. Enjoyed the visit."

"Me, too, Dick."

"And how did you find Two Six?" the Bull asked when I returned to our piece of the perimeter.

"In high spirits, Top."

"And the young lieutenant?"

"Surviving and doing fine with his new command. Still lessons to be learned, but it takes time."

It would, but in the end O'Brien would do well. As was the case with Sweet Willie, the war would serve him well. He would be a better man for having been part of it. Twenty years later, damn few other graduates of Brown University could tell about their experiences in a land called Indochina.

As Charlie Company, and other companies of the battalion, and other battalions of the division, worked the street to Hue, severing the enemy's supply lines to the city, the battle for the city raged on. By any account, it was the longest and nastiest of Tet's many battles. Solidly entrenched within the walls of the Citadel, Hue's inner city, the enemy fought on. Reluctant to destroy one of their few real cultural treasures, Saigon's government had initially demurred in employing air and artillery strikes against the Citadel, and our leaders had acquiesced to their desires. And while these powers dallied about the destruction of stone walls, North Vietnamese cadres methodically murdered three thousand men, women, and children—and Marines, paratroopers, ARVN soldiers, and Cav troopers continued to die.

In February's waning days, after air and artillery were finally brought to bear on the inner city, and after the Cav had fielded sufficient troops to stop the resupply of enemy forces therein, we began to notice a shift in our encounters with the enemy. Whereas before we had oriented our main effort northward, we now found our foe approaching us from the south. Charlie was no longer trying to sneak into Hue. He was trying to sneak out.

"Sir," Blair said, scurrying up beside me as we trudged along one of Thua Thien's winding rice-paddy dikes, accompanying Three Six on a business-as-usual search-and-destroy trek.

"Three's on the horn, right?" I answered.

"No, sir. Captain Carroll's been hit! They killed him, sir."

"What?"

"Just heard it. They got into something east of us, and his RTO said couple of their men were killed and Carroll was down. Next transmission, he told Major Byson their Six was dead."

"Let me listen in, please," I said, grabbing his handset.

"Runner, this is Arizona Six. What's the status on your Six? Over," Colonel Lich was saying in a very concerned voice.

"Runner Two Six . . . Uh, killed in action. Over."

There was a long pause before Colonel Lich again came on the air and, with a discernible sigh, said, "Okay. You're in command. I'm en route. Out."

Bob Carroll had been a close friend, and his death saddened me, as it did his soldiers. But he was not the first company commander, nor would he be the last, to die in a war that others would later call a company commander's war. Vietnam, unlike most of our nation's wars, was a war without fronts, a war fought in the enemy's lair by widely scattered infantry companies. Like cavalry troops on our western plains a century before, the soldiers of these companies fought alone.

A short while later we took a break next to another nameless and virtually deserted village. It had stopped drizzling, but the sky remained overcast, dark, and low. A misty wetness enveloped us.

"Too bad about Carroll," Lieutenant Halloway remarked as we sat on a low-lying mud-and-stone wall at village's edge.

"And his soldiers," I muttered in return. "Not too far from us—a couple, three klicks east of here."

"That's Blue Max supporting 'em now, sir," Moseley said, pointing to a pair of Cobra attack helicopters that were alternately making firing runs on an unseen target to the east of us. Moments after each completed its pass, we'd hear the muffled reports of their rockets and 40-mm impacting. "And they're not gonna be supporting them much longer if this ceiling keeps dropping," he added, dryly.

"Wonder what they ran into?" Halloway asked.

"Who knows," I replied. "Damn, wish *we'd* run into something. We're just not making contact up here like we did on the plain, Bob."

"That's 'cause the plain—the mountain—was *our* playpen. The street is Charlie's," he responded. "Just takes time to figure out the lay of the land, Six. Once we do, we'll be scoring same as we did down south."

"Hope you're right. Only concern is that Charlie's had a twenty-, twenty-five-year head start on figuring the lay of the land around here."

Lieutenant Moseley, changing the course of our conversation, commented, "Appears the Marines are about to wind it up in Hue. Least that's what the papers are saying."

"About time," Halloway said. "How long they been at it now? A month?"

"Nearly," I said.

"Got a letter from my wife yesterday. She said they must have a TV cameraman assigned to every other soldier and Marine fighting in Hue. Said it's as much a part of the evening news as the weather. You know, 'And now, turning to the battle for Hue' . . ."

As he talked, I idly watched his RTO clean his disassembled M-16. "That couldn't wait till tonight, Torres?" I asked.

"No, sir. Weather's hard on her. She needs a lot of TLC in weather like this."

Smiling, Halloway said, "Cleanest weapon in the United States Army, sir. Seems to always be in pieces before him. And every two, three days, he extracts, cleans, oils, and reinserts each of the three hundred rounds . . ."

"Two hundred and seventy, LT," Torres said, correcting his platoon leader. "Fifteen magazines, eighteen rounds per. Ought to always go two rounds shy if you want your magazine to feed properly."

"Whatever," Halloway said. "Anyway, I'm not faulting you for your paranoia. Hell, might save your life some day."

"Might save yours, Robert," I said.

As we got to our feet to continue our wanderings in and about Thua Thien Province, it started to drizzle again.

The following morning, after the log bird had departed and we were finishing up our C&D of hard-boiled eggs, bread, oranges, and coffee, Major Byson's command-and-control helicopter set down unannounced on our LZ.

Meeting him as he dismounted the communication-laden Huey, I saluted and said, "Ready, sir!"

Smiling, he returned my salute. "Tall Comanche, are you in a posture for a pickup?"

"Your timing couldn't have been better, sir," I said. "We were just about to split up and begin today's walk in the sand."

"Great. If the ceiling holds, got three hooks coming in here at 0900."

"Our LZ's gonna be green, sir?"

"Should be," he responded. "It's Evans."

"Evans, sir?" the Bull asked, joining us.

"Just for the day, First Sergeant," Byson replied. "The colonel wants to get you in for a shower and a little drying out. Then it's back to the war, okay?"

"Okay, sir!" Sullivan responded. "And please pass along my thanks to the colonel. Snuffie can sure as hell use a little drying out. Clean jungles, I suppose?"

"It's all taken care of. Trains will just do the uniform dump there instead of out here."

Then the major turned to more serious matters. "Listen, I know the weather's miserable, and the sun rarely shines, but your sufferings have not been for naught. The battle for Hue, for all practical purposes, is pretty much history. Marines are still mopping up in the Citadel, and they may be doing that for some time yet, but Charlie's beaten—royally! And the reason he lost the battle is because you and others in the Cav have been suffering out here, denying him the ability to reinforce. Of course, it's been costly. Battalion's taken some bad hits lately . . ."

"Yeah, sorry to hear 'bout Bob Carroll," I said.

He merely nodded and continued his discourse. "Anyway, as you probably know, the traffic out of Hue is heading north now, so I want you all to keep yourselves oriented south. Within the next couple days or so, we're gonna start working the middle of the street. Gonna get into Charlie's twenty-year lair and pacify the street like we did Bong Son's plain."

This was all well and good, but at the moment a shower and a change of uniforms were top priority.

Thirty minutes or so after Major Byson took off, we heard the inbound CH-47s. Twenty minutes later we were at Evans, and soon after that, with our feet ankle deep in mud, we were in a GP medium tent, under a shower head dispensing cold water. And it was great!

Outside the tent, Willie and our trains folk busied themselves outfitting us with clean, dry uniforms. After donning these, we were trucked to battalion's portion of Evans and fed a hot lunch. Then, after cleaning their weapons and caring for their gear, the soldiers of Charlie Company were given the run of the camp for a couple of hours to visit the PX, steam bath, special services, and so forth. Many simply napped the day away.

At three-thirty that afternoon we were trucked back to the camp's pickup zone, where we were to board three hooks, which would fly us to a secure LZ astride Highway One a couple kilometers from our NDP of the night before. But there were only two hooks on the PZ— and four slicks and Major Patrick J. Byson, map in hand.

"Change of mission, Jim," he said, as I jumped from the deuce-and-a-half. "Navaho's got a good contact going to the southeast of us. Probably more of Hue's recent visitors trying to find their way home."

As we unfolded our maps, I signaled Moseley and Halloway to join us. Moseley, as the attached FO, had to be apprised of the company's tactical scheme, and, *reserve* Reserve or not, Halloway was my senior lieutenant and must be able to assume the reins of command at a moment's notice. Sergeant Sullivan joined us because he wanted to.

"They're in the foothills a couple klicks west of the highway, right about here," Byson said, pointing to his map. "Ran straight into Delta Company, which was working that side of the big red. They're trying to disengage—pretty much succeeded in doing so. My concern is that with Delta in the high country west of 'em, they'll try to work their way around them and then get back on their trek through this next valley to the north."

My two officers and I nodded in agreement. The Bull grunted.

"So," Byson continued, "gonna put your folk in blocking positions up the valley 'long about here." He pointed to the plot of our blocking position and then to an LZ a short distance north of it at a higher elevation.

"If there are no questions, let's get this show on the road," he concluded. He raised his arm and, with his index finger extended, began rotating his hand in a circular motion, signaling the helicopters' pilots to start their engines.

"Now?" I asked a bit frantically, hearing the Hueys begin their prestart whining.

Major Byson looked at me in surprise and said, "Of course, now. Get your people on the helicopters."

"Uh . . . yes, sir, but can't we have a little time to put an assault order together?"

"I'll take care of it, sir," the Bull said, interrupting me. "Who does the assault?"

"Uh . . . One Six," I responded. "It's their turn, right?"

Lieutenant Halloway nodded.

Then, turning from us and walking toward a loosely assembled Charlie Company, Sullivan yelled, "Platoon sergeants, front and center, on a run!" He talked to his sergeants for perhaps ten seconds, and in not very much more time than that our soldiers were loading their assigned helicopters in an orderly fashion.

Walking toward our slick alongside Lieutenant Norwalk, I commented, "Goddamn, Top can put an air-assault order together in a hurry. Wonder what he says to 'em?"

Norwalk knowingly, somewhat dryly replied, "Sir, I think he says, 'Get on the helicopters.'"

Our touchdown in Thua Thien's foothills above Highway One was without mishap, and after the hooks had off-loaded the remainder of the company, we began moving downward from the hill's pinnacle, Two Six leading. The valley lay before us. Arriving on a gently sloping, horseshoe-shaped ridge overlooking the upper valley, we stopped and established a hasty perimeter. Then we sat down to plan how best to accomplish the task given us.

The offshoot of this hurried planning session was that we would block in much the same manner that we had on Binh Loc's outskirts months before. Two Six would position themselves on the right—southern—prong of the horseshoe; One Six on the left; and Three Six, Four Six, and the headquarters section in the center.

While the line platoons set about preparing their elongated defensive perimeters, Four Six began clearing an area large enough to land a single Huey. Although we doubted we'd be logged that night, we needed an LZ in case we suffered wounded or required class V resupply. In truth, we'd probably have cleared an area anyway; Cav troopers just don't feel comfortable without an LZ close at hand. Besides, it was no great feat to chop out an LZ. The entire ridge line was only lightly vegetated with low-lying shrubbery and elephant grass. In fact, from our position at the middle of the horseshoe, we could see several of One Six's and Two Six's soldiers to the north and south of us, digging their holes.

Dusk settled over the valley. A short time later, we were pleasantly surprised when Dubray, monitoring the log net, announced, "Log bird inbound, Top."

"Well, sonofabitch! Will wonders never cease?" the Bull said.

Turning to Anderson, I said, "Andy, give One Six and Two Six a call and tell 'em to start getting their people over here as soon as possible. Want to get 'em fed and back in position before dark."

They came, a squad at a time, wolfed down their meals, picked up their rucks, and trudged back to their positions so others in their platoon could come forward to do the same. They were wet again and muddy from digging their defenses in Vietnam's soil, and tired, because you're always tired in the Nam. As the men walked by me at the end of a three-mermite chow line, they'd smile and say things like, "How's it going, sir?" and, "Good evening, sir," and, "When we gonna go back to our mountain, sir?"

The Bull's right, I thought. You gotta love 'em.

That night the Bull was in a happier frame of mind than he had been lately. It might have been because of the shower and the six- or seven- hour stand down at Evans. Or perhaps it was the weather; the skies had cleared somewhat shortly after dark, and now and then we saw stars appear between the fast-moving clouds above us.

"Shit, I don't know what your young lieutenant's complaining about. This ain't so much different from camping. Want to sing a song, sir?" he jested as we sat atop our mermites, watching the sky. Parachute flares were being dropped from an unseen aircraft orbiting to the south of us. As one flare would burn itself out shortly before touching ground, another would pop above us, releasing its canister, which would make a ghostly whistling sound as it fell to the earth below. The flare, suspended from its parachute, would then drift downward with the wind until it burnt itself out, and the cycle would then be repeated.

"Can't think of anywhere else I'd rather be tonight, Six—unless it was back home, or in Australia, or Bangkok, or Egypt, or Bong Son's plain," he said, grinning. "On the other hand, it's not so bad here. We're wet again, but we're clean, and our poncho liners are reasonably dry. And the weather looks like it might be breaking up."

"Hope so, Top."

"And we're gonna get a good night's sleep because of the weather and because Charlie, assuming he's trying to evade us like the major says, is hardly gonna wander straight up that draw there. Hell, he had an hour or more of daylight to watch us dig in. If he didn't see us then, he'll see us now, what with those flares off and on turning the landscape to day."

"Often wondered if anybody ever got hit with one of those flare canisters," I remarked. "Wonder if the Air Force knows we're down here. You know, if they have some sort of no-drop zone plotted around friendlies."

"Why, of course they do," Sergeant Sullivan said mockingly. Then, in a serious tone, he said, "Come on, sir. You know better than that.

Our boys in blue simply get a mission to light an area, and they plot wind drift and so on and start dropping flares. They don't know or care who's under their canisters."

"Guess not."

"But why use them, sir? That's what I was getting at. I mean, it sounds like a good idea, right? Enemy's trying to evade us in the dark, so you pop flares so you can see him, right?"

I nodded.

" 'Course, then he can also see you, right?"

I nodded again.

"So, when you think about it, really think about it, it doesn't make a whole hell of a lot of sense. I mean, here's Charlie, who was able to disengage and hide himself from Running Navaho in broad daylight, and now we're gonna pop flares to find him in the dark? Shit!"

"Well, goddamn it, Top! You're right! Want me to call Tolson and put a stop to it?" I said, grinning at him.

"Naw, don't bother. The good general is probably in the sack by now."

We sat in silence for a few minutes; then I got up. "Top, think I'll go over and talk to our new FO for a few minutes. Remiss for not doing so sooner. Join me?"

"Naw . . . uh . . . sir. Think I'll just stay right here and count stars."

I walked the short distance between our CP and where Lieutenant Moseley and his recon sergeant were sharing a piece of the country's sod. Moseley, on radio watch as his recon sergeant slept close by, was alternately studying his map under the glare of a red-filtered flashlight and then gazing out at the valley floor below. Seeing me approach, he rose to his feet, saying, "Sir?"

"Evening, Mark," I said, motioning him to sit back down as I did the same. "Uh . . . thought we might chat a while. We haven't done a lot of that. My fault. Sorry."

A bit uncomfortably, he said, "If it's about what's expected of me, Slim filled me in on that quite thoroughly, sir. What with that and our little talk at Phu Cat, well, thought I'd been . . ."

"No! Hell, no. Nothing like that, Mark. Shit, couldn't be more pleased with your performance—company couldn't be more pleased." Then, smiling, I said, "Hey, Mark, even though we all know that Slim's gonna make general someday, and of course Lieutenant . . . uh . . . Captain

Brightly knows it better than any of the rest of us, we've all noted that you're firing your registrations quicker than he did."

He brightened.

"You know, it's a small thing," I continued, "timing how long it takes to adjust on an RP, but it gives snuffie something to do before he settles in for the night. Hell, for him it's entertainment, and he has very damn little of that. Same as with Wester and his shotgun. You heard about our point man in Two Six who can pump out a fully loaded twelve-gauge faster than an incoming replacement can fire a twenty-round magazine through an M-16?"

He nodded.

"Well, anyway just wanted to chat for a while. Uh . . . what you doing with the map this time of night?"

"Just playing, sir. You know, figuring the lay of the land. Didn't have that much time to read the terrain before dark." Pausing, then pointing down the valley, he said, "Fired the RP 'bout six hundred meters out, center of sector. See that little knoll on the floor down there?"

I nodded. I'd seen his three rounds impact earlier, the third one hitting dead atop the knoll.

"Wanted to fire it closer, but the lay of the guns precluded me from bringing rounds in any nearer One Six and Two Six. But that's no problem. I can work off the RP in any direction, at any range."

"Fine. How long you been over here now, Mark?"

"Six, nearly seven months."

"Oh? Where were you assigned?"

"Eighth Field. They couldn't find an observer slot, so they went along with my transfer to divarty. You know, got to make sure all our artillery lieutenants have an opportunity to do their time with snuffie."

I smiled. "Yeah, one of those necessary 'career-enhancing moves,' huh?"

He nodded, grinning.

"Where'd you go to school?"

For the next half hour or so, we talked of that trivia that soldiers in combat talk about—families and friends, women and wives, R&R, the war, careers, the Army, the company, and the Nam. The flares, swinging to and fro under their parachutes, continued to cast eerie, bobbing shadows across the valley's landscape below us.

Suddenly a stream of twenty or so speeding red tracer rounds slammed into the side of a hill a short distance to the north of us, exploding on impact.

I jumped! Then relaxed.

"Nervous, sir?" Moseley asked, tongue in cheek.

"Yeah, stay nervous. Uh . . . what was it? Forty mike-mike?"

"Yep. Dusters. Got a pair of 'em on the highway south of Evans. They're just throwing rounds down range, H&I."

"Well, hell, hope they know we're up here."

"You don't have to worry about that, sir. They're in the net and have our plot. Guarantee it."

He was right. They must have our plot, and so there was nothing to worry about. But I said, "Check it out, will you, Mark?"

"Sir?"

"The dusters. *I* know and *you* know they know we're up here. I just want make sure *they* know, okay?"

"Sure, sir. No problem," he said, turning to his radio.

The Bull, reclining on his back, fingers interwoven behind his neck, was still gazing skyward when I returned. "Enjoy your little tête-à-tête with our cannon cocker, Six?"

"Yes, I did, Top. Bright young lad," I replied as I wrapped myself in my poncho liner.

He lay in silence for a while and then suddenly, buoyantly, remarked, "Damn, look at that sky, sir! Clear as a bell. Tomorrow's gonna be a bright and sunny day, same as if we were back on the plain."

"Hope so, Top."

The next morning, destined for other parts of Thua Thien Province, we walked off our horseshoe ridge because Evans' helicopters were socked in. It was raining.

One evening in early March, we set up our NDP on an old French plantation several klicks east of Highway One adjacent to the river Giang, which at that juncture was actually more canal than river. From here, Major Byson had told us, we would be picked up early the next morning and air-assaulted across the river into the village of Thon Can Nhi, which was supposedly infested—as indeed they were all *supposedly* infested—with enemy or enemy sympathizers.

It continued to rain, usually that irritating drizzle we had become accustomed to. The sun rarely emerged. We were always wet and chilled to the bone, wondering if I Corps' winter monsoon would ever end.

Shortly after the evening log bird departed, I walked the company's perimeter, as was my custom each night just before dark. This nightly ritual gave me an opportunity to check our defensive arrangements and, perhaps more important, to see and chat with the soldiers of Charlie Company.

Entering Two Six's area, which was closest to the river and obscured from most of the company by a grove of palms intermingled with banana trees and other tropical vegetation, I saw, twenty or thirty meters forward of the platoon's perimeter trace, a picturesque two-story French plantation house. It was an imposing brick-and-stucco structure, now badly in need of a coat of whitewash, with a red-tile roof. The roof was also in dire need of repair. Still, the house looked very out of place in a land of thatched and mud-walled hutches.

I left our perimeter and entered the house from the rear. It was, of course, deserted and was devoid of furniture, with the single exception of an old rocking chair in the middle of what probably had been the downstairs parlor. I wondered why the rocker hadn't been "liberated" along with the other furnishings. Maybe the Viets don't like rocking chairs?

Exiting the front door, I walked out onto a weathered veranda and gazed across what had undoubtedly once been a beautifully landscaped lawn that descended gently to a small canal running inland from the Giang. Although the lawn was now hopelessly overgrown, there were still several giant tamarind trees forming an archway from the veranda to the canal.

Reentering the house, I sat in the chair and rocked myself for a while, savoring the surreal tranquility of the moment. I tried to imagine what the house had been like in its heyday and found myself pondering the fate of the family that had lived within its walls years, perhaps a decade or more, ago.

Then I got up and walked back to the war. It was nearly dark.

Approaching the CP, I noted a somewhat disgruntled first sergeant anxiously awaiting his evening parley. I sat down beside him, and before I could query him on the state of the command, he blurted out, "Sir, the state of the command sucks! I Corps and this goddamn weather suck! Troops are wet, cold, and miserable!"

"Well, Top, as you very well know, neither of us can change the weather. Uh . . . as to the state of the command, is it your considered opinion, then, that the troops are no longer so very excited about our move to I Corps?"

"Excited? Six, next to a quick flight back to the States or a second R&R, the troops would rather be back in Binh Dinh right now than anywhere else they can think of!"

He paused and then said in a calmer tone, "Aw, shit, I know we can't do anything 'bout the weather. Just wish the sun would come out again, you know, even for a few hours. Give us a chance to dry out."

"Me too, Top. Just like to know it's still up there somewhere, huh?"

"Yeah, ain't seen it so long, shit, not more than a couple times since we left Binh Dinh. Uh . . . platoon sergeants think it might be a good idea to have field jackets shipped out. What's your feeling on it?"

"Don't know, Top. They'd be nice at night, but what with the log birds not flying that often up here, it'd be a pain in the ass carrying wet field jackets 'round with us all day."

"Yeah, that's what I told 'em. You know, just hold off a while, 'cause the sun's *gotta* shine again. If it don't, the whole goddamn company's gonna go bugfuck!"

"Hey, Top, you worry too much. Hell, I know the weather's depressing, but snuffie understands there's nothing we can do about it. And I think morale's still good in spite of it. Least that's my sounding. How do you see it?"

He smiled and said, "You're right, Boss. Snuffie's fucking miserable, but he's joking about it. You know, 'Gonna *swim* my way back to the world, Top. And, 'Got a can of ham and limas for a dry pair of socks, Top.' And, 'Where's my fucking diving pay, Top?' But what we really need is to get a couple of kills in the sunshine. Then morale would soar!"

Figuring we'd covered the issue of troop morale, I told the Bull about the deserted plantation house.

"Probably some fat old French fart now living in the lap of luxury somewhere in France," he speculated. "You know, sipping his grape in Paris, Marseilles, or some such place."

"I kind of hope he is, Top," I said, surprised at my own comment.

"What? Uh . . . why do you say that, sir?"

"I don't know," I responded, suddenly laughing. "Sonofabitch, I really don't know."

He shrugged his shoulders and changed the subject.

"Well, what's the plan for tomorrow, Six? How we gonna attack the ville?"

"We're gonna do it like Benning taught us, First Sergeant, two up and one back: One Six on the left, Two Six on the right, and Three Six following. Way I see it—and by the way, I've already passed this on to our platoon leaders during the perimeter walk—Three Six will conduct the air assault. Then we'll bring One Six and Two Six in on the hooks. They'll move off the LZ toward Thon Can Nhi, we'll follow right behind them with Four Six, and then Three Six will fold in behind us. Inasmuch as you *are* the company air-movement officer, Top, how 'bout whipping up a quick air-assault order 'long those lines and getting it down to the platoons?"

He smiled at me and said, "Sir, it's time you knew."

I looked at him, perplexed.

"Think about it, Six. If you've already told Three Six they're on the slicks, you've given your air-assault order. I mean, if they're not the assault element, One Six and Two Six know they take the hooks. Platoon sergeants know how to get their people on the helicopters and know what their people have to do when they land. Four Six knows they always board the hooks, as do Willie, Doc Heard, and I. Andy, Blair, and our cannon cocker know they always accompany you on the slicks.

"And, Six, that's the fucking company air-movement order!"

Sonofabitch! He's right.

"Ah, Top," I said, laughing, "at last I understand what you meant that first day when you said air-movement officer was the least taxing of your responsibilities."

"Absolutely!" he said, smiling broadly. "God almighty, sir, I still can't believe all that plastic you went through on the bridge just to tell us how to get on helicopters. I mean, stick orders, ACL, cross-loading, contingencies en route, air density! I said to myself, Benning's done warped this young captain's mind."

We were both laughing now.

"I mean this *is* the Cav, Six! Those helicopters are our horses, and any good trooper knows how to mount his fucking horse without a five-paragraph field order telling him where to find the stirrups!"

"I know, Top, I know," I said, wiping at my eyes. "Thought at the time it was the best goddamn air-assault order ever written! Thought *you all* were screwed up for not recognizing it as such."

Regaining my composure, I said, "Shit, Top, the bridge seems like a hundred years ago, huh?"

"Yeah, know what you mean. But actually, it don't seem that long to me. See, you're still counting backwards, while I'm counting forward."

"That's right, isn't it. How long now before you start teaching others how to make war? Two more months?"

"Sixty-three days and a wake-up. Got my countdown figured just as close as any other snuffie."

As we sat there in the mud with our ponchos about our shoulders, me on my upturned helmet and the Bull atop an empty mermite, conversing idly, Dubray approached us—coffee in hand.

"Got here what's the last of the fresh brewed, Top, sir," he said, handing us the still-lukewarm coffee. "Heared you laughing. Wondered what's funny."

"Ah, Willie," the Bull responded, "we were merely discussing the many facets of airmobile tactics. Far above you, I'm afraid, but many thanks for the java."

Java! Who but the Bull would still refer to coffee as java? I thought, amused. He's sitting here in Quang Tri's mud while this miserable drizzle forms little rivulets of water on his poncho, but he would have been just as much at home in the mud of France nearly a quarter of a century ago.

I sensed that Willie felt mildly rejected by Sergeant Sullivan's somewhat callous remark. Then, suddenly brightening, he blurted out, "Hey, Top, guy on the log bird, he say the Seventh got back their dead what they buried in the boonies!"

"What dead in the boonies?" the Bull asked. "What are you talking about, Willie?"

"Uh . . . don't rightly know everything 'bout it. Say something 'bout burying 'em in the field after a big firefight, and the Man, he makes 'em go back and get 'em . . . or something."

"You know anything about this, sir?" Sullivan asked, turning to me.

"Not much," I responded, trying to recall what little I'd heard. "But, Willie, I think you, or maybe your friend on the log bird, might be a bit confused on when all this took place. A week or more ago—think it was the night 'fore we left Evans—I was up at the TOC when the commanding general announced the Cav was approaching the west wall of the Citadel, severing the enemy's supply lines into Hue. Anyway, same time, during the course of the evening brief, they mentioned that the Seventh had recovered their dead from a firefight a day or so before. As I understand it, they had no choice but to bury or leave several of their dead in the field, then go back and get 'em the next day. Hard choice, but shit, none of us here had to make it, and it probably saved lives. Any event, don't think we should point fingers."

"No, sir! Nothing like that," the Bull said. "Mean, could've just as easily been us. And there ain't no outfit in the division what's kicked Charlie's ass any harder than the Seventh. But every now and then, they just wade into something like this. I mean all the way back to LZ X-Ray in the Ia Drang. Must be the ghost of the Little Big Horn looking over their shoulders."

"What's a little big horn, Top?" Willie asked.

"Ah, Willie, I'm afraid that too is far above your head, but thanks for the java."

As Sweet Willie Dubray walked off into the darkness, the Bull commented, "Hate to hear that 'bout the Seventh. Losing too many of our people in this war, too many of our NCOs. Good NCOs, irreplaceable NCOs, goddamn it!"

Uh oh! Here we go again on the NCO thing.

"I tell you, Six, we can't keep fighting this fucking war alone! Peacetime Army ain't supposed to fight a war by itself! Mark my words, we're gonna wake up one of these days and find we got all of those soldiers and officers out there, but no one left to teach either of 'em a fucking thing. Oh, we'll have a bunch of people walking 'round with stripes on their sleeves, but the old hard-core professionals will be gone. I mean, damn it, you just don't produce an NCO overnight!"

"Well, that may be true, Top—shit, probably is—but if the powers that be are correct, we've turned the corner, and this thing's gonna be history pretty soon; so we're gonna save our NCO corps."

"Yeah, perhaps so, if indeed victory's now at hand. But you know how I feel about that. I'm telling you, Six, this thing's turning sour! And what if it goes on another two, three years, huh?"

"Well, in that case, we'll just have to keep on . . ."

"No, sir! Can't just keep on for another two or three years by ourselves! The Army—the infantry—'cause it's all over here now, will turn itself inside out. You'll take the best goddamn Army the country ever fielded and turn it fucking inside out!"

Not knowing how to respond, I said nothing, hoping he might change our conversation's course. He didn't.

"Hell, you know how long it takes to grow a good NCO, Six. You used to wear stripes, right?"

"Right, Top."

"Served in the 82d Airplane Division, right?"

"Right, Top."

"Right! 'Course I never cared much for anything airborne, never understood why anybody would want to jump out of an airplane—just never made any sense to me. But the 82d's a good outfit, and their NCOs are sharp! Worked with one of their battle groups ten, twelve years ago down in Panama and never seen sharper sergeants. I mean you could ID 'em as NCOs even if they weren't wearing stripes.

"But the point is, Six, if this war goes on another two, three years, the fucking 82d 'Airplane' is gonna be 'bout the only infantry division left with its NCO corps intact, 'cause its 'bout the only walking infantry that ain't yet over here! Right?"

Oh, to hell with this. We've got to get some sleep.

"Top, you're probably right, though I honestly think you're overly concerned about it. But whether you're right or not, it just doesn't matter, 'cause there's nothing you or I can do about it. I mean, like they say, 'Ours is not to reason why, ours is but to take Thon Can Nhi.' In the morning, early in the morning."

Grinning, he said, "Yeah, guess you're right, Six. See you at first light."

Getting to his feet, he noticed he was nearly ankle deep in water. "Well, shit we may be seeing you before that. I'm fucking soaked, and ain't nobody can sleep soaked."

The Bull wandered off toward his piece of the Nam. Sixty-three days and a wake-up. I'll really miss him, I thought to myself. I've learned a lot from him, and it'll be difficult, uncomfortable, bringing a new first on board.

And I would miss him, but not in the context I then thought. Because, although I had no way of knowing it, I only had three days and a wake-up before leaving the Nam.

"Six! Six! This is Two Six! Got a man hit! Got a man down. Over."

"Roger, Two Six," I replied, speaking into Andy's handset. "How bad? Do you need dust off?"

"This is Two Six. Yeah, think so. Oh, yeah, absolutely. Doc's working on him now. Stomach . . . uh . . . chest wound. Bleeding badly. Over."

"This is Six. We'll get a dust off en route. Hold tight! Out."

Quickly changing handsets between Andy and Blair, I called for a medevac.

"Arizona Three, this is Comanche Six. Need a dust off. Got a WIA. Got friendly wounded on the ground at our objective. Serious. LZ is . . . will be green. How copy? Over."

Arizona acknowledged the request, promising to have a medevac en route within minutes.

Up to that point the attack on Thon Can Nhi had gone as planned. But now, just minutes after leaving the LZ, approaching the outskirts of the village, Two Six was obviously in trouble. Moreover, since the village's periphery was a maze of hedgerows and stick fences, intermingled here and there with an occasional mud hutch, we couldn't see O'Brien and had little idea where the contact had occurred.

Moving with Four Six, we were nearly on line with, and between, the two attacking platoons. As I passed the handset back to Blair, I noted that One Six's soldiers on our left were continuing to push forward, while Two Six on the right had evidently stopped in place. Turning to Andy, I once again changed handsets.

"One Six, this is Six. Need a quick sitrep. Over."

"This One Six, Roger. We're moving into the ville now. No contact. Uh . . . monitored Two Six's transmission."

"This is Six. Okay. Two Six appears to be stopped in place. Want you to do the same till we can get their man out."

"This is One Six. Wilco."

"This is Six, Roger. Out . . . break. Two Six, this is Six. Dust off en route. Have you got an LZ, and are you green at this time? Over."

"This is Two Six. Roger on the green. Must have been a sniper, single burst of AK fire. Stand by on the LZ . . . wait. Roger, we'll bring it on the paddy to our rear. Over."

After our injured soldier had been evacuated, we moved on through Thon Can Nhi, discovering nothing of any consequence except for a wounded child about seven or eight years old. Although no interpreter or Kit Carson accompanied us, it was obvious from the villagers' gestures that the young boy had been hit by a stray piece of shrapnel during Blue Max's prep of our LZ. The wound was serious but not life threatening. Doc Heard patched it up, assuring the young boy's hysterical mother that her son would be okay. I hoped he was right. Civilian casualties distressed me. Wounded children sickened me.

That night we set up our NDP in a cemetery on the far side of the village. After the log bird had departed and a wet, watery meal had been consumed, the Bull opened our nightly ritual by saying, "Sir, I know you don't believe in omens, so I ain't gonna say it. But today was a bad . . ."

"Don't say it, Top! As you just pointed out, I don't believe in omens."

"Okay, but our wounded man was a bad . . . sign."

We spent the next couple of wet and dreary days working the area east of Highway One in the vicinity of Thon Can Nhi. Then, on the evening of 8 March, Byson sent a warning order informing us we would air-assault the village of Xom Dong My the following morning. Locating the encoded coordinates on our maps, we discovered the village was nearly midway between Highway One and the coast of the South China Sea—right in the middle of Fall's "street." With this bit of information in hand, we found ourselves anticipating the attack with a certain relish, feeling that we would finally find I Corps' elusive enemy.

As we were discussing the operation, the sun suddenly emerged from the overcast sky, preparing to set over the Annamese cordillera to the west of us. In silence, almost reverence, we looked up into its fading, warming rays.

Ah, this is a good omen, I said to myself.

But it wasn't.

That early March morning began like so many mornings before it. We stood to at first light, fired a short but violent mad minute, washed and shaved, emptied our helmets of the pint of water needed to accomplish both these toilets, and then awaited the C&D bird. It arrived an hour or so after dawn, off-loaded several cases of C rations and some ammunition, and picked up our rucks, water cans, and mermites. But on this occasion it unexplainably failed to bring us our customary C&D. As might be expected, this caused some grumbling among Charlie Company's rank and file. This quickly subsided, however. By now, we had resigned ourselves to the fact that life in I Corps wasn't going to be as pleasant as it had been on Bong Son's plain; and it really wasn't any cup of tea on the plain.

Some of the men ate a quick charlie rat or a portion thereof, while others decided to wait for a hot that night—a mistake on their part, since there was to be no hot that night. I had a can of fruit cocktail with peanut butter and crackers.

Shortly after the log bird departed, Blair passed me his handset, saying, "And he's on the horn, sir."

"Tall Comanche, this is Arizona Three. Inbound your location with four, plus two, plus two in zero six. How copy? Over."

"This is Comanche Six. Solid copy and standing by for pickup."

After passing word to saddle up, I watched as the company prepared to board the incoming helicopters. C rations were hurriedly discarded, holes covered, shoulder harnesses and pistol belts donned and adjusted, weapons readied, and a final radio check conducted. Troops then formed into lift-off sticks.

As was customary in an extraction, the hooks landed first, picking up One Six, Three Six, and Four Six. When these double-rotary-bladed giants lifted off, the remainder of us, Two Six and the headquarters, quickly folded our defensive perimeter and ran toward the four Hueys that set down just as the hooks took off. The orbiting Cobras covered our extraction.

Our formation of eight helicopters initially flew in a westerly direction, away from the street, so as to gain altitude and allow Major Byson time to set up his artillery prep of the LZ. In a few minutes, however, we began a gradual easterly turn and then flew back across Highway One, en route to what would be my last combat air assault of the war. Others were not so lucky. They would be dead before the sun set that evening.

As we had hoped the night before, the day had dawned without a cloud in the sky. A bright, beautiful sunny day, so very different from those of the seemingly endless northeastern monsoon, with its surreal darkness and continuous drizzle. It felt good to be warm and dry again and about to engage the enemy on what we felt would be our terms, beating him as we had always done on the plain. We had had enough of those cold wet nights penned up inside Camp Evans waiting for a nameless, faceless enemy to loose his rockets upon us. We had had enough of those meaningless, fruitless searches for an enemy we could not find in the villages straddling Highway One. It was time to take the offensive, time to teach Charlie here in I Corps what his friends on the plain knew only too well—you don't fuck with the Cav. No, sir!

Sitting on the floor of the doorless, seatless helicopter with my legs dangling outside, I was momentarily distracted by the funny fluttering waves the aircraft's slipstream was making in my jungle fatigues as we clipped along at ninety knots. I looked down at the landscape slipping past us and was suddenly impressed with its simple beauty. Composed primarily of rice paddies, it was the most vivid green I could ever recall seeing and, with the exception of an occasional water-filled bomb crater, seemingly untouched by the war. I noticed the peasant farmers working these paddies behind their water buffaloes.

Hell, they were doing the same thing yesterday, and the day before, and the day I first arrived in this country back in 1962, and, for that matter, for five centuries before that. And regardless of what happens at Xom Dong My today, they'll be working these paddies in the same medieval fashion tomorrow, oblivious to or not caring about what might have happened to us such a short distance away.

The exhilaration I had felt earlier suddenly lost some of its flavor. What the hell are we doing here? What lasting importance will the outcome of today's operation have on that peasant down there, or me, my men, or anything or anyone else? Dangerous thoughts, I told myself. Who am I to question the importance of this or any other operation? Captains of infantry, and the soldiers they command, do not question. Theirs is not to reason why, theirs is . . .

Byson's penetrating voice in the headset quickly returned my wandering mind to the present.

"Comanche Six, Red Rider, this is Arizona Three. Insert in zero four. Standard two-minute prep with last round smoke. Smoke on fifteen-second final. Blue Max will cover the insert. How copy?"

"This is Comanche Six. Good copy. Over."

"Roger, this is Red Rider, and I copy that. Go."

"This is Arizona Three. Okay, good hunting, Comanche. Out."

I gave a four-finger heads ups to those aboard, signifying four minutes until touchdown.

At two minutes out, we saw the artillery begin plastering our LZ, providing Lieutenant Moseley and me an opportunity to confirm its location on our maps.

Soon after that, Byson began his final insert countdown. "Eighteen, seventeen, sixteen. I have smoke on the LZ. Rider Six, make your insert."

Now on fifteen-second final, we were coming in low and fast at treetop level. Discarding my headset, I and the others aboard shifted our weight, assuming our customary position on the aircraft's skids. As we skimmed across the paddies, we saw the smoke from the artillery marking round rising lazily from the LZ. Suddenly, we heard the *whoosh, whoosh, whoosh* of an accompanying Cobra's aerial rockets as they jetted passed us and impacted on the LZ's perimeter in brilliant white-and-red flashes.

Nearing the landing zone, the slicks began flaring, tails down, preparing to land. A second Cobra passed us, laying a blanket of minigun and 40-mm grenade fire on the flanks of the LZ. Simultaneously, our door gunners began raking the zone's periphery with their M-60 machine guns.

When the helicopter's skids were within two or three feet of the ground, we leaped, and our Huey pulled away without touching the paddy in which we now found ourselves. Quickly picking up speed and gaining altitude, the four slicks disappeared over the treetops as the Cobras continued to fire around the landing zone's perimeter, covering our hurried movement to secure it.

There was no return fire. The LZ was green, and within a matter of minutes the hooks had off-loaded the rest of the company. It had all gone like clockwork. A piece of cake.

Once the company was assembled, we began moving in a northeasterly direction, Two Six leading, followed by Four Six, the headquarters section, and Three Six. One Six accompanied us on a separate route, a hundred meters or so to our left, protecting the company's northern flank, which was dominated by a wood line of bamboo and other tropical shrubbery. If we should run into any trouble on the way to Xom Dong My, we felt it would come from that quarter, since there was nothing to the south of us except open rice paddy as far as the eye could see.

We did not have far to go, perhaps a klick or so. In the distance the village looked larger than indicated on our maps. Noting a church steeple towering above the bamboo and palms surrounding the village, I remarked to Lieutenant Moseley that he had a super registration point should he need it.

With a couple hundred meters of open paddy to cross before entering the southwest corner of Xom Dong My, I passed the word to Lieutenant Norwalk to clear the distant wood line that dominated our left flank before the rest of the company proceeded further. He did so and then continued moving along the wood line toward the northwest corner of the village, as Two Six and headquarters began crossing the paddy. Reaching the far side, Two Six postured itself defensively, preparing to cover the rest of the company's crossing.

That's when Charlie hit One Six! It was a hastily established but well-executed ambush, and Norwalk and his men found themselves right in the middle of it.

At the same moment, enemy fire began popping over our heads, high and ineffective but loud and unnerving. Caught midway across the paddy, we in headquarters dove for what cover a paddy can provide—which is very little. Anderson, holding his handset above the putrid water in which we had immersed ourselves, yelled, "Sir, Two Six on the horn!"

Two Six? They're hitting One Six. Aren't they?

"Comanche Six, this is Two Six. The dinks are hitting One Six! Over."

"This is Six. Get off the goddamn radio, Two Six. Break. One Six, this is Six. Over."

No reply.

"One Six, One Six, this is Six. Over."

Still no reply.

"One Six, One Six, this is Six. Give me something, now! Over."

Lieutenant Norwalk's RTO, obviously frightened, probably somewhat disoriented, but still soldiering, replied, "This is One Six Alpha! One Six is down! He and the point are dead! Need help! Over."

"This is Six. Pop smoke and hang tight! We're on the way. Out. Break. Two Six, Three Six, go perimeter where you are and stand by to assist. I'm moving to One Six now! Out."

While talking to One Six, we had crawled our way to the paddy dike. From there I saw they had marked their position with red smoke, which was now drifting over a large embankment approximately seventy-five meters and two rice paddies to the north of us.

Charlie Company's headquarters section, composed of Blair, Anderson, Moseley and his recon sergeant, and me, began moving toward the red smoke. We covered each other as we crossed the paddies separating us from Norwalk and his platoon. The enemy's fire was light and sporadic.

First Platoon had taken a swift and violent hit that had all but eliminated its chain of command. Bill Norwalk was not dead, but he had been shot through the neck and was unable to speak coherently. Sitting upright, bleeding profusely, he was obviously going into shock. However, being the good officer—the leader—he was, he was still commanding his soldiers through gestures. His platoon sergeant, who had been at the rear of their formation, had also been hit, and his RTO had been killed. Their point man, I was told, lay somewhere atop or on the other side of the embankment along which the platoon had been moving. The remainder of One Six was crouched at the bottom of this embankment, seeking what cover it afforded.

And Charlie was on the other side.

While Anderson struggled to get a battle dressing around Norwalk's neck, I attempted to ascertain that everyone was at least accounted for. One of the platoon's squad leaders, taking charge as good squad leaders do, assured me that everyone was behind the embankment except the point man, who was dead.

"Sir, he's dead! I was right behind the LT. I saw them both get hit, the LT in the throat and the point right smack in the face. Goddamn, sir, the whole of his head just burst open! He's dead!"

But what if he wasn't? I crawled up the embankment and looked across its crest. The point man was lying face down in a great pool of blood about ten meters or so to my right front. As I slithered toward him on my belly, I stared fixedly at the soles of his jungle boots, noting that they looked brand new. And he never suspected that when he put them on they would outlast . . .

But maybe not, maybe he was just . . .

No, his squad leader was right. One Six's point man was very dead. And shame on you, Captain Estep, because you can't remember his name. Shame on you, indeed!

War is not at all like Hollywood depicts it in movies. You do not effortlessly toss the dead or dying soldier across your shoulder and run merrily along, firing a submachine gun with your free hand. Dead and dying soldiers are so very heavy. I pulled, tugged, and rolled our nameless point man to the edge of the embankment, where Moseley helped me drag him on down to One Six's covered position.

Now, having our dead and wounded on the friendly side of the embankment, all that remained were to move ourselves across the open paddies, rejoin the rest of the company, and then bring down all the artillery in the free world on this ambush site and the enemy that had killed our soldiers. Unfortunately, the rest of the company, positioned as it was, could not provide covering fire, so we would have to cover our own withdrawal.

We assigned two uninjured men of the leaderless 1st Platoon to each of their dead and wounded and then, after tossing hand grenades over the top of the embankment, sent them scurrying across the paddy while we fired a "mini–mad minute" at a foe we could not see.

It worked! They reached the far paddy dike and were out of harm's way. Charlie hadn't fired a round in return.

I felt it best to next send what remained of the leaderless and somewhat shaken 1st Platoon. After collecting their grenades, we sent them sprinting toward safety, covering them the same way—with grenades over the embankment followed by an earsplitting volley of automatic-weapons fire.

Again it worked. Again Charlie's weapons remained silent.

Now it was our turn. I told Moseley, his recon sergeant, Blair, and Andy to each toss a grenade and run like hell. The grenades exploded! They ran. I fired a final twenty-round magazine at our unseen enemy, an enemy that I secretly suspected no longer opposed us. Looking over my shoulder, I saw the others nearing the safety of the paddy dike. I had one grenade left. I pulled the pin, threw it over the embankment, and ducked.

Whoom!

As dust and debris from the explosion fell around me, I jumped to my feet. Now run like the wind, Comanche!

I nearly made it.

I was fully two-thirds of the way across the paddy when Charlie opened up, first with small arms and then with a machine gun. And I was the only one left to shoot at!

Oh, shit! Twenty-five, thirty meters to go. Run!

The sordid paddy water was perhaps a foot deep. Each time a round struck, and there were many of them, the water burst ten to twelve feet into the air, showering me like a tropical downpour. I was soaked. The paddy's soft, sucking mud pulled at my feet, slowing my passage to safety. My legs began to feel as if they were made of lead.

Just ten or fifteen more meters! I'm going to make it. Gonna conduct this little ado without suffering a single additional casualty. Gonna . . .

It did not hurt. Not at first. It merely felt like a giant iron-fisted hand had reached up from the depths of the paddy, grabbed my leg, and then in one swift violent motion snapped my entire body as if it were the cutting end of a bullwhip. My head flew back, and suddenly I was gazing at the cloudless blue sky above, watching my CAR-15 fly end over end, up and to the right, as my helmet followed a similar path of flight, up and to the left. I began falling from what seemed to be a great height. And then, briefly, there was darkness.

Choking on the putrid paddy water, I looked up to see Lieutenant Moseley and his recon sergeant lying behind the paddy dike, firing over my head at the enemy beyond. Another ten meters or so, and I'd lie in safety with them. I started to crawl forward. But something was very wrong. My right leg wouldn't work. There was no feeling in my leg!

Okay, we'll just drag it along behind us, Comanche. No sweat. But they're still shooting at me! They're still trying to kill me! Don't they know, haven't they been taught, that it's better to wound a man than kill him? Isn't that what they told us at Benning? "Kill a man, and you only take out one of your enemy; wound him, and you take out three. Him and two others to care for him." 'Course, Charlie didn't go to Benning. Silly thoughts. Keep moving.

Finally, I reached the edge of the dike. Moseley grabbed my outstretched hand and pulled me over it, into the foul water of the next paddy. As he did so, one of Charlie's rounds hit the top of the dike between us, taking out a full foot of its mud wall.

Lying there exhausted, I looked down and saw the ugly white bone sticking through my torn jungle pants. I also saw the sole of my right boot angling crazily, staring back at me.

Something is amiss here, Comanche. I fear your tenure of duty with Charlie Company, Fifth Cavalry, is nearing its end. For if you cannot walk, you cannot command. Not in the infantry.

We were still receiving fire; in fact, it seemed to have intensified. Charlie, sensing we were in trouble and still separated from the rest of the company by a second paddy, was obviously maneuvering to cut us off. It was a wise decision on his part; he knew that as long as he "hugged" us, we couldn't bring our artillery to bear upon him. Movement across the second paddy appeared impossible unless Moseley and his sergeant left me behind. But being the brave soldiers they were, they refused to do that.

However, Charlie had a surprise in store for him. Blue Max was en route.

Blair and Andy had already reached the company's perimeter, as they were told to do. Hence, I was without my communications link with battalion—an unforgivable sin on the part of a rifle company commander. Shame on me again.

Using the recon sergeant's radio, I attempted to contact battalion through the fire-control net.

"Arizona Three, this is Comanche Six. Over."

"Comanche, this is Lime Light. Go to Arizona push. Out."

Twisting, struggling, the recon sergeant and I managed to maneuver ourselves into a posture that allowed me access to the frequency knob atop the radio on his back. I quickly changed the set's frequency to battalion's push, wondering in the process just who the hell Lime Light might have been.

"Arizona Three, this is Comanche Six. Over."

Colonel Lich responded immediately.

"This is Arizona Six. Roger, we have dust off and Blue Max on the way. How bad are you hit?"

How does he know that?

"This is Comanche Six. Uh . . . don't really know, but don't think I'll be doing much humping for a while."

"This is Arizona Six. Okay, hang on. I'm en route. Out!"

Then the leg started to hurt! Oh, God, it started to hurt! It was like every single nerve ending was on fire. And, I casually observed, my arms were covered with the leeches that inhabit the Nam's paddies.

Leave 'em alone and let 'em suck. They're probably all over you anyway, and there's no bug juice handy.

Lieutenant Moseley, in the meantime, began bringing red leg in behind Charlie, creeping the rounds forward toward us. Before the day was over, the enemy of Xom Dong My would dearly wish this young lieutenant had never been born.

"Tall Comanche, this is Blue Max Lead inbound. Request smoke. Over."

Moseley's recon sergeant tossed a yellow smoke across the top of the paddy dike, and within a matter of seconds Blue Max was back on the air.

"Roger, Comanche. I see your banana. Where are the bad guys?"

"This Comanche Six. We're hugging the smoke. Other friendlies to our southwest. Enemy dug in across next paddy dike to our northeast. Uh . . . about forty, fifty meters at forty-five degrees. Copy?"

"This is Blue Max, and that's a Roger. See the dike and flashes. We'll be coming in west to east with rockets and minigun. Keep your heads down."

Whoom! Whoom! Whoom!

Give it to 'em, Blue Max! Tear 'em apart! Kill those sonofabitches!

As the Cobras began their second firing run, the three of us started crawling along the edge of the dike toward the company's perimeter. Our progress was slow, painful! Suddenly Sergeant Naple, Two Six's platoon sergeant, was kneeling at my side.

Naple! What the hell is he doing here? He's with Two Six, a world away.

Smiling down at me, he said, "Sir, if it won't be bothering you too much, I'm gonna get you out of this shit."

He grabbed the back of my suspenders and began running across the paddy, dragging me behind him as the enemy's rounds popped over our heads. God, it hurt! Then, passing a clump of bamboo adjacent to the dike, I saw Wester jump out of the foliage, fire two quick rounds from his M-79, and fall in behind us.

Wester! What's he doing here? Brave men, Naple and Wester. Brave men, indeed!

We made it. And then Doc Heard pounced on me. "I told you, sir! Again and again, I told you. Always want to travel with the point. Always want to see what's happening. Well, I told you sooner or later something like this was gonna . . . goddamn it, I *told* you!"

And I suppose he had.

After giving me a shot of morphine, which did absolutely nothing to relieve the pain, he pulled my right leg straight and tied it to my left leg. As he was filling out a casualty card, I asked, "How about it, Doc? Will I be coming back?"

He shook his head. "Sir, you know better than that."

Arizona Six landed moments later with a new captain at his side. My replacement? Colonel Lich and I talked briefly, the two of us agreeing that it was best to hit Charlie hard with artillery before sending the company back in. I told him he must get new leadership to 1st Platoon quickly, before they began feeling sorry for themselves. He said he would. After a short and somewhat awkward lull, he told me I mustn't worry about the company; I'd be back. But he also knew better than that.

Then, looking up, I saw the Bull kneeling beside me. He was smiling but had concern in his eyes. "Like I say, Six, sometimes you eat the bear, and sometimes the bear eats you."

"I'll be back, Top," I said, forcing a smile. "Just hold it together till I get back."

He looked at my leg, shook his head, and said, "No, you won't be back, sir. And we'll miss you; company will miss you."

Seeing the dust-off Huey coming in on final, he got to his feet. Looking down at me, he said, "Good luck, Six. See you in the world."

I was loaded aboard the Huey, and we took off. The helicopter gained altitude quickly and then, banking sharply to the left, overflew the company's perimeter on its way back to Evans. From atop my stretcher, I was able to look over my shoulder and see the men of Charlie Company digging their defenses on the edge of Xom Dong My.

I'll miss you so very much.

TOUR'S END: 9 MARCH 1968

As I was taken from the helicopter and rushed into the Cav's forward evacuation station at Evans, I noticed that the sun was still shining. It was a beautiful day.

Everyone began working on me at once. Someone removed my left boot, while others cut away my uniform and right boot. Suddenly I was naked, filthy, and covered with leeches. These were quickly removed. Meanwhile, someone inserted an IV in my right arm, while others straightened my leg—a dreadfully painful experience—cleaned it, stuffed some gauze in the open wound, and then splinted it with wire and ace bandages.

Throughout this ordeal, yet another party kept asking me questions.

"Name and rank?"

"Estep, James L., Captain."

"Service number?"

"05322246"

"Unit . . . next of kin . . . home of record . . ." And so forth.

After giving me a general wipe down to remove most of the mud, they gave me another shot of morphine, covered my nakedness with a blanket, wrote up what they had done, and put me back on the helicopter.

It had all taken less than twenty minutes.

My next stop was one of the Corps' evacuation hospitals, a major medical facility located at Hue–Phu Bai. Here things did not go nearly as quickly as they had at Camp Evans. After being hurriedly transported from my Huey into a spacious warehouselike structure, I was placed on a concrete floor—and left there.

It was a dark, dreary place, but there was still enough light to see that I was not alone. Stretchers such as mine, with wounded soldiers atop them, literally covered the building's floor. Many of the men were in pain. Some of them moaned, a few called for their mothers or divine intervention, while one simply screamed over and over. There was one other who loudly cursed everything and everyone imaginable. Taken together, these many expressions of pain produced an eerie, morbid "oversound" that Hollywood could never recreate in its most macabre horror films.

I didn't like it. I missed the security of my company. I missed sitting atop my mermite and discussing the state of the command with the Bull.

The hours passed. Oh, how my leg hurt! The pain began coming in waves, the crests of which brought tears to my eyes. Occasionally a medic would check my wound and vital signs.

"How's it going, buddy?"

"I'm in pain. Lots of pain."

"Sorry, buddy, can't give you anything yet. Too soon. Hang in there."

Don't call me "buddy," goddamn it! I'm a captain, captain of infantry, queen of battle! Address me as "sir."

But he had already left.

They continued to hurry stretchers out one end of the building, while bringing them in the other just as quickly.

I know what we have here, I thought to myself, remembering my Special Forces training. This is the triage process, the process of determining priority of treatment when confronted with mass casualties. Those with life-threatening wounds, but who can be saved, go first. Serious but non-life-threatening wounds are treated next. Those so seriously wounded that treatment would probably be of no avail—well, you put them in the corner and call the chaplain.

This is a good sign! I'm not in a corner, and I'm obviously not being treated as first priority in their sorting process.

Sometime later the medical attendant returned.

"How's it going, buddy?"

"Are you gonna give me a shot?" I asked. You can call me buddy if you'll give me a shot.

"Yes, but only if you feel you really need it."

You pompous sonofabitch! Who made you keeper of Uncle Sam's medicine chest?

"Yes, I really need it, goddamn it! And if you call me buddy again, if you don't address me as sir, I'm gonna have you up on charges!"

I must have drifted off for a short while. Suddenly, I awoke to find myself being moved. It was my turn. Lifting me from the stretcher, they placed me on a gurney and wheeled me through the double swinging doors at the end of our "warehouse." The next room was a brightly lit operating facility, a large one composed of several cubicles. I was wheeled into one of them.

"Okay, what do we have here?" someone asked.

"High-velocity gunshot wound, lower right leg. Compound fracture, tibia-fibula. He's stable," someone else replied.

Stable, my ass. I've never been so unstable in my entire fucking life.

"Roll him on his side. We can handle this with a spinal," the first party replied.

As they rolled me over on my side, a third party said, "This won't hurt at all, and it'll take the pain completely away."

He, or she, was 100 percent correct. It didn't hurt, and, like magic, the pain disappeared! For the first time in the six to eight hours since Moseley had pulled me over that paddy dike, my leg didn't hurt. I felt absolutely nothing from the waist down. Now, with the pain gone, I could feel the effects of the morphine, or Demerol, or whatever I was shot up with—and it felt good.

All right, Doc, let's get on with this operation. Piece of cake! Like we say in the Cav, "Ain't no big thing."

A bit fuzzily, almost mindlessly, I watched as they did a quick prep and then went to work trying to clean up the mess Charlie had made of my leg. A modern high-velocity projectile, regardless of its caliber, destroys a lot of tissue as it passes through the human body. An AK-47 round is no exception. Hence, the team's first order of business was the debridement, or removal, of this dead meat, which they accomplished quickly and efficiently. A drain was then inserted in the open wound, the wound sutured around it, and the leg set and plastered around the drain. Then I was whisked away as one of the surgical team yelled, "Next!"

Later that night or early the following morning, when the effects of the spinal had worn off, I awoke in one of Hue–Phu Bai's holding wards to find the searing pain once again attacking me in throbbing waves. A nurse gave me a shot and a sleeping pill, and I drifted off for another couple of hours. This was the first night of a sleep, wake, pain, wait, shot, pill, sleep again ritual that would be part of all my nights for weeks, indeed months, to come.

Sometime after the new day had dawned, a doctor came by to tell me of my postop prognosis.

"You lost a lot of bone there, Captain. About two inches. That'll never come back, so we'll probably be looking at footwear buildup and a leg brace somewhere down the line. You also have some nerve damage."

"What about the leg, Doc? Am I gonna walk on it, run on it again?"

"I honestly think so," he said, "but, of course, I can't guarantee it. We'll be watching closely for any infection in the coming weeks. You know, you really shouldn't lie in a rice paddy with an open wound."

He smiled at me a moment and then continued: "Although amputat . . . loss of the leg, or a portion of it, is within the realm of possibility, there's no medical reason for worrying about that at this time."

I could not have asked for a more honest or forthright opinion. I thanked him and never saw him again.

After he departed, a chaplain from the First Cavalry Division came by to talk to me about those things that chaplains get paid to talk to wounded soldiers about, none of which interested me very much. Instead, I wanted news of my company. How are the wounded? Did they take Xom Dong My? What did they find? Where are they now? Who's in command? Of course, he was unable to answer any of my questions, but he did write them down and promised to get back to me just as soon as possible. I thanked him—and never saw him again.

That night many of us on the ward were loaded stretcher to stretcher on a C-141 StarLifter to begin our long flight home. As we went "wheels up," leaving Vietnam and the war behind us—or so we all thought—my thoughts remained with Charlie Company.

Let it go, Comanche Six; let it go. It's over!

Indeed it was. I was no longer Comanche Six. Or Comanche anything. I was just another wounded soldier.

War's End

March's cold damp air felt foreign, unfamiliar, as we were carried from our StarLifter to the awaiting ambulance buses at Andrews Air Force Base in Maryland. It was a clear, frigid night, and the temperature couldn't have been much above freezing, manifest evidence that the Nam was indeed behind us and we were home!

But there was no celebration, no kissing of our native soil, or screams of joy, or tears of relief. There were no wives or girlfriends, no bands, no flag-waving masses, no grateful citizenry throwing flowers at our feet—those of us who still had feet. Nor did the government that had sent us forth to do battle have a single representative, uniformed or otherwise, there to greet us on our return. Only the bus drivers, standing by idly with cigarettes dangling from their mouths and hands in their pockets, waited planeside. Once our stretchers were unceremoniously strapped into their vehicles, we began the last leg of our twelve-thousand-mile trip home.

"Where are we going now?" I asked the nurse as she rolled me into the hospital's orthopedics ward.

"To the pit, Captain," she responded, looking down at me as I lay on the gurney looking up at her. "This portion of the ward is referred to by its occupants as the 'snake pit.' But don't let that scare you.

235

They're a good bunch, officers and gentlemen all . . . uh . . . most of the time."

Inasmuch as it was fairly late at night, I assumed the pit would be shrouded in darkness with its inhabitants in a sound sleep, drug induced or otherwise. After all, this was a military hospital.

As the nurse pushed the gurney through a set of double wooden doors, I saw that the snake pit was anything but in slumber. Its windows' blinds were closed and drapes drawn, perhaps to shield the scantily clad go-go girl dancer from any inquisitive soul who might happen by on the sidewalk bordering the building's exterior. This very attractive young lady stood atop a table in the middle of the eight- to ten-bed ward, swaying seductively to the music of a portable radio.

While the nurse and a medical attendant transferred me from the gurney to a corner bed, I took notice of my roommates. As with the beds, there were eight to ten of them, nearly all of whom looked a bit younger than me and all of them amputees, some twice so. Those not confined to their beds sat around the table, smoking, joking, and drinking, as they watched the dancer above them trying to separate her pelvis from her lower torso. Most were dressed in standard blue hospital garb that in some cases was covered by striped robes bearing the initials WRGH on the left pocket. A couple, however, were clad in slacks and sweaters.

"Now you just make yourself comfortable and hang tight while I go get you some water and your kit," the nurse said, departing.

"Hi. Name's Stan," one of the two patients in civilian attire said, shaking my hand. "Want a beer?"

"Yeah, I'd appreciate that. Uh . . . name's Jim."

Returning to my bedside, beer in hand, he asked, "What outfit? Where, when, and how bad?"

"Cav, Fifth Cavalry. Two, three days ago, north of Hue, and I don't know."

"Well, Jim, you can bet your sweet ass it's more than just superficial, or you wouldn't be joining us in the pit. As you might have noticed, most of us are missing assorted parts of our anatomy."

"Yeah, so I see. But you look whole," I commented, although I had noticed he limped badly while fetching my beer.

"Ah, but looks can be deceiving," he said, knocking loudly on an artificial leg hidden by his slacks. "Lost it just above the knee nearly a year ago. Transferring me over to Forest Glen tomorrow." (Forest Glen was Walter Reed's recuperation annex.)

We were briefly interrupted by the nurse's return. She deposited my water bottle and "kit" (a stainless steel urinal and bedpan, toothbrush, soap, and washcloths) at bedside, checked my IV, plugged a fresh bottle of whatever into it, and said, "Got to get some fluids into you, Captain, and I want you to drink plenty of water. It's *good* for you."

"What have we here, fresh meat?" a somewhat gaudily dressed middle-aged woman said, approaching the bed.

"Jim, meet 'Sweet' Mary," Stan said, grinning. "Sweetest angel in the city of Washington. Knows how to take care of us poor crippled folk, so much so she makes Florence Nightingale look like the goddamn enemy! Young lady atop the table over there, by the way, is courtesy of Sweet Mary here."

He paused and gave Mary a peck on the cheek.

"I mean it, Jim. This lady makes Florence look like Ho Chi Minh's old-maid aunt! So I'm gonna let the two of you get acquainted while I get back to the festivities. Hell, it's my going-away party!"

He turned to go and then, over his shoulder, said, "Hang tight there, partner, and remember, it's always darkest just before they wheel you into preop."

Returning to his place of honor at the table in the center of the ward, Stan sat down, gazing contentedly at the young lady above him.

Sweet Mary was perhaps in her late thirties or early forties, a little on the chubby side and a bit overly made up. But Stan was right. She was indeed a princess in every respect.

"I know you're in pain," she said. "They tell me these first few days are the hardest. Would a drink help?"

"Drink? Drink of what, Mary?"

Reaching into a large vinyllike shopping bag, she retrieved a nearly full bottle of Wild Turkey bourbon.

"Only the best for our fighting forces," she chimed, smiling. "Water okay?"

"Water's fine. Hell, it's *good* for you. But just a tad, please."

Using the ice water the nurse had so conveniently set at bedside minutes before, she quickly mixed a potent bourbon and branch. Then we talked, but not of the war or anything of importance. Mostly just chitchat about families and friends, likes and dislikes. In fact, Mary's ramblings were very much like those of the chaplain, but coming from her these same trite utterances were far more interesting, entertaining. And, I thought to myself, if our straight and true of God's squad carried a bottle of Wild Turkey in *their* kits, they might very well find a whole new world in chaplain-patient relationships opening up to them.

Mary introduced me to a couple of my fellow patients, while others, at one point or another, introduced themselves. Later, her seductive protégé from atop the table came over, and we talked for awhile. Her name was Susan, and *her* bedside manner was light-years ahead of that of our chaplain brethren.

"Looks like you're running on empty there, Jim," Mary said. "Would you like another?"

"Uh . . . a tad, please."

The evening wore on and eventually, finally, wore out. Before Mary departed, I asked her why she did this, why make these time-consuming and, I would imagine, somewhat expensive visits to the different wards at Walter Reed.

She merely smiled, winked, and said, "Well, it keeps me off the streets. See you in a week or so. Hang tight."

Yeah, just gotta hang tight, I told myself. I'll survive this tour; it's no different from any other. Just another tour of duty.

Within a short time, I discovered Walter Reed's orthopedics ward to be similar to any other well-functioning military organization. The doctors were without question the best in their profession, as was the nursing staff. And the nurses would do anything in the world for us—well, almost anything, although even on that score some of the alcohol rubs were pretty exciting. As in any well-run military unit, the ward's underlying philosophy was "work hard, play hard." The staff tolerated no action on our part that might compromise an early recovery and release. If we were scheduled for two hours of torture in physical therapy, we had no choice but to endure those two hours of pain. If we were granted a pass or placed on convalescent leave, we were wise to return to the ward on time and without having reinjured our wounds in some drunken fall.

However, we were allowed to come and go pretty much as we pleased; there were no staff-imposed curfews, visiting hours were essentially all hours of the day and much of the night, and the nurses rarely took notice of our private class VI (booze) stocks.

Time passed relatively quickly. There were the good days—those days between operations, the most mobile and pain-free time. And the bad days—those immediately following an operation, the ones in which you slept with the animal pain.

Roommates came and went, some spending only weeks on the ward, others remaining for a year or more. One of those who had been there the longest was a seasoned but young infantry captain named Steve. Although missing only a single foot, due to prosthesis problems and a nagging on-again, off-again bone infection, he was still a member of the "pit crew" a year or so after having been wounded. Ivy League educated, he was looked upon as the pit's intellectual.

Dave, a young first lieutenant, was another of the ward's long-term patients. Once a warrior with the famed 173d Airborne Brigade, he had lost his arms and a large portion of his face in a one-sided encounter with a "bouncing betty"—a land mine triggered to explode at chest level.

On the last day of March, a Sunday, the three of us lay in the pit, listening to our commander in chief, President Lyndon Johnson, address his fellow Americans on national television. During the course of his speech, he made two startling announcements, the first being that he had decided to *unilaterally* deescalate our involvement in the war, hoping this initiative would lead to meaningful peace talks. He told us that as a first step in his strategy of deescalation, he had ordered the immediate cessation of nearly all air action against North Vietnam. He emphasized that this was but a first step and that the United States would substantially reduce "the present level of hostilities."

"Now what the fuck does that mean?" I asked, angrily.

"Means he's throwing in the towel," Steve replied dryly. "Means we've lost the war, my friend."

"My ass! Hey, you all been here too long. I mean, having just returned from Nam, I can tell you we're kicking Charlie's ass up one side and down the other. This peace talk thing ain't gonna do anything but give Charlie breathing room to recoup."

I paused as the two of them stared at me, seemingly unable to comprehend what I had just said. For a moment, it was as if we might have fought in two different wars. On reflection, I decided we had. They'd spent the last year or more watching the evening predictions of gloom and doom on television while our country's "vocal minority" marched on the Pentagon and across our colleges' campuses. I had missed all of that. I, along with other recently inducted members of the pit crew, had seen our soldiers rout General Giap's army in its last-ditch attempt to militarily turn the tables on us.

"Hey, guys, I mean it! We're winning big time. Uh . . . at least before hearing our commander in chief just now, I thought we were winning."

"Well, Jim," Steve said, smiling, "you're in notable company on that score, 'cause that's exactly what Walter Cronkite recently said."

"Know what I think it is?" I said, still trying to grasp a glimmer of hope from the president's pronouncement. "It's a ploy! That's what it is, and a goddamn good one, too, now that I think of it. See, LBJ and his people aren't dumb. They know we kicked the shit out of Charlie during Tet, know we virtually eliminated the Cong. It's a brand-new war, one with opportunities we never had before, and he's going for the win!

"In the meantime, however, he's got this domestic mess on his back, which means he's gotta go about this thing with a bit of finesse. So today he up and announces to the American people—whole world in fact—that all he really wants is peace, and in pursuit of peace, even though Charlie violated the Tet truce, even though they committed all those atrocities in Hue and so forth, he's gonna unilaterally stop the bombing and invite North Vietnam to negotiate an 'end to this long and bloody war.' See, he puts the ball in their court, and we all know that Uncle Ho ain't about to negotiate his way out of South Vietnam, so he just keeps on fighting.

"Then, say a month or so from now, LBJ comes back on television and says, 'Ma fellow 'Mericans, I've tried, Lord knows I've tried. I've taken every avenue in search of peace, given our vicious and uncompromising enemy every opportunity, all in my undying quest for a just peace, but alas' . . . so on and so forth. Then he gets to the 'I therefore have no alternative but to' part of his speech and tells us he's gonna bomb 'em back to the Stone Age and then send in the 82d to police up the rubble!"

I paused, letting their subtle laughter subside, and then asked, "Well, what do you think?"

"What do I think?" Steve asked. "I think you're either grasping at straws or out of your goddamn mind!"

I noted that our newly assigned, legless helicopter pilot didn't share in our assessment of the president's announcement or my fantasies regarding the reason for it. He lay there with stony tears on his cheeks and mumbled, as if to himself, "Then what was it all for?"

Our commander in chief's second startling proclamation was that he would not seek his party's nomination for another term as our president. This was fine with us.

One pleasant early summer afternoon, I awoke from a short nap to find Captain, ex–Sergeant Major Cooper, dressed in hospital garb, sitting in a chair next to my bed.

"Hi there, Big Jim," he said, grinning.

"Well, sonofabitch!" I said, astonished at seeing him. "We heard you bought it just after getting that iron coffin company of yours."

"Nearly did. Charlie put one right through the center of my chest. Missed the ticker by a quarter of an inch, missed my spine by 'bout as much. Collapsed a lung and tore up some other stuff. But, shit, Charlie should've known he can't kill a captain, ex–sergeant major! I mean, he's dusted off quite a few sergeant majors and a whole slew of you captains, but I'll just bet he ain't never yet got a captain, *ex–sergeant major!*"

"Well, I'm just happy as hell to see you . . . uh . . . Top."

"Yeah," he said, smiling uneasily, "don't really know what happened to Russell. Heard he bought it up in the A Shau." He paused, visibly shaken, then with uninvited tears forming in his eyes, added, "He was a hell of a good officer. Twice the officer I'll ever be."

After an uncomfortable lull, I said, "Well, shit, how the hell you doing? Look great!"

"Feel great, Jim. It was touch and go for a while in the Nam, but once I went stable and they decided I wasn't a candidate for Arlington's marble orchard, they shipped me out to the Philippines. Spent some time there, and then, after I raised some sergeant major–type hell in Angeles City one night, the medical powers decided it was time to forward me to Walter Reed for 'additional tests.' Got in yesterday."

"Super! They got you in the pit here?"

"Naw, ain't nothing orthopedic 'bout me. I'm upstairs, just a stone's throw from Ike, as a matter of fact."

"Great!" I replied, smiling. "Ex-president of the United States and ex–sergeant major of the best goddamn outfit in the Army up there rubbing elbows."

"Well, we ain't exactly that close yet, but give me a couple days, Jim. Hell, always wanted to talk to Ike, wanted to ask him how he got us out of Korea so quick after becoming our commander in chief. Thought I might be able to pass this info along to our present commander in chief, who don't seem to have a fucking clue 'bout how he's gonna get us out of the Nam."

"Yeah," I replied, "think we missed a good bet by not taking it to North Vietnam right after Tet. Hell, we had Charlie on the ropes . . ."

"And going down for the count, Jim," he chimed in. "But we didn't have to invade the north to win. Didn't have to change much of anything. All we had to do was lock old LBJ in a woodshed somewhere and keep plugging away at Charlie, north and south, 'fore he had a chance to get his second wind."

"Well, I agree. But maybe . . . hey, what do I call you now, anyway? Sergeant Major is hardly appropriate."

"Call me Coop, and there ain't no maybe about it. If we hadn't thrown in the towel, if we'd kept bombing up north—really bombing 'em—if Uncle Ho thought we were still in there for the win after the losses he suffered in Tet . . . well you can bet your sweet ass the peace delegation in Paris would have been talking 'bout something besides the shape of the fucking table!"

"You're preaching to the choir, Coop."

"But we didn't lock our commander in chief in the woodshed," he continued, an anguished look about him. "And if the message he sent to Uncle Ho was the wrong one, the message he sent to snuffie was a hell of a lot worse. I mean what's snuffie supposed to think when his supreme commander, the president of these United States, says, 'Hey, guys, I'm calling it quits. Ain't gonna be no victory, 'cause we're getting out soon as I can find a way to do it without winning. In the meantime, I'd like you to just keep on fighting and dying same as if I weren't saying any of this, okay?'

"Well, Jim, you cannot expect an American field army, any field army, for that matter, to fight very well or very long on guidance like that. Mark my words: the Army's gonna tear itself apart in Vietnam."

"Yeah," I responded, "Sergeant Sullivan said it'd turn itself inside out if something like this happened. And, Coop, he predicted it would happen, right after Tet!"

"Well, the Bull was right," Cooper said. "Hey, by the way, you hear that Naple got hit?"

"Yeah, but don't know much about it. What happened?"

"Not sure myself. Heard the U.S. Navy put a salvo of rockets in Charlie Company's NDP not long after you caught your dust off. You know our Navy. Probably mistook your company for a Viet Cong submarine lurking about a mile or so inland. Understandable mistake.

Anyway, Naple got hit bad, but last I heard he still had all his limbs and all his senses and was on the mend. Uh . . . remember that black point man of his, Wester? Think the two of 'em, Naple and Wester, pulled you out of the paddy north of Hue."

I nodded, fearing the worst.

"He got hit bad a short time later, think it was up in the A Shau. Head wound, heard he lost his eyesight."

"Fuck," I said, suddenly wishing I could be the one to lock our commander in chief in a woodshed.

"Yeah, the blind ones are the worst," Coop commented.

In May of 1969, a year and two months after being felled in that putrid rice paddy, I departed Walter Reed. As the taxi wound its way through Silver Springs, I suddenly realized I'd been mistaken in my initial assessment of duty at the hospital. It had not been "just another tour." It had been a tour of unpleasant excesses. Too much pain, trauma, tears, blood, and drugs. Too many saddened mothers and fathers, uncomprehending children, shocked—and in some cases adulterous— wives, and plainly disinterested but duty-bound relatives. And too many crippled warriors who would have to go through life wondering if their sacrifice had been in vain.

However, if not an uplifting experience, it had in many ways been a positive one. I had seen my fellow patients, the pit crew, daily display a bravery, a heart-rending courage, that one only occasionally sees on the battlefield. And I had witnessed a hospital staff routinely demonstrate a compassion and dedication that would have put Florence Nightingale to shame.

Nearly three years after limping out of Walter Reed's front portals, on the eve of my fourth and final tour in the Nam, I received an invitation from the hospital's staff asking that I attend the formal closing of the snake pit. The war, for all practical purposes, was over, and there was no longer a need for the pit.

I did not attend. I wish I had.

FORT BENNING, GEORGIA: SPRING 1970

I spent the next couple of years doing what many other Indochina returnees were doing—recuperating from wounds, ending marriages, and pondering what in the hell had happened to the world we once knew. These were harsh years—harsh on those of us who remained in uniform and just as harsh, perhaps more so, on those who returned to America's civilian community. Collectively, we searched in vain for something meaningful to hang onto. However, contrary to what most of our fellow countrymen now believe, we were not looking for some mythical meaning to the war we had fought or wishfully seeking a grateful nation's thanks for having done so. We knew the meaning of the war, if not the reason for it. We were searching instead for some purpose in the society we had served, a society that seemed to be casting asunder what many of us thought of as rock-solid, eternally enduring values.

Unable to find what we sought, our malaise often turned to bitterness, and many of us distanced ourselves from an American populace that somehow seemed foreign to us. Of course, our society had not changed—we had. The war had put us in touch with those values others merely speak of. That is the way of war and is perhaps one of its few positive consequences.

Soon after reentering the military's mainstream, I discovered that our Army, as an institution, was beginning to exhibit many of the same symptoms of apathy and purposelessness that its Vietnam returnees were experiencing as individuals. In 1970, the military's outlook on the war was undergoing a dramatic change. "Can do, sir!" was rapidly becoming "don't make waves, sir."

Not surprisingly, the sentiments of those soldiers preparing to go to war and of those training them to do so had also changed. An atmosphere of inertia and indifference, a "wait-and-see" attitude, had begun to settle over much of the Army's rank and file. There was little talk of kicking Charlie's ass. Younger soldiers talked instead of surviving their tour, while older ones spoke of resignation and early retirement before their next tour. Both looked in vain for some direction from above.

For whatever reasons, the Army was in trouble. As the Bull had predicted while sitting atop his mermite two years before, the Army was indeed "turning itself inside out."

AUBURN UNIVERSITY: SPRING 1972

I don't quite know how it happened. I never intended to return to Vietnam. Still, in the spring of 1972, while finishing up my bachelor's work at Auburn and after having spent a brief tour as a battalion S-3 at Fort Benning and undergoing its officer's advanced course, I found myself on the phone with Infantry Branch, once again requesting duty in the Nam.

"Well, Jim, I quite candidly don't advise that," the assignments officer, a major whom I had never seen or talked to before, said in response to my request. "I mean, frankly speaking, we no longer look upon duty in Vietnam as career enhancing, especially repeat tours. And this would be your fourth."

"Major," I replied, "I quite candidly don't give a tinker's damn about career enhancement at the moment. At the moment, I want to go to Vietnam."

"Well, Major, if that's what you really want, I'll get the orders working this very morning. We still honor voluntary requests for Southeast Asia, and if you insist on so callously ignoring my advice, it'll just save me from sending some reluctant major back involuntarily on a second tour. Okay?"

Okay. Once more into the breach.

When I made that call, North Vietnam was once again wreaking havoc on its southern neighbor. This time it was the Eastertide offensive, and although I could do little to change the battle's course, it seemed only fitting that I again heed the trumpet's call—or so I told myself at the time.

Later I concluded that the call was not nearly so noble. In reality, I had simply suffered a mild recurrence of "yellow fever" and wanted to go back because the Nam, if not the most stable, was the most comfortable environment for me. I had spent most of my previous ten years in Vietnam, training or training others to go to Vietnam, or recuperating from having been in Vietnam. And we all feel most comfortable in that world with which we are most familiar. Moreover, it seemed to me that inasmuch as combat was a rarity in a thirty-year career, one ought to spend as much of his time in it as opportunity afforded.

However, as I was soon to discover, this thesis simply no longer applied to duty in the Nam. In the summer of 1972, American combat forces were no longer in the fray.

SAIGON, VIETNAM: JULY 1972

As the Eastertide offensive faded into but another footnote on Indochina's long and troubled history, I arrived, again via World Airways, at Tan Son Nhut, the same airfield upon which I had landed ten years earlier when first setting foot on Vietnam's soil.

We have come full circle, I thought to myself as we deplaned. In '62 we were all advisors, of one sort or another, and we all landed at Tan Son Nhut. Now, ten years later, we're again all advisors, of one sort or another, entering the country at Tan Son Nhut. Cam Ranh must be a ghost town.

Although the war was over for most Americans serving in Vietnam, there were some advisors who were still very much in the thick of it, none more so than those attached to Vietnam's only airborne division. By a fortuitous stroke of fate, coupled with some politicking and a bit of deviousness on my part, that's where I was going! Or so I thought.

"I'd like to see the general!" I snapped, glaring at the lieutenant colonel, one of the general's minions, as he sat behind his desk with a surprised look on his face.

"Whoa there, Major! What's the problem? Hell, you just got here. Got a plum of an assignment, too."

"The assignment *is* the problem, sir."

All had gone well and according to plan the first two days after my arrival. AAG's (Army Advisory Group's) personnel section had confirmed my assignment to the airborne division's advisory team and, after in-processing me, had sent me on down to the team's rear detachment in Saigon. There, after meeting the team's RDC, a captain, I was in-processed a bit further, drew my weapon and field gear, and was told to report to Tan Son Nhut at 0800 hours the following morning to catch a flight north and join the team on the outskirts of Quang Tri.

At 0745 hours the next day I stood on the airfield's flight line, rucksack at my feet and CAR-15 in hand. That was as close as I ever got to hearing a round fired in anger on my fourth and final tour in the Nam.

At that point a captain from AAG's personnel section arrived and informed me that the group had a new commander, who had a new assignment philosophy, and that I was being sent to the National NCO Academy in Nha Trang. He had my orders in hand.

Well, we'll just have to go and get this misunderstanding straightened out, I said to myself, catching a ride with the captain to AAG's headquarters compound.

By the time I got there, after listening to the captain's discourse on his new commander's assignment philosophy, I was steaming. It was very much like reliving my encounter with Lieutenant Colonel Know five years before, but this time there was no Colonel Lich to turn to. I was on my way to Nha Trang.

NHA TRANG, VIETNAM

The National NCO Academy sat astride Highway One on the South China Sea's coast. Earlier in the war, the academy's primary task had been to school ARVN's noncommissioned officer corps; however, at this juncture it was mainly involved in producing new lieutenants for an army that had been bled white in Giap's Eastertide offensive.

Housed in a small oceanside villa, the U.S. advisory team consisted of four people—a colonel in command, myself, a captain, and one NCO. Our job was to advise and assist the academy's commandant. In these waning days of America's involvement in Indochina, that's what we did—taught second lieutenants to fight a war that had become exclusively theirs. Most of these young officers—those who survived—would go on to become first lieutenants. Few, however, would be promoted to the rank of captain, because when that rank was due there would no longer be an army of the republic—nor would there be a republic.

By early October, rumors of war's end ran rampant. On the twenty-sixth, rumor seemingly became fact when presidential advisor Henry Kissinger announced that "peace is at hand." But Doctor Kissinger's pronouncement was a bit premature. In Paris, North Vietnamese negotiators continued to quibble over the smallest of points at the peace talks.

The U.S. Air Force was finally, mercifully, unleashed on a strategic, no-holds-barred aerial offensive against North Vietnam. Referred to as Linebacker II, or the Christmas bombings, it was a bombing campaign that the Air Force had pleaded for—and we who fought in the paddies had hoped for—since the war's beginning.

And it worked. Just eleven days later our enemy called it quits. We who remained found it ironic, and tragically sad, that what had eluded our negotiators throughout five fruitless years of "peace talks"— while our fellow soldiers were dying—was finally brought about by an *eleven-day* bombing campaign, a campaign our country could have conducted with impunity at any point in the war.

With the signing of the Paris Accords, the United States had sixty days to get the remaining twenty-three thousand of us out of Vietnam.

In mid-February we closed the door on the team's villa for the last time, bid farewell to the academy's commandant and his staff, and hitched a ride on an ARVN Huey to Long Van. From there we'd catch a C-130 and fly south to Saigon and points beyond.

While waiting at Long Van for our C-130, I suddenly experienced an intense feeling of déjà vu.

This is where it all started, at least for me. I first landed here ten years ago, nearly to the day! Across the strip there, the vacant and plainly deteriorating frame structures of the Fifth Special Forces Group's headquarters still stand . . . appears the Viets are using what's left of them for firewood. Can it be eight years since we processed through those buildings, heading for all our misadventures in a place called ARO? What had it all been about? A decade of my life, the best one, has passed, and I suddenly can't seem to find purpose.

To hell with it! Like we used to say in the Cav, it ain't no big thing. Just get on the plane and go home.

SAIGON, VIETNAM: MARCH 1973

On the eve of my departure from Saigon, I left one of the Army's contract hotels on the outskirts of Tan Son Nhut's main entrance and walked a bit.

I passed the villa in which—behind which—we youngsters of the "seventy-six trombones" had spent our first night in the Nam so many years before. The massive cypress trees straddling its walled entrance had changed little; however, the villa looked much older, much smaller, and was in obvious need of paint.

Strolling on down the street, I stopped in one of the many bars that now dotted the area around the air base's main gate and bought a Saigon tea for a completely disinterested young lady—a lady who knew the terms of the Accords—those that applied to her—far better than I did. All U.S. military personnel must be out of Vietnam by midnight on the twenty-ninth of March, an hour and date that were quickly approaching. Our era had ended. We were no longer the saviors of her country or the providers of her welfare.

The following morning, thirty or so of us were bused to Tan Son Nhut for the last time. Out-processing was quick and efficient, and, after a shorter-than-usual wait, our flight's departure was announced. This time, many civilian passengers were boarding with us.

Walking across the airport's tarmac, I noted a North Vietnamese officer standing next to our aircraft, pencil in one hand and what I presumed to be the flight manifest in the other. He wore the all-too-familiar khaki uniform and pitched helmet, red star affixed thereto. He was the enemy!

Who's responsible for this, goddamn it? Who has permitted our enemy to inflict this final insult upon us? This bastard was fair game; he was "good hunting" a very short time ago. Now he's allowed to solemnly, condescendingly check off our names as we . . .

Upon reaching the aircraft, I stopped and stared defiantly at my foe, momentarily holding up the boarding passengers behind me. He gazed back at me, an arrogant, triumphant look in his eyes.

I would like to kill you, I thought. If I had a weapon, I would. Then it would all end right. There would just be the two of us, and you'd die, and I'd place a Cav patch on your chest and leave this country. Fulfilled.

I boarded the plane.

After we were airborne, I spent a few brief minutes gazing out the window, watching Vietnam quickly slip away below me. In no time we were over the coast, and Vietnam's jade green rice paddies gave way to the South China Sea's cobalt blue waters. Turning back in my seat, I was suddenly aware of a striking difference between this flight and the three that had preceded it. Always before, even while lying in a stretcher aboard my C-141 medevac, I had had a gut feeling I'd be back. I had no such feeling this time. I felt nothing at all.

What was it all about? Where is the meaning, the purpose in all of it? Ten, nearly eleven years of my . . .

"Can I get you something to drink?" an attractive flight attendant asked, interrupting my thoughts.

"Well . . . how about a virgin Mary, with just a touch of vodka in it, please."

She smiled, mixed the drink, handed it to me, and continued to work her way down the aisle.

What were the good and bad about it, the worth and waste of it all? Hell, I don't know, probably a little of—no, a lot of—both. Too deep for me; let someone else sort it all out in the future. I'm too tired to think about it right now.

Yeah, eleven years' tired.

But it had been exciting! Good or bad, right or wrong, it had been exciting! Life is always better at the edge.

Finishing my drink, I leaned back in my seat, closed my eyes, and let my thoughts drift.

"Comanche Six, this is Arizona Three inbound in zero five with four, plus two, plus two. There's good hunting in the high country today . . ."

Glossary

AK-47 The enemy's standard automatic weapon (of Soviet or Chinese origin—7.62 mm).

AO Area of operations.

APC Armored personnel carrier.

ARA Aerial rocket artillery (rocket-laden Cobra helicopters).

Arclight B-52 bombing strike.

ARVN Army of the Republic of Vietnam.

Blue Max 20th Aerial Rocket Artillery Squadron.

BMNT Before morning nautical twilight. That time of day when the sun is twelve degrees below the horizon, allowing enough light for small units to move unhindered.

C&C ship (bird) Command and control helicopter. A communications-laden HU-1D helicopter used by commanders and their S-3 operations officers to control ground operations.

C&D Coffee and doughnuts. An austere breakfast of coffee, usually doughnuts, and at times other entrees such as oranges, apples, hard-boiled or powdered eggs, and toast.

Cami stick Facial camouflages.

CAR-15 Shortened, carbine version of the M-16 rifle.

CEOI Communications-electronics operating instructions. The RTO's bible, it contains unit call signs, transmission procedures, secure codes, helicopter landing instructions, and so forth.

Charlie The enemy. Initially Charlie referred to the Viet Cong or VC; later the term encompassed North Vietnamese regulars. Also "Chuck."

Charlie rats   Combat rations. Also called C rations.

CIB   Combat Infantryman's Badge.

CIDG   Civilian Irregular Defense Group.

Class I   Rations.

Class V   Ammunition.

Class VI   Liquor (booze).

Claymore   U.S. antipersonnel mine.

CO   Commanding Officer.

Commo   Communications.

CP   Command post.

Divarty   Division artillery.

Dust off   Helicopter medical evacuation.

E tool   Entrenching tool, a small collapsible shovel.

Fast movers   Jet aircraft. Fighter-bombers of the Air Force's Tactical Air Command, the Navy, or the Marine Corps.

FO   Forward observer. An artillery officer attached to an infantry company to coordinate artillery fire.

FRAGO   Fragmentary or frag order. Shortened version of a lengthy operations order. Used in a fast moving, fluid situation to maneuver forces quickly.

Gun target line   The path along which an artillery projectile travels from firing until it impacts.

Gunship   Armed helicopter.

H&I   Harassment and interdiction. Artillery fire directed at suspected, but unconfirmed, enemy locations.

HE   High explosive.

Hook   CH-47 helicopter, the Chinook.

KIA   Killed in action.

Kit Carson   North Vietnamese defectors in the employ of U.S. forces as guides, scouts, and, at times, interpreters.

Klick   Kilometer.

LAW   Light antitank weapon.

Log bird   Resupply helicopter.

LP   Listening post.

LT   Lieutenant.

LZ   Landing zone. LZ Green is a secure landing zone—one not occupied by the enemy. LZ Red, or a "hot" LZ, is one defended by the enemy.

M-16   U.S. soldier's standard infantry weapon (5.56 mm).

M-60   U.S. infantry's standard machine gun (7.62 mm).

M-79   40mm grenade launcher, often referred to as a "thumper."

MACV   U.S. Military Assistance Command, Vietnam.

MIA   Missing in action.

NDP   Night defensive position.

NVA   North Vietnamese Army.

OP   Observation post.

Point of origin   Method of referencing a location on a map.

Punji stakes   Bamboo spikes emplaced as booby traps by the Viet Cong.

Push   Radio frequency.

PZ   Pickup zone.

R&R   Rest and recuperation.

RDC   Rear detachment commander. The officer—usually the S-1—in charge of the battalion's rear area while the rest of the command fought Charlie.

Red leg   Artillery.

Red line   Highway or road. (Rivers were indicated by blue lines.)

RON   Remain overnight.

RP   Registration point. A pre-fired reference point from which an artillery forward observer could rapidly adjust artillery fires in an emergency.

RPG   Rocket-propelled grenade (launcher).

RTO   Radio telephone operator.

Ruff Puffs   Regional-Popular forces. Montagnard peasant militia—a paramilitary force fighting on the side of South Vietnam.

S-1   (Staff) personnel officer.

S-2   (Staff) intelligence officer.

S-3   (Staff) operations officer.

S-4   (Staff) logistics officer.

Search   Army postal service's code word for "killed in action."

Sitrep   Situation report.

Six   Commander of a unit.

SKS   The enemy's standard semiautomatic weapon (7.62mm).

Slick   HU-1D troop transport helicopter, the "Huey."

Snuffie   U.S. infantry soldier.

Starlight scope   Optical instrument capable of intensifying low light, allowing its user to see at night.

Strike Force   Offensive arm of the CIDG program.

Striker   Strike Force soldier.

TOC   Tactical operations center.

TOT   Time on target. A devastating artillery strike in which the firing batteries of several units are concentrated simultaneously on a single target.

Train fire   Infantry marksmanship training.

Trick or treat   An ambush or ambush site.

VC   Viet Cong.

WIA   Wounded in action.

XO   Executive officer.

Z   DMZ, demilitarized zone.